SWIFT'S POETRY 1900–1980

GARLAND REFERENCE LIBRARY
OF THE HUMANITIES
(VOL. 335)

SWIFT'S POETRY
1900–1980
An Annotated Bibliography of Studies

Compiled, with a Critical Introduction,

by David M. Vieth

GARLAND PUBLISHING, INC. • NEW YORK & LONDON
1982

Library of Congress Cataloging in Publication Data
Vieth, David M.
  Swift's poetry, 1900–1980.

  (Garland reference library of the humanities ; 335)
  Includes indexes.
  1. Swift, Jonathan, 1667–1745—Bibliography.
  2. Swift, Jonathan, 1667–1745—Poetic works.   I. Title.
  II. Series.
  Z8856.V54   [PR3728.P58]   016.821'5   81-48492
  ISBN 0-8240-9393-3   AACR2

Printed on acid-free, 250-year-life paper
Manufactured in the United States of America

CONTENTS

PREFACE

This is the first full-scale bibliography of studies of the poetry of Jonathan Swift ever assembled. It is primarily a record of criticism of his poetry from 1900 to the present. Because the criticism is intertwined with publications of other kinds, however, especially editions of the poems, the scope of the volume has been enlarged to include scholarly studies of a biographical, bibliographical, and textual nature. Thus Sections I and II consist of editions, the concordance to the poems compiled by Michael Shinagel, "Primary Bibliography" (of the poems themselves), and "Secondary Bibliography" (lists of secondary sources).

Section III, "General Studies of the Poetry," lists significant studies of Swift's poetry as a whole, as well as essays on groups of poems that cut across the categories in Section IV. That section, "Specialized Studies," consists mostly of single poems or groups of poems which have attracted a well-defined body of publication. Section V, "Miscellaneous," is just that: it includes large numbers of sharply focused scholarly studies, some general studies too tangential to be included in Section III, and several very distinguished critical studies of individual poems that do not fit into Section IV. Section VI, "Background," comprises items whose relevance to Swift's poetry is indirect.

The arrangement of Section IV, "Specialized Studies," which is roughly chronological, follows a perhaps eccentric scheme that at least has the virtue of being easy to remember. Beginning with poems of youth and the dawn (the early odes, the *Description* poems), it continues with five categories representing mid-life crises, one of them a fable (*Baucis and Philemon*) and four reflecting Swift's relations with women. The first three women are actual persons (Vanessa, Stella, Lady Acheson), while the fourth is the composite Celia, Corinna, or Chloe of the "scatological" poems. The series concludes with damnation (*On Poetry: A Rapsody*), death

(*Verses on the Death of Dr. Swift*), and judgment (*The Day of Judgement*). If there were a category for *The Legion Club*, it would represent hell. I do not offer any further interpretation of this suggestive scheme; I assume it is natural for authors like Swift to write on matters of interest to their particular age-group.

The titles of Swift's poems are normalized and italicized to accord with the practice in the index of the three-volume edition by Sir Harold Williams, although he is not always consistent. Williams's format has been adopted for spelling and punctuation, but capitalization has been modernized in conformity to twentieth-century practice. To a surprising degree, the titles of Swift's poems were already standardized in the eighteenth century.

The poems have been indexed by titles rather than by first lines, because that is the way in which students of Swift customarily think of them. Attention should also be paid to the cross-references at the end of each of the eleven categories in Section IV, the "Specialized Studies." Particularly for poems in groups, such as the "scatological" poems, these cross-references may provide relevant information beyond that available in the index. For any specific poem by Swift, the use of the index in combination with the cross-references should enable a reader to locate every significant discussion published since 1900.

Most of the publication on Swift's poetry has come since 1965, which was the cut-off date for the two most recent bibliographies of Swift studies, those compiled by James Stathis and Claire Lamont. Hence the items listed under "Secondary Bibliography," including the earlier bibliography by Louis Landa and James Tobin, have afforded minimal assistance in assembling the present volume. The annual bibliographies consulted in its preparation included *PMLA*, *Philological Quarterly* (now *The Eighteenth Century: A Current Bibliography*), and the Modern Humanities Research Association, but the most useful publication of the kind proved to be *The Scriblerian*.

This volume owes much to the Morris Library of Southern Illinois University at Carbondale, whose resources are organized ideally for the production of bibliographies. Special thanks are due to Alan Cohn, the Humanities Librarian, and to D. Kathleen

Eads and Angela B. Rubin of the library staff. Thomas K. Pasch assisted in assembling the list of M.A. theses and Ph.D. dissertations. Richard Rodino called attention to several items. For help in obtaining copies of out-of-the-way items and transliterating an item in Russian, I am grateful to my daughter Carolyn. For the time and care they devoted to retyping my manuscript, I am indebted to Pauline Duke and the staff of the Department of English, Southern Illinois University at Carbondale.

SWIFT'S POETRY: THREE CENTURIES OF CRITICISM

Nearly three centuries have elapsed since Dryden allegedly re-marked, "Cousin Swift, you will never be a poet." As recently as fifteen years ago, the idea that Swift wrote any poetry was dismissed as ridiculous.[1] As a result of the extraordinary shift of opinion that is documented in this bibliography, however, Swift is now widely regarded as a major English poet, second only to Pope in the eighteenth century and equal at least to William Blake.

Since the mentality of earlier decades may already be difficult to recapture, a passage from a letter by Maurice Johnson, addressed to me not long before his death, may be instructive. Professing himself "delighted" with the Special Session on Swift's poetry that was being planned for the annual meeting of the Modern Language Association in New York City in December 1976,[2] he continues,

No one knows better than I do how outrageous such a proposal would have seemed twenty-five or thirty years ago. Even Harold Williams seemed puzzled that anyone would try to find matter for an extended study in the poems—though he was generally very kind and expressed himself as surprised by my finished MS, [sic] when he read it. Herbert Davis, though I found his interest in the poems to be of a very limited sort, was of course encouraging; he told me in conversation that he doubted whether Williams found any pleasure at all in the poems despite his years spent in editing them. Joseph Wood Krutch was somewhat amused at my undertaking; John Crowe Ransom wrote that it was a waste of time: there was nothing in the poems. Jim Clifford, always friendly and critically loyal, must have known what a real book on Swift's poetry should be like and must have known that I didn't write it. Perhaps no one was ready to do so at that time. The Sin of Wit is an extended essay arguing that individual poems by Swift are worthy of close exam-

ination and that general study of the corpus is rewarding in a
number of ways.[3]

Thirty years after *The Sin of Wit* was published in 1950, Swift's
poetry has a higher reputation than at any time in the past,
including Swift's own lifetime. Like the Boswell of the *Journals*,
Swift the poet is as much an author of the twentieth century as of
the eighteenth. Although *The Sin of Wit* was not followed for more
than a quarter-century by any similar book-length critical study of
the poems, five such volumes have appeared in five years: the
books by Nora Crow Jaffe (1977), John Irwin Fischer (1978), Peter
J. Schakel (1978), A. B. England (1980), and Louis K. Barnett
(1981), as well as the collection of essays in *Contemporary Studies of
Swift's Poetry* (1980), with other volumes soon to follow.[4] Coming
with a suddenness that must disconcert readers accustomed to
thinking of him as a great prose writer who also wrote verse—
Swift is his own stiffest competition—the recent success of Swift's
poetry amounts to a revolution in taste that calls for fuller explanation than is possible in this introduction. One may speculate
that for American readers suffering from post-Vietnam disillu-
sionment (English readers are scarcely better off), the sordid,
fragmented world of Swift's poetry seems to mirror their reduced
personal expectations and the myriad ills that beset their country.
Swift's battered whore Corinna, striving desperately to "recollect
the scatter'd Parts" of her "self" to face each new day, may be
Everyman for the 1980s.

The history of criticism of Swift's poetry is unusual in that
despite superficial differences of opinion and occasional acri-
mony, it does not consist of a succession of "schools" or rival
factions whose interpretations are mutually incompatible. Every
important approach to the poems, however one-sided, possesses a
measure of truth that is descriptively, if not evaluatively, accurate.
Even an apparent aberration like the prudish horror of Huxley,
Lawrence, and Middleton Murry at Swift's "scatological" poems
comes closer to the current view of them as "vexatious" satires
than do attempts to explain them away as Freudian anality, Christian moralizing, conventional antifeminist satire, or lighthearted

comedy; Swift expected his readers to be shocked. It is tempting to assume teleologically that earlier opinions, many of which represent criticism of a high order, are segments of the more nearly inclusive response to the poems which we now possess, and which we can expect to broaden in the future.

Swift's poetry has been undervalued for almost three centuries, and the reason can be given in a word: Romanticism. Evident in its first stirrings during Swift's lifetime, the effects of Romanticism linger to the present day. In the line of poets that runs from Spenser, Shakespeare, and Milton (as the Romantics understood them) to Wordsworth, Coleridge, Shelley, and Tennyson, Swift found no place.[5]

The Romantic refusal to consider Swift a poet stemmed not only from his subject matter and philosophical attitude but from his treatment of poetry itself. The task of the poet, as the Romantics saw it, was to transform humdrum reality by escaping into a Platonic realm of truth and beauty. Swift, by contrast, dwelt obsessively upon the seamy particulars of everyday living. Where the Romantic goal was to idealize experience, Swift saw little in human nature but the Yahoo. Equally bad, he appeared determined to subvert and thereby destroy the conventions and traditions (such as pastoral, epic, elegy, and the forms of romantic love) that lend continuity and meaning to poetry and to culture generally. The deliberately cacophonous rhythms of his verse mocked the desire to sing and soar. Curiously, even those who denied Swift the name of poet attributed his failure, not to lack of ability—he was credited with "imagination"—but to conscious choice. A period that valued the expression of emotions in poetry naturally regarded Swift's verse as intellectual. The poems to Stella were, however, respected for their sentiments, and one poem that enjoyed sustained popularity during the eighteenth and nineteenth centuries was *Cadenus and Vanessa*, perhaps for the same reason that Pope's *Eloisa to Abelard* continued to be read, memorized, and recited.

Even at the height of Romanticism, Swift's poetry never lost its appeal for the common reader—a circumstance all the more remarkable in that for a long time there was no satisfactory edition. Probably because of disapproval from the official arbiters of taste and morality, no reliable collection appeared until the monumental three-volume work by Sir Harold Williams in 1937, available in a revised second edition in 1958 and in the alternative one-volume edition by Herbert Davis in 1967. Earlier in the twentieth century, readers had to makeshift with the Aldine edition or that of William Ernst Browning in the Bohn Standard Library, both based on Sir Walter Scott. Even with the basic problems solved, editions aimed at a popular market, such as the Muses' Library collection by Joseph Horrell, have not fully reached their intended readers.[6] Moreover, as interest in Swift's poetry has grown, the Williams edition, which reviewers at the time considered so good that it would never have to be done over, has proved faulty on some points of canonicity as well as seriously deficient in textual accuracy and the quality of its annotations.[7] A new edition of the poems is currently being prepared by James Woolley, John Irwin Fischer, and Donald C. Mell under contract to the University of Delaware Press, and a Penguin edition by Pat Rogers will appear soon.[8]

According to a well-known story, Swift customarily had his publisher read the proof-sheets aloud both to him and to two men servants, "Which, if they did not comprehend, he would alter and amend, until they understood it perfectly well, and then would say, *This will do; for I write to the Vulgar, more than to the Learned.*"[9] No author knew better than Swift how to reach an audience. In the eighteenth century, his verses were praised universally for their wit, humor, and satire, although from the start there was an ominous tendency to deny their status as poetry by trivializing them. "In the poetical works of Dr. Swift," wrote Dr. Johnson in his *Life of Swift*, "there is not much upon which the critic can exercise his powers."[10] Complaints of indelicacy, often directed against *The Lady's Dressing Room*, were parried with the excuse that Swift's purpose was moral reform. By the beginning of the nineteenth century, accusations of triviality and indelicacy coalesced into the Romantic view that Swift's verses lacked sublimity and were therefore not poetry.

For readers from the eighteenth century to the twentieth, the most striking quality in Swift's verses has been their realism. Although Swift appeals memorably to all five senses, the dominant impression is pictorial vividness resulting from an abundance of concrete details, the pungent particulars of ordinary experience. As early as 1709, Richard Steele said of *A Description of the Morning* that instead of indulging in "fantastical Descriptions," the poet has "describ'd Things exactly as they happen: He never forms Fields, or Nymphs, or Groves, where they are not, but makes the Incidents just as they really appear." So unique are the details that the poem is not only "a Description of the Morning, but of the Morning in Town; nay, of the Morning at this End of the Town, where [the poet] at present lodges." Echoing Steele's words (if they were not written by Swift himself), Oliver Goldsmith praised Swift for depicting nature "just as it was, with all its deformities."[11] In the twentieth century, Swift's descriptions have reminded countless critics of the passionately squalid urban scenes in the early poems of T.S. Eliot. Swift's realism also appears in the uncanny skill with which his verse reproduces the qualities of everyday conversation. The poem invariably cited is Frances Harris's *Petition*, but his colloquial style is equally well illustrated by *Mary the Cook-Maid's Letter* and the card-playing passage in *Verses on the Death of Dr. Swift.*

An aspect of Swift's poetry that has drawn astonishingly favorable comments, from readers of varying critical sympathies over a span of three centuries, is the excellence of the verse. This is one feature Dr. Johnson chose for commendation, despite his inclination to dismiss Swift's poems as trivial. Praise is frequently lavished on the ingenuity of Swift's rhymes, his deft handling of meter, and the precision and appropriateness of his diction. Several critics, including Coleridge, pronounce his verse style "perfect," especially his rhymes. This extreme consciousness of Swift's craftsmanship, which for some readers extends to his ability to construct whole poems, is specially impressive because of circumstances that might have conspired to conceal it, such as the casualness of the style itself, the relatively little care Swift gave to the publication of his poems, and his pose of indifference toward them, as in his remark to a friend that "I have been only a Man of Rhimes, and that upon Trifles."[12]

A more elusive feature of Swift's verse, though often mentioned by critics, is its dramatic quality. Many of his poems, to be sure, are narratives that include characters, dialogue, and dramatic conflict. For a gesture of flamboyant theatricality, it would be difficult to match *Verses on the Death of Dr. Swift*. Still, those who discuss the point seem strangely unable to document their responses or to specify where Swift's dramatic quality resides— whether in the vivid concrete detail, in the tautness of the verse and its colloquial realism, or in narrative structure generally. All seem agreed that it involves the reader in an experience of "peculiar emotional intensity."[13] Writing in 1906, one critic saw this dramatic quality as Swift's sublimation of a thwarted drive toward Romantic lyricism that gives his verse "its only artistic value."[14] What these readers are responding to, one may conjecture, is Swift's skill at reader entrapment, which is a topic of current critical interest. A corollary feature, noted increasingly as the twentieth century proceeds, is the frequency with which Swift's dramatization is self-dramatization.

Surprisingly, in view of the fascination the Swift biography has long inspired, there was little awareness of the personal quality of his poems until F. Elrington Ball's book on *Swift's Verse* in 1929 and Sir Harold Williams's edition in 1937. Ball's words were widely quoted:

> Without knowledge of his verse a true picture of Swift cannot be drawn. In his verse he sets forth his life as a panorama, he shows more clearly than in his prose his peculiar turn of thought, and he reveals his character in all its phases from the most attractive to the most repellent. Before the testimony of his verse the work of many of his biographers cannot stand.[15]

Not yet suspected was the possibility that Swift might be projecting a semi-fictitious impression of his identity for rhetorical purposes. Ball's statement anticipates current interest in the "biographical presence" in Swift's poetry.

In the same year (1929) as Ball's recognition of its personal quality came one of the more ludicrous episodes in the criticism of Swift's poetry, the shocked reactions of D.H. Lawrence and Aldous Huxley to the "scatological" poems and what they saw as Swift's insane inability to accept the coarser functions of the human body. Similar views were repeated by John Middleton Murry in 1954. All three were scolded for their squeamishness by Norman O. Brown, who in 1959 advocated Swift's "excremental vision," the term Murry had coined, as a healthy Freudian attitude toward anality and sublimation. Answering Brown, Donald Greene in 1967 interpreted the "scatological" poems as a Christian rebuke to the sin of pride. Although it is difficult to imagine how a distinguished critic could be more wrong, the effect of Greene's essay was enormously salutary. One of the strongest efforts of a gifted controversialist, it simultaneously put amateur psychobiography in its place and restored the "scatological" poems to the rapidly swelling mainstream of criticism of Swift's poetry. The many subsequent discussions of these poems have concentrated upon typically literary concerns such as "outside" and "inside," the question of positives, the pattern of extremes without a mean, unreliable narrators, and "vexatious" satire.

Interest in Swift's poetry came with a rush during the decade of the 1960s. After barely a half-dozen critical discussions in the 1950s and no more than two or three in any preceding decade, dozens of essays appeared in the 1960s, followed by more than double that number in the 1970s. One welcome sign of a newly broadened response was a series of essays reasserting qualities that eighteenth-century readers had enjoyed in Swift's poetry, above all his humor.[16] If Swift is one of the gloomiest of the world's great poets, he is also the funniest. Any interpretation of his poems that ignores their humor runs a risk of serious distortion.

Just why the burst of interest should have come in the 1960s remains somewhat mysterious. Possibly it was stimulated by the publication of the Williams edition but artificially retarded by the Second World War. Certainly it gained impetus from the numerous volumes celebrating the tercentenary in 1967 of Swift's birth.[17] The affluence and expansionist mood of the academic profession during the 1960s must have made Swift's poetry attractive to younger scholars seeking topics for research: the Ph.D. dissertations of A.B. England, John Irwin Fischer, Jae Num Lee, Peter Schakel, Charles Scruggs, Barry Slepian, James Tyne, Robert Uphaus, and Charles Waller all date from the years 1962–1969. The principal cause, however, was probably the delayed impact of the New Criticism and allied forms of rhetorical analysis, which expended their energies during the 1950s on familiar areas like Swift's prose and then turned to the unexplored territory of his poetry.

Although slow in coming, the effect of the New Criticism was massively beneficial as well as maddeningly ambiguous. It took two directions, one of which was emphasis upon closer reading of the Swiftian text. A justly admired example is Charles Peake's analysis in 1962 of *A Satirical Elegy on the Death of a Late Famous General*. Peake achieves convincing results with Swift's precise, intricate language, but he is brought up short by the limitations of his method. "For exact discussion of those very aspects of poetry in which Swift excels," he concludes, "we may still lack adequate critical tools."[18] This was partly true, but the real trouble, paradoxically, may have been the other feature of the New Criticism, its conception of a work of literature as a "closed," autonomous structure, in contrast to the "open" forms usually used by Swift. The "closed," self-reflexive structures favored by the New Critics embody a circularity that makes their major themes and image-patterns easier to discern. Lacking this circularity, "open" forms require even more of Peake's kind of detailed analysis to bring out their structural disjunctions.

The New Criticism took Swift's poetry seriously and therefore collided in the mid-1960s with the notion that what Swift wrote was "anti-poetry." This notion, prevalent for the past fifty years, originated as a quiet protest against the Romantic designation of Swift's verse as non-poetry. Altered to "anti-poetry," by which was understood the realism of the verse, especially its use of coarse physical details for shock effect, the term was adopted as a slogan of approval—perhaps with the implication that "anti-poetry," something like antimatter, is not inferior to its opposite, merely different. The idea will not bear theoretical scrutiny, but it was rhetorically useful, and its prevalence registers the growing popularity of Swift's poetry, which gained in inverse proportion to the waning influence of the Romantic sensibility. Expressions of the "anti-poetry" position have come from Herbert Davis (1931), Ricardo Quintana (1936), Oswald Johnston (1962), Martin Battestin (1974), and in an attenuated and sophisticated form, Clive T. Probyn (1977).[19]

The incipient clash between the "anti-poetry" conception and the New-Critical demand for "whole" poems surfaced in 1965 in a curious article by E. San Juan, Jr., titled provocatively "The Anti-Poetry of Jonathan Swift." Recognizing, with the "anti-poetry" critics, "the extraordinary mass of details in Swift's poetry," San Juan went further to insist like a New Critic upon its "meaningful relationships" and "aesthetic pattern imposed on the discordant qualities."[20] The same dichotomy, between miscellaneous details and ordering pattern, was picked up by A.B. England the following year in his superb essay "World Without Order" and developed in a series of publications leading to his book in 1980, where the polarities of concrete and abstract, particular and general, matter and form are subsumed in the twin terms in his title, *Energy and Order in the Poetry of Swift.*[21] Probably the most notable critic of Swift's poetry during the past fifteen years, England emphasizes, as too few of his contemporaries have done, the characteristic "imbalance" between "energy" and "order" in most of Swift's poems. Significantly, the notion of "imbalance," which is an aspect of "open" form, challenges the very premises of the New Criticism which separate England from the "anti-poetry" position. The notion appears in a nearly legendary article published in 1970 by Gareth Jones, who maintains that proper reader response to *Cadenus and Vanessa* requires the balance to be tilted away from "positives" and "generalising abstraction" toward "the multiple and baffling particularities of experience." [22]

Another aspect of Swift's verse that has been invoked against the "anti-poetry" view is his use of allusion, which promises results as illuminating and ambiguous as the New Criticism but has not yet realized its potential. Taking allusion in a broad sense to include poetic conventions, this is the approach adopted by Geoffrey Hill (1968) and Robert Uphaus (1972), who argue that although Swift subverts these conventions, as the "anti-poetry" critics claimed, he returns them to traditional functions.[23] Besides Peter Schakel's book-length examination of Swift's classical, biblical, and contemporary allusions (1978), there have been brief studies of allusions in (to name only a few) the two *Description* poems, *Baucis and Philemon, Cadenus and Vanessa*, and of course the imitations of Horace. Even an "anti-poetry" critic like Oswald Johnston has contributed substantially to the subject.

If the net accomplishment of these many studies of allusions seems diffuse and inconclusive, the difficulty, as with attempts to apply the methodology of the New Criticism, may be an unexamined assumption that Swift uses "closed" structures. Allusion functions very differently in the "open" forms Swift actually employs. With a "closed" structure, the effect of allusion is convergent, tending toward integration of the elements of the literary work. With "open" form, the result is divergent, tending toward a multiplication of discontinuities—hence the oversimplified inference by the "anti-poetry" critics that Swift wished to destroy all conventions. Swift's techniques of allusion range from full-scale imitations, parodies, and fables down to the connotations of single words such as Charles Peake explored in *A Satirical Elegy*. Because it involves comparison, allusion is part of Swift's analogical technique, which includes his very striking metaphors.

Most of Swift's verse is occasional. This truism disturbed no one until the 1960s, when the New-Critical emphasis upon the essential autonomy of a work of art reminded readers that Swift's occasional poems are not self-contained. They were "stimulated by a specific occasion and planned in some way to change it," observed Edward Said in a timely article in 1969, adding that Swift's special purpose was to project his own personality into the future as a historical event.[24] This radically refined interpretation of the personal element in Swift's poetry, restated in 1971 in an influential essay by Maurice Johnson that labeled it Swift's "biographical presence," figures prominently in subsequent discussions by Robert Uphaus and Louise K. Barnett.[25] It is a noteworthy manifestation of the "sense of self" that currently engages much scholarly attention in eighteenth-century literature.

Having come so far so fast during the 1970s, in decidedly *avant-garde* directions, criticism of Swift's poetry seems likely to continue at a similar pace along similar lines. Little clue to the future, unfortunately, is provided by the essays in *Contemporary Studies of Swift's Poetry* (1980), which, despite the youth of most of the fifteen contributors, tend merely to reaffirm positions formulated earlier in the decade. At least five areas for future investigation can, however, be identified.

First, there are Swift's techniques of reader entrapment, which represent varieties of "open" form. The primary purpose of a work of entrapment is not to convey thematic content but to perplex, provoke, entice, manipulate, or otherwise trick the reader into a response whose intensity seems out of all proportion to its cause. In current investigations of these techniques, such as Richard Rodino's studies of Swift's "vexatious" satire, Swift is emerging as the all-time master of literary entrapment.[26] Besides the anticipations of the notion of entrapment in earlier discussions of the dramatic quality of Swift's poetry, including its "biographical presence," Padraic Colum in 1962 commented on its ability to elicit "audience participation."[27]

Second, more attention must be paid to the quality of asymmetry or, as England calls it, "imbalance" in Swift's poetry. Asymmetry is fundamental in Swift's writing, governing everything from large structures like the relationship of man to Lilliputian or Brobdingnagian down to the rhetorical arrangement of his style in prose and verse.

Third, asymmetry carries far-reaching philosophical overtones, for it implies a universe in which nothing really matches or is comparable to anything else. Here we can recognize the fundamental premise of twentieth-century Existentialism, namely that existence precedes essence, an insight first made explicit in modern times by Søren Kierkegaard more than a century after Swift. We have seen how the prose account of *A Description of the Morning*, which Swift himself must have written, insists upon the uniqueness not only "of the Morning, but of the Morning in Town; nay, of the Morning at this End of the Town, where [the poet] at present lodges." Such anticipation of a philosophical development in a literary work is not unparalleled. In the seventeenth century, the Cartesian dualism was preceded by nearly a half-century in *Don Quixote*, which dramatizes the dichotomy of thought and extension in the dilemma of whether a giant is merely a windmill, a castle merely an inn, or Dulcinea merely the peasant girl Aldonza Lorenzo.

These three considerations lead to a fourth area that should reward future investigation, Swift's analogical technique. His use of analogy, which takes many forms, is best illustrated by his wildly asymmetrical metaphors, as in *A Tale of a Tub* or, to cite just one poem, *The Progress of Beauty*. The technique may involve "literalization of metaphor," in which the vehicle overwhelms the tenor and usurps its function. A distant descendant of the Renaissance doctrine of "correspondences" gone awry, Swift's analogical technique conveys his amused view of a world that simultaneously does and does not make sense. To the extent that his skewed metaphors are plausible, they imply meaningful relationships in the universe; to the extent that they strain credibility, they deny such meaning.

The ambiguity of Swift's analogical technique, teetering between meaning and non-meaning, truth and falsehood, faith and doubt, virtually defines a fifth area that should clarify his philosophical stance: the Absurd, whether in a twentieth-century sense or that of Erasmus. In practical terms, the Absurd means observing the imperfect rules, routines, conventions, rituals, institutions, and other game-like activities of daily life as if one believed they were true, even with the knowledge that in any ultimate sense they do not exist and may at any moment collapse into hilarious ruin. The Absurd requires awareness of three cosmic realities: Nothing, the Finite, and the Infinite. For the Christian Absurdist, the Finite, though ultimately Nothing, offers the only access to the Infinite. For the atheistic Absurdist or existentialist, all possible meaning is confined to the Finite.

Concepts of the Absurd may help to explain two partially

extra-literary aspects of Swift's poetry, his social and religious views, that are glaringly absent from the foregoing account.[28] For an age whose first concern was man in society, this prominent element in Swift's verse has attracted amazingly little comment. Almost every poem he wrote has a social dimension. His portrayal of the Absurd in social usages, as in *Cadenus and Vanessa* and *The Journal of a Modern Lady*, is scarcely outdone even by Pope. The Absurd subtly pervades the poems he wrote after 1720 for his Irish friends, which are surely the finest things of their kind anywhere in literature. A start on Swift's social verse has been made by David Sheehan, in his Ph.D. dissertation and in an article on raillery in the poems to Stella.[29]

Swift's religious views remain as enigmatic in his verse as in his prose. Among the recent books on his poetry, Fischer's is a thoroughgoing Christian interpretation, whereas England's is resolutely secular. The answer to the riddle may lie in the Christian Absurd, which combines amused skepticism toward the Finite with tacit faith in the Infinite. Like Kierkegaard, Swift may have preferred to keep his "leap of faith" a matter of silence. Or, writing as a sincere Anglican clergyman in a partly secularized age, Swift in works like *Gulliver's Travels* may have felt obliged to choose a secular envelope for attitudes that are compatible with Christianity—a secular vehicle for a religious tenor, in terms of his analogical technique, with the whole of *Gulliver* an extended "literalization of metaphor." The currently fashionable notion of "indeterminacy" may be apt: Swift's poems at their best may be designed to tolerate both a secular and a much richer Christian reading. For comparable cases, we may have to go to the *Encomium Moriae* or to *Fear and Trembling*.

Carbondale, Illinois
July 1981
Revised May 1982

NOTES

1. Items 52 and 54 in the bibliography.

2. The five papers from this Special Session were printed together in *Papers on Language and Literature* (see item 118) and reprinted in *Contemporary Studies of Swift's Poetry* (see item 68).

3. Letter dated 22 January 1976; permission to publish granted in a letter dated 25 May 1976.

4. Items 47A, 62, 69, 78, 105, and see 68. A completed book-length manuscript by David Sheehan, on Swift's social verse, is in the hands of readers. A delay in the publication of this bibliography has permitted me to list the Barnett volume, the Clark Library lectures by Robert C. Elliott and Arthur H. Scouten (see items 61A, 91A, 105A), and several reviews of recent books.

5. A similar, though independent and much briefer account of the reputation of Swift's verse over the past two centuries is provided by Arthur H. Scouten in the concluding pages of his paper "Jonathan Swift's Progress from Prose to Poetry," read at the Clark Library Seminar on 20 January 1979 (see item 105A). Scouten calls attention to forward-looking remarks about Swift's poetry during the mid-1920s by the left-wing journalist Edgell Rickword, an author I did not consider important enough to include in my bibliography.

6. See items 1, 3, 10, 16.

7. See items 19, 249, 337, 413, 426.

8. Both editions are announced in item 19, which describes the Delaware project somewhat inaccurately.

9. Quoted from the Introduction to the Williams edition (item 16), p. xxxiv.

10. Quoted from Kathleen Williams's useful compilation *Swift: The Critical Heritage* (item 490), p. 203, from which and from the similar survey by Donald M. Berwick (item 434), much of the information in this and the surrounding paragraphs is taken.

11. These remarks, whether by Swift or Steele, introduce the poem in *The Tatler*, no. 9. Goldsmith is quoted from the section of Critical Comments in Horrell's edition (item 10), p. liv.

12. Quoted from the Williams edition of Swift's correspondence (item 488), 4:52.

13. The phrase is quoted from F.R. Leavis's essay "The Irony of Swift," which does not deal specifically with Swift's poetry but influenced many younger critics represented in this bibliography, especially those who have written on Swift's "vexatious" satire. Published in 1934, it is reprinted in *Swift: A Collection of Critical Essays*, ed. Ernest Tuveson (Englewood Cliffs, NJ: Prentice-Hall, 1964), pp. 15–29. Another writer who has exercised similar influence upon younger critics is Claude Rawson.

14. Mary Suddard, item 110, p. 245. I have relied heavily on this essay, which is an admirably sensitive and articulate enumeration of attitudes toward Swift's poetry at the beginning of the twentieth century.

15. Item 45, p. viii.

16. Items 51, 58, 75, 88.

17. Also, the first two volumes of the Ehrenpreis biography were published in 1962 and 1967.

18. Item 378, p. 88.

19. Items 57, 83, 95, 315, 384.

20. Item 104, p. 389. I say "curious" because San Juan seems to lack the courage of his convictions, which include a fleeting recognition of Swift's "open" form. Remarking that a typical Swift poem "effects a synthesis of disparities," he adds that "as a rule the resolution of attitudes remains manifold, inexhaustible, and susceptible of limitless interpretations" (pp. 388–89).

21. Items 62, 63, 64, 130, 131, 170.

22. Item 172, p. 248.

23. Items 73 and 115. This argument was anticipated forty years earlier by Herbert Read in item 98.

24. Item 275, p. 51.

25. Items 46, 82, 114, 283.

26. See especially item 238.

27. Items 2, 52, 54.

28. Also absent are the many discussions of Swift's attitudes toward women, which generally reveal more about their authors than about Swift.

29. Items 185, 560.

BIBLIOGRAPHY

I. EDITIONS OF SWIFT'S POEMS

1. Browning, William Ernst. *The Poems of Jonathan Swift,*
   D.D. Bohn Standard Library. 2 vols. London: G. Bell
   and Sons, 1910. Pp. xxii + 351; xiv + 415.

   Reviewed in *The Living Age*, vol. 266, no. 3453 (10 September 1910): 670-74 (see item 44).

   Browning's two volumes remained the standard edition of
   Swift's poetry from their publication in 1910 until they
   were totally superseded by the Sir Harold Williams edition
   in 1937 (see item 16).

2. Colum, Padraic, ed. *The Poems of Jonathan Swift*. New
   York: Collier Books; London: Collier-Macmillan, 1962.
   Pp. 126.

   Intended for the common reader, this inexpensive paper-
   back reprints forty of Swift's poems. Explanatory notes
   are not provided. In his concise, provocative critical
   introduction, Colum emphasizes salient features of the
   verse, such as Swift's ability to elicit audience participation and to project his own personality.

3. Davis, Herbert, ed. *Swift: Poetical Works*. Oxford
   Standard Authors. London: Oxford University Press,
   1967. Pp. xxx + 682.

   Reviewed in *London Times Literary Supplement*, 21 December 1967, p. 1237; by Maurice Johnson in *The Scriblerian*,
   vol. 1, no. 1 (Autumn 1968): 27-28; by W.A. Speck in
   Notes and Queries 214 (October 1969): 395-98.

   Based on the definitive edition of the poems by Sir
   Harold Williams (see item 16), Davis's edition provides
   a handsome single-volume "reading" text in contrast to
   Williams's somewhat cumbersome three-volume format.
   Omitted are Williams's detailed textual apparatus, his
   headnotes and explanatory footnotes except those approved
   by Swift himself, and a few poems such as some of the

Trifles. Balancing these omissions are compensating
benefits. The poems are printed in order of their composition as nearly as this can be ascertained, a useful
alternative to Williams's arrangement. From Williams's
textual apparatus, later corrections by Swift himself are
incorporated directly into the text. Indeed, substantive
variants were incorporated at the last minute from the
uncancelled copy of Volume II of Faulkner's 1735 edition
described by Margaret Weedon (see item 33). Because of
the Siamese-twin relationship between the Davis and
Williams editions, students of Swift's poetry should
always consult both.

4. Daw, C.P., introductory note by. *Jonathan Swift, "Miscel-*
   lanies in Prose and Verse," 1711. Menston, Yorkshire,
   Eng.: Scolar Press, 1972. Pp. 416.

   A photographic facsimile of the 1711 edition of the
   Miscellanies, which contains many of Swift's best-known
   poems written during 1698-1710.

5. Eddy, William Alfred, ed. *Satires and Personal Writings*
   by Jonathan Swift. Oxford Standard Edition. New York
   and London: Oxford University Press, 1933, pp. 449-95.

   Reprints sixteen poems, with minimal explanatory notes.
   Some amusingly outdated criticism of Swift's verse can be
   found in Eddy's introduction (pp. xx-xxii) and on p. 450.

6. Greenberg, Robert A., and William Bowman Piper, eds.
   The Writings of Jonathan Swift: Authoritative Texts,
   Backgrounds, Criticism. Norton Critical Editions. New
   York: Norton, 1973, pp. 511-79.

   Reprints twenty poems, with a notably good representation of the "scatological" poems. Other works selected
   include *Verses on the Death of Dr. Swift* and *On Poetry:*
   A Rapsody but not *Cadenus and Vanessa.* Though guided by
   the Sir Harold Williams edition (see item 16), which preferred manuscripts and the earliest printed versions as a
   basis for copy-text, the careful, sensible textual procedures in this volume tend instead to favor Faulkner's
   edition of 1735. Explanatory material, provided in footnotes, is minimal but helpful.

7. Hayward, John, ed. *Gulliver's Travels and Selected*
   Writings in Prose and Verse. London: Nonesuch Press;
   New York: Random House, 1934, pp. 739-824, 858-68.

   Includes fifteen of Swift's poems, the majority of
   which "have been reprinted from the volumes in which they

first appeared" (p. 746). Also included are an "Introduction to the Poems," mostly bibliographical and biographical, a "Note on the Text of the Poems," and textual
notes. Explanatory notes are limited to those provided
by Swift himself.

8. Heath-Stubbs, John, ed. *A Selection of Poems by Jonathan
    Swift*. London: Grey Walls Press, 1948. Pp. 64.

    Reprints all or part of twenty-seven of Swift's poems.
    Heath-Stubbs provides an introduction but no explanatory
    notes.

9. Horne, Colin J., ed. *Swift on His Age: Selected Prose
    and Verse*. Life, Literature, and Thought Library.
    New York: Barnes and Noble; London: Harrap, 1953.
    Pp. 283.

    Reprints twelve poems from Faulkner's editions of
    1734-1735 and later. Horne's introduction is historical,
    biographical, and critical. Explanatory notes and a
    select bibliography are placed at the back of the volume.

10. Horrell, Joseph, ed. *Collected Poems of Jonathan Swift*.
    The Muses' Library. 2 vols. London: Routledge and
    Kegan Paul; Cambridge: Harvard University Press, 1958.
    Pp. lxvi + 401; xi + 403-818.

    Reviewed by James Reeves in *Time and Tide*, 17 May 1958,
    p. 618; in *London Times Literary Supplement*, 30 May
    1958, pp. 302-03; by John Raymond in *New Statesman*,
    vol. 55, no. 1421 (7 June 1958): 735-36 (see item 97);
    in *The Listener*, vol. 60, no. 1529 (17 July 1958): 98;
    by Marius Bewley in *The Spectator*, 29 August 1958, pp.
    283-84 (see item 48); by Maurice Johnson in *Philological
    Quarterly* 38 (July 1959): 354; by Ralph M. Williams in
    College English 22 (October 1960): 57; by Hannah Buchan
    in *Review of English Studies* n.s. 12 (February 1961):
    88-89.

    Horrell's two volumes are the most ambitious attempt
    thus far to provide an edition of all of Swift's poetry
    at a reasonable price. Although not a specially signifi-
    cant contribution to the study of Swift's text, Horrell's
    edition reprints, from early sources, all the poems he
    regards as authentic. Following the Sir Harold Williams
    edition (see item 16) in matters of the canon, Horrell
    uses as copy-texts the Faulkner edition of 1746 and
    other eighteenth-century collections. His preliminary
    matter includes a biographical and critical introduction,
    with a note on canon and text; a select bibliography;
    and a section of critical comments. Since few editions

of Swift's poetry provide adequate explanatory notes,
Horrell's notes at the back of each of his volumes are
helpful. A possibly objectionable feature is the arrangement of the poems, not in chronological order, but according to "kind" or subject matter.

11. Pollard, Arthur, ed. *Silver Poets of the Eighteenth
     Century*. London: Dent; Totowa, NJ: Rowman and Little-
     field, 1976, pp. 1-63.

     Reprints fourteen of Swift's poems from the Sir
     Harold Williams and Herbert Davis editions (see items
     16, 3) or "the most reliable text deriving from or near
     the poet's own time" (p. xix). The Introduction includes
     brief remarks on the poems and a Note on Texts. Explana-
     tory notes are placed at the back of the volume.

12. Reeves, James, ed. *Selected Poems of Jonathan Swift*.
     The Poetry Bookshelf. London: Heinemann; New York:
     Barnes and Noble, 1967. Pp. vi + 146.

     Reviewed by Philip Roberts in *Notes and Queries* 213
     (June 1968): 231-32.

     Reprints twenty-eight of Swift's poems from the Sir
     Harold Williams edition (see item 16). Reeves provides
     a biographical and critical introduction. Explanatory
     notes are placed at the back of the volume.

13. Roberts, R[ichard] Ellis, ed. *Miscellaneous Poems by
     Jonathan Swift, D.D., Dean of Saint Patrick's Cathe-
     dral, Dublin*. Decorated with engravings on wood by
     Robert Gibbings. London: Golden Cockerel Press,
     1928. Pp. viii + 69. (Edition limited to 375 copies.)

     Reprints thirty-four poems from the Reverend John
     Mitford's edition of 1833. No explanatory notes are
     provided. The introduction, which includes some criti-
     cism of Swift's poetry, is identical with the latter
     half of Roberts's essay "Jonathan Swift in his Poems and
     Minor Writings" (see item 101).

14. Sisson, C.H., ed. *Jonathan Swift: Selected Poems*.
     Manchester: Carcanet, Fyfield Books, 1977. Pp. 91.
     Reprint. 1979.

     Reviewed by Merritt Eugene Lawlis in *Journal of English
     and Germanic Philology* 80 (January 1981): 138-40.

     Reprints forty-one of Swift's poems, without explana-
     tory notes. Sisson provides an introduction, mostly

biographical, a portion of which appears in his essay
"The Early Poems of Jonathan Swift" (see item 148), and
which is reprinted in his volume of collected essays,
The Avoidance of Literature (see item 403).

15. Tillotson, Geoffrey, Paul Fussell, Jr., and Marshall
    Waingrow, eds. *Eighteenth-Century English Literature*.
    New York: Harcourt, Brace, and World, 1969, pp. 359-
    404.

    This anthology reprints a generous selection of fifteen
    poems, including longer works such as *Cadenus and Vanessa*,
    Directions for a Birth-day Song, *Verses on the Death of
    Dr. Swift*, and *On Poetry: A Rapsody*. Although guided in
    some measure by the Sir Harold Williams edition (see item
    16), textual procedures involved the independent consulta-
    tion of eighteenth-century sources, with the first edi-
    tion generally chosen as copy-text and with accidentals
    preserved. Explanatory material is provided in headnotes
    and footnotes.

16. Williams, Harold, ed. *The Poems of Jonathan Swift*. 3
    vols. Oxford: Clarendon Press, 1937. Pp. lxii + 354;
    xii + 357-766; vii + 769-1242. 2d ed. (rev.). 1958.

    Reviewed in *London Times Literary Supplement*, 21 August
    1937, pp. 597-98; by Stephen Potter in *The London
    Mercury*, vol. 36, no. 215 (September 1937): 477-78;
    by M.J. MacManus in *The Dublin Magazine*, vol. 12, no. 4
    (October-December 1937): 52-54; by Lord Rothschild in
    The Cambridge Review 59 (3 December 1937): 147-48; by
    Shane Leslie in *The Nineteenth Century and After* 122
    (1937): 495-96; by Herbert Davis in *Modern Philology*
    35 (February 1938): 335-38; by Robert K. Root in *Philo-
    logical Quarterly* 17 (April 1938): 206-07; by E. Pons
    in *Études Anglaises* 2 (October-December 1938): 404-07;
    by Frederick A. Pottle in *Yale Review* 27 (1938): 427-
    29; by A.L. Rowse in *The Criterion* 17 (1938): 305-11
    (see also item 103); by Ricardo Quintana in *Modern
    Language Notes* 54 (January 1939): 59-61; by Max A. Korn
    in *Beiblatt zur Anglia* 50 (February 1939): 52-54; by
    John Sparrow in *Review of English Studies* 15 (April
    1939): 225-29; by James R. Sutherland in *Modern Language
    Review* 34 (April 1939): 264-66; by Paul Meissner in
    Englische Studien 73 (1939): 285-87; by Irvin Ehren-
    preis in *Modern Language Review* 54 (April 1959): 260-
    61; by Helmut Papajewski in *Anglia* 79 (1961/62): 504-
    05; by Mario Praz in *English Studies* 44 (February 1963):
    55-57.

Since its publication in 1937, and especially in the
revised second edition of 1958, Sir Harold Williams's
three volumes have remained the standard edition of
Swift's poetry, although Herbert Davis's more recent
Clarendon Press volume should also be consulted (see item
3). Williams's monumental achievement made intelligent
criticism of Swift's poetry for the first time possible
on an extended scale. From out of the approximately 400
poems which have been attributed to Swift, Williams prints
some 250 as genuine. For the poems omitted, the section
of notes on "Poems Attributed to Swift" (pp. 1053-1154)
is an indispensable source of information. Careful
scrutiny of manuscripts and early printed editions enabled
Williams to improve the text in some instances. Wherever
possible, the date and other circumstances surrounding
the composition and publication of a poem are specified
in a headnote. Proper names and unfamiliar terms are
explained in footnotes, although it must be recognized
that Williams's relatively light annotation is perhaps
the weakest feature of his editorial labors.

See also items 183, 254.

II. BIBLIOGRAPHY

A. Concordance

17. Shinagel, Michael. *A Concordance to the Poems of
     Jonathan Swift*. Ithaca and London: Cornell University
     Press, 1972. Pp. xxiii + 977.

     Reviewed by Paul J. Korshin in *Computers and the
     Humanities* 7 (1972-73): 219-20; George P. Mayhew in
     The Scriblerian, vol. 5, no. 2 (Spring 1973): 100-01.
     This computerized concordance to Swift's poems, ninth
     in the series of Cornell Concordances under the general
     editorship of Stephen M. Parrish, is based on the standard
     three-volume edition by Sir Harold Williams, second edi-
     tion, 1958 (see item 16). Shinagel's volume consists of
     three parts: a Preface, which includes a list of very
     common words omitted, together with their frequencies;
     the Concordance proper; and, as an Appendix, a list of
     the index words in order of their frequency. The disad-
     vantage of choosing the Williams edition as base text is
     that it includes some works of doubtful authenticity, a
     difficulty that could have been avoided by using instead
     the more convenient, as well as more recent (1967),
     single-volume edition by Herbert Davis (see item 3).

B. Primary Bibliography

18. Davis, Herbert. "Remarks on Some Swift Manuscripts in
     the United States." *Jonathan Swift: A List of Critical
     Studies Published from 1895 to 1945*. Compiled by Louis
     A. Landa and James Edward Tobin. New York: Cosmopolitan
     Science and Art Service Co., 1945, pp. 7-16. Reprint.
     New York: Octagon Books, 1974.

Lists manuscripts of poems by or relating to Swift in the Huntington and Pierpont Morgan Libraries. A footnote (p. 8) identifies additional poetical manuscripts included in an exhibition at Cambridge University (see item 23).

19. Downie, J.A. "Editor Extraordinaire." *The Scriblerian*, vol. 13, no. 1 (Autumn 1980): 2-4.

   This reappraisal of Sir Harold Williams as a scholar notes deficiencies in his edition of Swift's poems (see item 16). Williams's annotation is inadequate and occasionally incorrect. Transcriptions from manuscripts are not always reliable, a problem that became more acute as Williams's eyesight weakened during his later years. Downie calls attention to Pat Rogers's new Penguin edition of the poems and, somewhat inaccurately, to the multi-volume set now in preparation by James Woolley, John Irwin Fischer, and Donald C. Mell.

20. Dustin, John E. "The 1735 Dublin Edition of Swift's 'Poems.'" *Papers of the Bibliographical Society of America* 54 (First Quarter 1960): 57-60.

   Irregularities in the last two-thirds of Faulkner's 1735 edition of Swift's *Poetical Works*, especially the numerous cancels, cast doubt on the accuracy of the dates which were supplied for some poems by the printer.

21. Friends of the Library of Trinity College, Dublin. *Catalogue of the Exhibition held in the Library from October 19 to November 23, 1945 to Commemorate the Bicentenary of the Death of Jonathan Swift.* Dublin: Printed at the University Press by Ponsonby and Gibbs, 1945. Pp. 16.

   Many of the items listed are poems.

22. *Guide to Literary Manuscripts in the Huntington Library.* San Marino, CA: Huntington Library, 1979, pp. 449-50.

   Indexed alphabetically by author. The Huntington is among the world's leading repositories of manuscripts of Swift's poems.

23. [Hayward, John, comp.] *A Catalogue of Printed Books and Manuscripts, By Jonathan Swift, D.D. Exhibited in the Old Schools in the University of Cambridge. To Commemorate the 200th Anniversary of his Death, October 19, 1745.* Cambridge: At the University Press, 1945. Pp. 45.

   Many of the items listed are poems.

24. Jackson, W. Spencer, comp. "Bibliography of the Writings of Jonathan Swift." *The Prose Works of Jonathan Swift.* Edited by Temple Scott. 12 vols. London: G. Bell and Sons, 1900-1914, 12:107-241.

    This bibliography lists items chronologically from 1700 to 1808, without attempting to classify them. It was superseded in 1937 by the Teerink bibliography (see item 31).

25. Leslie, Shane. "The Script of Jonathan Swift." *The Script of Jonathan Swift and Other Essays.* Philadelphia: University of Pennsylvania Press, 1935, pp. 1-21.

    Includes discussion of the manuscripts of Swift's poems in relation to the difficulty of establishing the canon.

26. Leslie, Sir Shane. "The Swift Manuscripts in the Morgan Library." *Studies in Art and Literature for Belle da Costa Greene.* Edited by Dorothy Miner. Princeton: Princeton University Press, 1954, pp. 445-48.

    Discusses the Morgan Library manuscripts of *Vanbrug's House* (1703) and the later version *The History of Vanbrug's House* (1706); *The Discovery*; *Stella at Wood-Park* (*Stella's Distress*); *Apollo to the Dean* (*Apollo, to Dean Swift*), one page of which is reproduced photographically; and *Baucis and Philemon*.

27. Mayhew, George P. "The Swift Manuscripts at the Huntington Library" and Appendix, "A Brief Description of the Swift Manuscripts at the Huntington Library." *Rage or Raillery: The Swift Manuscripts at the Huntington Library.* San Marino, CA: Huntington Library, 1967, pp. 3-25, 157-83.

    The Swift manuscripts at the Huntington Library include important poetical manuscripts, both holograph and in other hands.

28. Schulz, H.C. "English Literary Manuscripts in the Huntington Library." *Huntington Library Quarterly* 31 (May 1968): 251-302.

    The section on Swift lists manuscripts of more than a dozen poems in the Huntington Library.

29. Sherburn, George. "The Swift-Pope *Miscellanies* of 1732." *Harvard Library Bulletin* 6 (Autumn 1952): 387-90.

    A document in Swift's hand, now in the Harvard College Library, helps to clarify the proceedings surrounding the

publication in 1732 of the final volume of the Swift-Pope
Miscellanies, which includes ten poems by Swift. In this
document, printed in full by Sherburn, Swift assigns the
rights in several unnamed works to Matthew Pilkington,
who intends to give them up to William Bowyer. (The
volume was published, not by Bowyer, but by Benjamin Motte
and Lawton Gilliver.) See item 30.

30. Sherburn, George. "The Swift-Pope *Miscellanies* of 1732:
     Corrigendum." *Harvard Library Bulletin* 7 (Spring 1953):
     248.

     Sherburn concedes that the document in Swift's hand
     reproduced in item 29 was not "hitherto unknown," as
     claimed, but had been published both by John Nichols and
     by Sir Walter Scott. Sherburn's conclusions are not
     otherwise affected.

31. Teerink, H., comp. *A Bibliography of the Writings in
     Prose and Verse of Jonathan Swift, D.D.* The Hague:
     Martinus Nijhoff, 1937. Pp. xi + 434. 2d ed., rev.
     A Bibliography of the Writings of Jonathan Swift.
     Second Edition, Revised and Corrected by Dr. H. Teerink.
     Edited by Arthur H. Scouten. Philadelphia: University
     of Pennsylvania Press, 1963. Pp. xviii + 453.

     Although amateurish in many respects, even in the much-
     revised second edition by Teerink and Scouten, this book
     remains the standard bibliography of Swift's own works
     including his poems. As originally published, the Teerink
     bibliography was sharply criticized for the confused,
     overlapping categories adopted in arranging entries, for
     the absence of full bibliographical descriptions, and for
     failure to distinguish adequately between genuine and
     spurious items. The revised edition, while essentially
     retaining some features such as the numbering of the
     entries, corrects the deficiencies of the original as far
     as possible by, for example, supplying full bibliographi-
     cal descriptions.

32. Thompson, Paul Vern. "The Canon of Swift, 1674-1714."
     *Summaries of Doctoral Dissertations, Northwestern
     University* 5 (1937): 29-33.

     Thompson's dissertation includes a study of the
     authenticity of poems ascribed to Swift and written before
     the death of Queen Anne in 1714. See item 568.

33. Weedon, Margaret. "An Uncancelled Copy of the First
    Collected Edition of Swift's Poems." *The Library*, 5th
    ser., 22 (March 1967): 44-56.

    A set of George Faulkner's 1735 edition of Swift's
    collected writings, now in the English Faculty Library
    at Oxford, preserves Volume II in the uncancelled state.
    The original versions of the cancelled poems, including
    five poems which were completely left out, reveal that
    Swift's textual revisions and other alterations while
    the volume was in press were very drastic indeed.

34. Weitzman, Arthur J. "Addendum to Teerink and Scouten:
    Another Edition of Swift's Poems." *Papers of the
    Bibliographical Society of America* 67 (First Quarter
    1973): 62-64.

    Bound together with two unrelated duodecimo editions
    in a copy in the Boston Athenaeum is a 1731 edition,
    unmentioned in the Teerink-Scouten bibliography (see item
    31), of three of Swift's poems: *Cadenus and Vanessa*,
    Baucis and Philemon, and *The Journal of a Modern Lady*.
    The first two poems follow the text of the 1727 *Miscel-
    lanies*; the *Journal* differs from the original Dublin
    printing of 1728 but agrees with later editions. The
    collection is probably pirated or at least unauthorized.

35. Wiley, Autrey Nell, comp. *Jonathan Swift, 1667-1745:
    An Exhibition of Printed Books at The University of
    Texas, October 19-December 31, 1945.*

    Many of the items listed are poems.

36. Williams, Harold. "Swift: Miscellanies in Prose and
    Verse. Second Edition. 1713." *Bibliographical Notes
    and Queries*, vol. 2, no. 11 (November 1938): 10.

    Points out that the "second edition," 1713, of Swift's
    Miscellanies in Prose and Verse, which includes many of
    his early poems, consists of two wholly different print-
    ings, set in different fonts from end to end. One of
    the two 1713 editions was set from the first edition,
    1711, and then served as copy-text for the other.

See also items 45, 128, 139, 144, 177, 178, 194, 207, 249,
252, 254, 255, 263, 268, 277, 278, 281, 282, 292-296, 300,
301, 302, 304, 305, 307, 308, 311-314, 316, 317, 319, 320,
324, 326, 330, 334, 335, 337, 338, 341, 343, 346, 347, 350,
353, 355, 357, 359, 360, 362-368, 372, 373, 375, 376, 377,
379, 380, 383, 394, 397, 398, 400, 401, 404, 406, 407, 408,
413-429, 456, 459, 482, 489, 549, 562, 568.

C. Secondary Bibliography

37. Lamont, Claire, comp. "A Checklist of Critical and
     Biographical Writings on Jonathan Swift, 1945-65."
     *Fair Liberty Was All His Cry: A Tercentenary Tribute to
     Jonathan Swift 1667-1745.* Edited by A. Norman Jeffares.
     London: Macmillan; New York: St. Martin's Press, 1967,
     pp. 356-91.

     Covering the same twenty-one years as the bibliography
     by Stathis (see item 42), this checklist is similarly
     designed to supplement the earlier bibliography by Landa
     and Tobin (see item 38). Unlike Stathis, who classifies
     his entries under six major categories, Lamont arranges
     hers chronologically by year of publication. The use-
     fulness of Lamont's otherwise commendable checklist is
     limited by the absence of any annotation from most
     entries, so that a reader often cannot tell whether they
     relate to Swift's poetry or some other aspect of his
     career.

38. Landa, Louis A., and James Edward Tobin, comps.
     *Jonathan Swift: A List of Critical Studies Published
     from 1895 to 1945. To Which Is Added Remarks on Some
     Swift Manuscripts in the United States by Herbert Davis.*
     New York: Cosmopolitan Science and Art Service Co.,
     1945, pp. 51-53. Reprint. New York: Octagon Books,
     1974.

     The Landa-Tobin bibliography has hitherto been an in-
     dispensable source of information on studies of Swift's
     poetry published up to 1945. Nevertheless, the section
     on the poetry totals only fifty-one entries, including
     fourteen cross-referenced from other sections, and many
     of these are minor or tangential. The volume's usefulness
     is further reduced because it technically covers only
     critical studies (although the limitation is interpreted
     generously) and because it is a checklist rather than an
     annotated bibliography. Entries in each section are
     arranged alphabetically by authors' names.

39. Quintana, Ricardo. "A Modest Appraisal: Swift Scholar-
     ship and Criticism, 1945-65." *Fair Liberty Was All His
     Cry: A Tercentenary Tribute to Jonathan Swift 1667-1745.*
     Edited by A. Norman Jeffares. London: Macmillan; New
     York: St. Martin's Press, 1967, pp. 342-55.

     Lists the one book and seven articles that Quintana con-
     siders the best criticism published on Swift's poetry from

1945 to 1965. Although "far less has been done on the verse than on *Gulliver's Travels* and *A Tale of a Tub*," a "marked shift in opinion has occurred" in favor of Swift's poetry, and "the criticism which has appeared has been generally of a high order."

40. Schakel, Peter. "A Brief Bibliography of Recent Swift Studies." *Johnson Society of the Central Region: News Letter* (edited by Howard Weinbrot), March 1980, pp. 3-4.

Noting that nearly a hundred considerations of Swift's poetry--books, articles, dissertations, and a concordance-- have appeared since 1971, this well-informed review singles out more than thirty of the best. The most concentrated source of critical activity has been a series of MLA seminars first organized by David M. Vieth. *Verses on the Death of Dr. Swift* and the "scatological" poems have attracted almost an industry on their own.

41. Schakel, Peter J. Review of James J. Stathis, *A Bibliography of Swift Studies 1945-1965* (1967). *Philological Quarterly* 47 (July 1968): 436-38. Reprint. *English Literature 1660-1800: A Bibliography of Modern Studies*. Compiled by Curt A. Zimansky *et al.* Vol. 6 (1966-1970). Princeton: Princeton University Press, 1972, pp. 932-34.

This mostly favorable review includes a supplementary list of items omitted from the Stathis bibliography (see item 42).

42. Stathis, James J., comp. *A Bibliography of Swift Studies 1945-1965*. Nashville, TN: Vanderbilt University Press, 1967, pp. 55-61.

Reviewed by Hilbert H. Campbell in *Papers of the Bibliographical Society of America* 61 (Fourth Quarter 1967): 392-93. See also item 41.

An indispensable supplement to the earlier bibliography by Landa and Tobin (see item 38), Stathis's volume differs in scope from its predecessor by including all types of studies instead of merely criticism. The section on Swift's poetry, one of Stathis's six major divisions, lists entries alphabetically by authors' names--differing in this regard from the duplicating Lamont checklist, which groups entries chronologically by year of publication (see item 37). Even though Stathis's section on the poetry numbers only about eighty entries, including nearly forty items cross-referenced from other sections, a disconcerting number of these items have only a tangential

bearing on the poems. Also, useful though Stathis's
annotations are, they are usually brief and too often do
not indicate clearly which poems are covered in a particular item. The only index, of authors, provides no
further assistance in locating specific poems.

43. Voigt, Milton. *Swift and the Twentieth Century*. Detroit:
     Wayne State University Press, 1964, pp. 44-48.

     For Swift's poems, Voigt's survey of twentieth-century
     scholarship and criticism is of slight assistance because
     studies of the poetry have been almost wholly excluded
     in favor of concentration on studies of *A Tale of a Tub*,
     Gulliver's Travels, and the biography. Nevertheless,
     Voigt carefully evaluates Sir Harold Williams's edition
     of the poems and studies of the canon by Ball, Davis,
     Gulick, and Ehrenpreis (see items 16, 45, 263, 292, 139).

See also items 228, 517.

III. GENERAL STUDIES OF THE POETRY

44. Anonymous. "Swift's Poems." *The Living Age*, vol. 266,
     no. 3453 (10 September 1910): 670-74.

     Ostensibly a review of William Ernst Browning's edition
     (see item 1), about which it says almost nothing, this
     anonymous essay denounces Swift for not writing Romantic
     poetry like that of Keats and Shelley. Only one poem,
     Cadenus and Vanessa, receives high commendation for por-
     traying a beautiful girl's sincere love for "old, dis-
     illusioned, chilly Cadenus."

45. Ball, F. Elrington. *Swift's Verse: An Essay*. London:
     John Murray, 1929. Pp. xv + 402. Reprint. New York:
     Octagon Books, 1970.

     Reviewed in *Notes and Queries* 156 (16 February 1929):
     125-26; in *Philological Quarterly* 9 (1930): 207-08; by
     Emile Pons in *Revue Anglo-Américaine* 7 (1930): 343-45.

     Ball's volume, which was complete except for the index
     at the time of his death in January 1928, was seen through
     the press by E.M. Walker assisted by D. Nichol Smith and
     Harold Williams. Consisting essentially of prolegomena
     for an edition of Swift's verse, its principal concern is
     to establish the canon of the poems. It also represents
     the first real attempt to arrange the poems in chronologi-
     cal order, locate them in the context of Swift's biography,
     and illustrate the development of Swift's characteristic
     style.

46. Barnett, Louise K. "Fictive Self-Portraiture in Swift's
     Poetry." *Contemporary Studies of Swift's Poetry*.
     Edited by John Irwin Fischer and Donald C. Mell, Jr.,
     with David M. Vieth, associate editor. Newark: Univer-
     sity of Delaware Press; London and Toronto: Associated
     University Presses, 1980, pp. 101-11.

     Barnett amplifies the "biographical presence" approach
     associated with Maurice Johnson (see item 82). Unlike

Pope, whose first-person speakers consistently serve to
convey a satirical ethos ("the strong antipathy of good
to bad"), Swift generates a discontinuous variety of fictive
selves, with a growing tendency as his poetry develops
to make himself his subject. His fictive selves, though
assuming the factuality of biography, lead not to some
inner "real self" but to multiple refractions of Swift's
image by public opinion, implicitly questioning what the
truth is. His motive was to impose his self-image upon
circumstances, mastering private crisis by establishing
his own version of it, as in the Market Hill poems. In
poems like *Drapier's Hill* and *Verses on the Death of
Dr. Swift*, the self, something like Yeats's golden bird,
seeks to defeat time, death, and slander by transfiguration into the artifact it creates.

47. Barnett, Louise K. "'Saying the Thing That Is Not':
     Swift's Metalinguistic Satire." *Concerning Poetry* 12
     (Spring 1979): 21-27.

A number of Swift's satiric poems take as their subject,
not vicious or foolish actions, but linguistic offenses
ranging from foolish metaphors and affected diction to
the language of calculated deception. As always in
Swift's satire, the norm is reality, as opposed to lying
or false representation. Barnett discusses *The Progress
of Beauty*, *A Pastoral Dialogue* (1729), *His Grace's Answer
to Jonathan* [Smedley], *An Epistle upon an Epistle* [to
Delany], *A Quibbling Elegy on Judge Boat*, *The Description
of a Salamander*, *Whitshed's Motto on His Coach*, *On the
Words--Brother Protestants and Fellow Christians*, *The
Place of the Damn'd*, and *On Dreams*.

47A. Barnett, Louise K. *Swift's Poetic Worlds*. Newark: Uni-
     versity of Delaware Press; London and Toronto: Asso-
     ciated University Presses, 1981. Pp. 225.

Published after this bibliography was completed, Louise
Barnett's volume is the fifth of five book-length critical
studies of Swift's poetry to appear during 1977-1981,
following those by Nora Jaffe, John Irwin Fischer, Peter
Schakel, and A.B. England (see items 78, 69, 105, 62).
Her special emphasis is Swift's "biographical presence,"
as Maurice Johnson called it (see item 82), which figures
more prominently here than in any earlier book. Barnett's
worthwhile but flawed study seems almost to be two separate
monographs of differing value: after a substantial Introduction, it divides into Part I, "Ordering the Self: The
Poetry of Fictive Self-portraiture," and Part II, "Ordering

the World: The Satiric Poetry." The main thesis is developed at length in Chapter 1, "Strategies of Self-defense," followed briefly in Part I by Chapter 2, "The Vulnerable Self." Part II consists of Chapter 3, "The Verbal Universe"; Chapter 4, "'Foppery, Affectation, Vanity, Folly, or Vice': The Disordered World of the Gentlewoman"; Chapter 5, "Poetry of Excess: The Body and the Body Politic"; and Conclusion.

Principal poems discussed: Introduction: *Drapier's Hill*, *A Dialogue between an Eminent Lawyer and Dr. Swift*, *An Epistle to a Lady*. Chapter 1: the early odes, especially those to Sancroft, Temple, Congreve, and the Athenian Society; *Lady Betty Berkeley*; Frances Harris's *Petition*; the Market Hill poems, including *Lady Acheson Weary of the Dean*, *My Lady's Lamentation and Complaint*, *A Pane-gyrick on the Dean*, and *The Grand Question Debated*; imitations of Horace, *Epistles* 1.7 and *Satires* 2.6, and *The Author upon Himself*; *The Life and Genuine Character* and *Verses on the Death of Dr. Swift*. Chapter 2: *In Sickness, On His Own Deafness, Holyhead. Sept. 25, 1727*, the birthday poems to Stella, *Cadenus and Vanessa*. Chapter 3: *His Grace's Answer to Jonathan, A Quibbling Elegy on Judge Boat, The Description of a Salamander, Whitshed's Motto on His Coach, On the Words--Brother Protestants and Fellow Christians, On Dreams, The Place of the Damn'd, A Satirical Elegy*, the two *Description* poems, *Baucis and Philemon, An Elegy on Mr. Patrige, Vanbrug's House, On Poetry: A Rapsody, To Doctor Delany on the Libels*. Chapter 4: *Verses Wrote in a Lady's Ivory Table-Book, The Furniture of a Woman's Mind, The Journal of a Modern Lady, Cadenus and Vanessa, To Stella, Visiting Me in My Sickness* and *To Stella, Who Collected and Transcribed His Poems*. Chapter 5: the "scatological" poems, *The Character of Sir Robert Walpole, Traulus* (both parts), *Toland's Invitation to Dismal, Helter Skelter, The Legion Club*.

48. Bewley, Marius. "The Poetry of Swift." *The Spectator*, 29 August 1958, pp. 283-84. Reprint (in part). "The 'Romantic Imagination and the Unromantic Byron." *Masks and Mirrors: Essays in Criticism*. New York: Atheneum, 1970, pp. 77-103.

In the guise of a review article on Horrell's *Collected Poems* and Ehrenpreis's *Personality of Jonathan Swift* (see items 10, 329), Bewley provides a sensitive general essay on Swift's verse. There are comments on *To Lord Harley, on His Marriage, Helter Skelter, A Description of the Morning, On Poetry: A Rapsody*, and *The Legion Club*.

48A. Carnochan, W.B. "Augustan Satire and the Gates of
     Dreams: A Utopian Essay." *Studies in the Literary
     Imagination*, vol. 5, no. 2 (October 1972): 1-18.

     Includes brief but illuminating comments on the element
     of dream and reality in the early odes, *A Description of
     a City Shower*, *A Beautiful Young Nymph Going to Bed*, *The
     Day of Judgement*, and *On Dreams*.

49. Carnochan, W.B. "The Consolations of Satire." *The Art
     of Jonathan Swift*. Edited by Clive T. Probyn. London:
     Vision Press; New York: Barnes and Noble, 1978, pp. 19-
     42.

     Swift's satire is claimed to be therapeutic in that it
     hurts only to deny the pain, and dissects only to make
     whole. Paradoxically, it breeds "gain out of loss, life
     out of annihilation, something out of nothingness, tulips
     out of dung, a new creation from a confusion of waste and
     loss." The poems discussed include three riddles, *Cadenus
     and Vanessa*, *The Legion Club*, *Verses on the Death of Dr.
     Swift, Occasioned by Sir William Temple's Late Illness
     and Recovery*, and (two notably provocative analyses)
     Apollo: Or, A Problem Solved and *Death and Daphne*, the
     latter with special reference to Nora Jaffe's article
     (see item 191).

50. Clark, John R. "Embodiment in Literature: Swift's
     Blasted Pocky Muse of Poetry." Review essay. *Thalia:
     Studies in Literary Humor*, vol. 2, no. 3 (Winter 1979-
     1980): 23-33.

     Under the guise of a review essay on the books by Nora
     Jaffe, John Irwin Fischer, and Peter Schakel (see items
     78, 69, 105), Clark seeks to point the way for future
     interpretation of Swift's poetry by detailed analysis of
     illustrative passages from *Stella's Birthday, 1727*; *Verses
     on the Death of Dr. Swift*; *Part of the Seventh Epistle of
     the First Book of Horace Imitated*; *Phillis, Or, the Progress
     of Love*; *The Lady's Dressing Room*; *Holyhead. Sept. 25,
     1727*; *The Description of a Salamander*; *On Poetry: A
     Rapsody*; and *Verses Wrote in a Lady's Ivory Table-Book*.
     In many of Swift's poems, Clark concludes, "the text is
     regulated by two powerful and opposing currents; the
     content is abrupt, fierce, infernal, whereas the *form* is
     logical, cool, precise--almost serene. Such an internal
     friction is the source of much Swiftian combustible
     energy."

51. Clarke, Austin. "The Poetry of Swift." *Jonathan Swift 1667-1967: A Dublin Tercentenary Tribute.* Edited by Roger McHugh and Philip Edwards. Dublin: Dolmen Press, 1967, pp. 94-115.

A rambling, reminiscent, gracious essay that touches briefly upon many of Swift's best-known poems, from the early odes to *The Day of Judgement.* Clarke is sensitive to Swift's humor. See also item 325.

51A. Cohen, Ralph. "The Augustan Mode in English Poetry." *Studies in the Eighteenth Century: Papers Presented at the David Nichol Smith Memorial Seminar, Canberra, 1966.* Edited by R.F. Brissenden. Canberra: Australian National University Press; Toronto: University of Toronto Press, 1968, pp. 171-92.

Includes brief discussions of *A Description of a City Shower* as "a harmony of garbage" and *Stella's Birthday, 1719* as a "playful poem of dismemberment."

52. Colum, Padraic. "The Poetry of Jonathan Swift." *Proceedings of the American Academy of Arts and Letters and the National Institute of Arts and Letters,* 2d ser., no. 18 (New York, 1968): 3-19.

An address delivered at a dinner meeting on 31 January 1967. For the common impression of Swift as a non-poet or anti-poet, Colum adduces two historical causes: Swift fails to satisfy the romantic conception of poetry, and he is a poet of the city and court rather than of outdoor nature. Unlike the romantics, Swift in his poetry provides clear, exact statements, encourages audience participation, dramatizes himself, makes us feel present at the scene of action, and above all judges himself and the human race. Colum cites *The Author's Manner of Living, The Description of a Salamander, An Epistle to a Lady, The Legion Club, A Beautiful Young Nymph Going to Bed, Verses on the Death of Dr. Swift, The Day of Judgement,* and *Cadenus and Vanessa.* In a concluding exchange with Louise Bogan and others, Colum calls Swift a poet of "engagement" in the existentialist sense.

53. Colum, Padraic. "Return to the Poetry of Jonathan Swift." *Pennsylvania Literary Review,* Second Quarter, 1955, pp. 19-26.

For the younger poets of today, Swift as "anti-poet" provides a model that is free from the luxuriance of Romantic poetry, compact and orderly, capable of dealing

with the concrete, and acclimatized to city life. His
poems pass judgments, make us feel present at the scene
of action, cultivate "boldness" (Goldsmith's term), draw
upon contemporary street-songs, and dramatize Swift himself. Although *A Beautiful Young Nymph Going to Bed* is
heartless, *An Epistle to a Lady* develops a lighter, more
attractive tone. Other poems discussed by Colum include
The Day of Judgement, *The Legion Club*, *The Description of
a Salamander*, *Stella at Wood-Park*, *My Lady's Lamentation
and Complaint against the Dean*, and *Verses on the Death
of Dr. Swift*.

54. Colum, Padraic. "Swift's Poetry." *The Dublin Magazine*,
     vol. 6, nos. 3-4 (Autumn/Winter 1967): 5-13. (Swift
     Tercentenary Edition.)

     This paper is a variant version of Colum's "The Poetry
     of Jonathan Swift," item 52. Although the wording of his
     own text is different, Colum makes the same points and
     cites nearly the same passages from the same poems.

55. Davis, Herbert. "Alecto's Whip." *A Review of English
     Literature*, vol. 3, no. 3 (July 1962): 7-17. (Special
     issue on Swift.) Reprint. *Jonathan Swift: Essays on
     His Satire and Other Studies by Herbert Davis*. Galaxy
     Books. New York: Oxford University Press, 1964,
     pp. 249-59.

     Swift's verse reveals the prevalence of satire in his
     writings, not only in attacks on his contemporaries but
     in works more universal in scope. "He often gives the
     impression that he is a little too fond of Alecto's whip,
     a little too ready to take over the business of punish-
     ment as well as judgement and to enjoy his power and his
     triumph as he lashes his victims until they howl and
     wriggle and skip." Among the poems cited are several of
     the early odes, *The Fable of Midas*, *A Satirical Elegy*,
     The Beast's Confession to the Priest, and *The Legion Club*.

56. Davis, Herbert. "The Poetry of Jonathan Swift." *College
     English* 2 (November 1940): 102-15.

     An enthusiastic revaluation of Swift's verse, designed
     for the common reader but packed with incisive comments
     on individual poems and on Swift's poetry generally.
     Sir Harold Williams's recently published edition of the
     poems (see item 16), Davis asserts, gives us more new
     knowledge of Swift's life and works than can be found in
     any of the biographies that keep appearing year by year.

Among the poems briefly discussed are *Ode to the Athenian Society*, *Ode to the Honourable Sir William Temple*, Frances Harris's *Petition*, the two *Description* poems, *A Satirical Elegy*, the *Stella* poems (especially *Stella's Birthday, 1727*), *An Epistle to a Lady*, *On Poetry: A Rapsody*, and *Verses on the Death of Dr. Swift*.

57. Davis, Herbert. "Swift's View of Poetry." *Studies in English by Members of University College, Toronto*. Toronto: University of Toronto Press, 1931, pp. 9-58. Reprints. *Jonathan Swift: Essays on His Satire and Other Studies by Herbert Davis*. Galaxy Books. New York: Oxford University Press, 1964, pp. 163-98. *Fair Liberty Was All His Cry: A Tercentenary Tribute to Jonathan Swift 1667-1745*. Edited by A. Norman Jeffares. London: Macmillan; New York: St. Martin's Press, 1967, pp. 62-97.

An early expression of the notion that what Swift wrote is "anti-poetry." Swift, according to Davis, reacted against the heroic or romantic concept of the poet's function and the nature of art, which was generally accepted by such writers as Dryden and Pope; in contrast, his theory and practice show none of this professional pride and set little value on the business of writing poetry. His verses were written to gain a reputation and establish his influence, or to force his views on the public; hence they adopt the stance of a man of action rather than an artist, or of a gentleman amusing his friends. Davis discusses many poems briefly while analyzing few in detail.

58. Dobrée, Bonamy. "The Jocose Dean." *Fair Liberty Was All His Cry: A Tercentenary Tribute to Jonathan Swift 1667-1745*. Edited by A. Norman Jeffares. London: Macmillan; New York: St. Martin's Press, 1967, pp. 42-61. Reprint. *Swift: Modern Judgements*. Edited by A. Norman Jeffares. London: Macmillan, 1969; Nashville, TN: Aurora, 1970, pp. 28-46.

An entertaining, illuminating, admirably civilized essay making the point that in spite of Swift's *saeva indignatio*, almost everything he did was infused with a sense of fun. Dobrée draws his illustrations of the jocose and humorous from Swift's conversation with his friends, his correspondence, the poems, and the prose works. Among the many poems cited are several of the Market Hill group which banter Lady Acheson, the verses he exchanged with Sheridan, and *Verses on the Death of Dr. Swift*.

59. Donoghue, Denis. "The Sin of Wit." *Jonathan Swift: A
    Critical Introduction.* Cambridge: At the University
    Press, 1969, pp. 188-221. Reprint. *Jonathan Swift:
    A Critical Anthology.* Harmondsworth, Eng.: Penguin
    Books, 1971, pp. 285-314.

    In Swift's poetry, "even when he writes an occasional
    poem, he always keeps his mind focused on the object: to
    push things into the daylight of common sense, to force
    them into definition." Donoghue's thesis, unfortunately,
    is less precisely articulated than Swift's verses are
    said to be. He discusses *On Dreams, The Legion Club, A
    Satirical Elegy,* and several "scatological" poems: *The
    Lady's Dressing Room, The Progress of Love, The Progress
    of Beauty, A Beautiful Young Nymph Going to Bed, Strephon
    and Chloe,* and *Cassinus and Peter.* See item 60.

60. Donoghue Denis. "Swift as Poet." *Swift Revisited.*
    Edited by Denis Donoghue. Cork: The Mercier Press,
    1968, pp. 75-89.

    A shorter and presumably earlier version of Donoghue's
    essay "The Sin of Wit" (see item 59).

61. Ehrenpreis, Irvin. *Swift: The Man, His Works, and the
    Age.* Vol. 1. *Mr. Swift and His Contemporaries.*
    Cambridge: Harvard University Press, 1962. Pp. xi +
    294. Vol. 2. *Dr. Swift.* Cambridge: Harvard Univer-
    sity Press, 1967. Pp. xviii + 782.

    Ehrenpreis's two volumes, representing the definitive
    biography of Swift for the years up to 1714, regularly
    include discussions of Swift's more important poems under
    the dates at which they were composed. Because the index
    has been postponed until the third and concluding volume,
    these discussions, which should be consulted by anyone
    studying the poems, are sometimes inconvenient to locate.
    The following list may assist temporarily.

    Poems discussed: Vol. 1: the early odes (pp. 109-41);
    Apollo's Edict (p. 162). Vol. 2: *Verses Wrote in a Lady's
    Ivory Table-Book, The Problem, The Discovery,* Frances
    Harris's *Petition* (pp. 23-33); *A Ballad on the Game of
    Traffick* (pp. 91-92); *The Description of a Salamander*
    (pp. 162-65); *Verses Said to Be Written on the Union*
    (pp. 174-75); *An Elegy on Mr. Patrige* (pp. 205-06);
    Baucis and Philemon, A Description of the Morning
    (pp. 243-51); *Apollo Outwitted, To Mrs. Biddy Floyd*
    (pp. 306-09); *A Description of a City Shower, The Virtues
    of Sid Hamet the Magician's Rod* (pp. 383-88); *The Windsor*

Prophecy (pp. 478-79, 519-21, 633); *An Excellent New Song, Being the Intended Speech of a Famous Orator against Peace* (pp. 515-16); *Toland's Invitation to Dismal* (pp. 566-68); *Cadenus and Vanessa* (pp. 309-14, 635-51, 673); *To Lord Harley, on His Marriage* (p. 673); *Horace, Seventh Epistle of the First Book Imitated* (pp. 675-77); *Horace, First Ode of the Second Book Paraphras'd* (pp. 698-99); *The Author upon Himself* (pp. 521, 632, 735-37, 745); *Horace, Part of the Sixth Satire of the Second Book Imitated* (pp. 381, 575, 742-44).

61A. Elliott, Robert C. "Jonathan Swift: The Presentation of Self in Doggerel Rhyme." *The Poetry of Jonathan Swift.* Papers read at a Clark Library Seminar 20 January 1979. Los Angeles: William Andrews Clark Library, University of California, 1981, pp. 1-23.

An unfocused discussion of Swift's use of himself in his poetry, drawing upon the analogy of Horace and the theories of Patrick Cruttwell and especially Erving Goffman. Unfortunately, one of the poems cited most prominently is *A Panegyric on the Reverend Dean Swift*, which is spurious; Elliott rejects the case against Swift's authorship assembled by Aubrey Williams and James Woolley without offering any evidence of his own (see items 413, 426). Elliott discusses *An Epistle to a Lady*, the imitation of Horace's *Epistles* 1.7, and *Verses on the Death of Dr. Swift*, citing also *Toland's Invitation to Dismal*, *A Libel on Doctor Delany*, and *The Author upon Himself*. His essay is essentially a sequel to his earlier *Yale Review* article on "Swift's 'I'" (62 [March 1973]: 372-91) and makes no reference to other practitioners of the "biographical presence" approach such as Maurice Johnson (see item 82), Robert Uphaus, and Louise Barnett, although Edward Said is quoted in passing (see item 275). It is a shame that instead of dedicating the Clark Library papers to Elliott, the editor did not suppress this very weak essay in kindness to the memory of a critic and scholar whose previous work on Swift and satire we all honor (see item 91A).

62. England, A.B. *Energy and Order in the Poetry of Swift.* Lewisburg: Bucknell University Press; London and Toronto: Associated University Presses, 1980. Pp. 241.

Reviewed by Nora Crow Jaffe in *The Scriblerian*, vol. 13, no. 2 (Spring 1981): 112-14; by Richard B. Schwartz in *Studies in English Literature* 21 (Summer 1981): 522;

by Claude Rawson in *London Times Literary Supplement*,
4 September 1981, p. 1017; by John H. Middendorf in
Johnsonian News Letter, vol. 41, no. 3 (September 1981):
8-9; by David M. Vieth in *Eighteenth-Century Studies*.

A.B. England's volume is the fourth book-length critical study of Swift's poetry published during 1977-1980,
after the books by Nora Jaffe, John Irwin Fischer, and
Peter Schakel (see items 78, 69, 105). England's special
critical tool is the interplay in the poems of the two
terms in his title, "order" and "energy," which represent
familiar polarities: reason and passion, form and matter,
general and particular, abstract and concrete, permanence
and change. Typically, in a Swift poem, these two elements
are in a state of imbalance. England's perceptive interpretations of individual works, expressed in remarkably
deft critical prose, amount to a successful overview of
Swift's poetry that is not exhaustive but should stimulate
much future thinking. Unlike Fischer's religious approach,
England's is determinedly secular.

Principal poems discussed: Chapter 1: the early odes
and *On Poetry: A Rapsody*. Chapter 2: *The Problem*, *The
Description of a Salamander*, *The Fable of Midas*, *A Simile
on Our Want of Silver*, *Vanbrug's House*, *The Virtues of Sid
Hamet the Magician's Rod*, *A Serious Poem upon William
Wood*, and *The Bubble*. Chapter 3: *Baucis and Philemon*,
To Charles Ford on His Birth-day, *The Journal*, the two
Description poems, *The Furniture of a Woman's Mind*, *Direc-
tions for a Birth-day Song*, the imitation of Horace's
Odes 2.1, *The Legion Club*, and Frances Harris's *Petition*.
Chapter 4: *The Journal of a Modern Lady*, *An Apology to the
Lady Carteret*, *A Libel on Doctor Delany and a Certain
Great Lord*, *The Progress of Poetry*, the imitations of
Horace's *Odes* 1.14, *Epistles* 1.7, and *Satires* 2.6, the
birthday poems to Stella for 1719 and 1721, and *To Stella,
Visiting Me in My Sickness*. Chapter 5: *Cadenus and
Vanessa*, *Verses on the Death of Dr. Swift*, *Phillis, Or,
the Progress of Love*, *The Progress of Marriage*, *The Prog-
ress of Beauty*, *The Lady's Dressing Room*, and *Strephon
and Chloe*.

63.   England, A.B. "The Subversion of Logic in Some Poems by
      Swift." *Studies in English Literature* 15 (Summer 1975):
      409-18.

In several major prose works, Swift parodies the techniques of formal logic by ironically presenting a speaker
who attempts to apply them in situations too complex for

them to cope with. Similarly, in a few curious poems, Swift not only exhibits disrespect for rigid argumentative procedures but comes close to burlesquing formal, consecutive logic of any kind. This pseudo-logic relies upon extended debasing analogies. England discusses *The Description of a Salamander*, *The Fable of Midas*, *The Virtues of Sid Hamet the Magician's Rod*, and *A Serious Poem upon William Wood*.

64. England, A.B. "World Without Order: Some Thoughts on the Poetry of Swift." *Essays in Criticism* 16 (January 1966): 32-43.

The peculiarly disconcerting quality of Swift's writings is caused by their unresolved oppositions which must nevertheless be somehow held in tension--England's "world without order." In an interplay of order and disorder, Swift builds up patterns of antithesis without establishing his own preferences. Thus *The Lady's Dressing Room* (England's test case) juxtaposes two ridiculously oversimplified concepts of woman to insinuate that a right attitude lies somewhere in between, this somewhere not being precisely located. Swift's antithetical structures are frequently expressed in verse-couplet form, as in *Verses Wrote in a Lady's Ivory Table-Book*. Other poems covered in this brief but perceptive and historically important article are *On Dreams*, *On Poetry: A Rapsody*, *A Description of the Morning* (an especially incisive discussion) and the *City Shower*, and Frances Harris's *Petition*. *Cadenus and Vanessa* is mentioned.

65. Fabricant, Carole. "The Garden as City: Swift's Landscape of Alienation." *ELH* 42 (Winter 1975): 531-55.

Attempts--unsuccessfully, most readers will feel--to transform Swift's numerous descriptions of buildings and landscapes into a thoroughgoing expression of the formerly fashionable "gloom of the Tory satirists." Significantly no single poem is discussed in detail. Voluminous quotations from Swift's prose and poetry, instead of documenting the central thesis, reveal how selective these citations are. Despite her disclaimers, Fabricant seems incapable of responding to Swift's playful sense of absurdity.

66. Fairchild, Hoxie Neale. *Religious Trends in English Poetry*. New York: Columbia University Press, 1939, 1:26-32, 57-61.

An intelligent, generally well-informed, but perhaps unfairly negative assessment of Swift's religious views

as these are reflected in his poetry. Personally,
Swift "had his spiritual impulses, but he was not genuine-
ly religious"; none of his poems "reveals the slightest
trace of a reverent and loving personal faith in any sort
of Divine Power." Publicly, he was a High Churchman.
Fairchild briefly cites some twenty poems, including *Ode
to Dr. William Sancroft*, two or three of which may be
spurious.

67. Fischer, Alan S. "Swift's Verse Portraits: A Study of
     His Originality as an Augustan Satirist." *Studies in
     English Literature* 14 (Summer 1974): 343-56.

     Portraits, though they may seem biographical, are really
     a specially rich kind of metaphor. Swift's satirical
     verse portraits are distinguished by three features:
     treatment of their subjects in terms, not of essence, but
     of process; the process of devaluation as itself a kind
     of truth; and, presiding over the process of devaluation,
     a critical, detached, free-standing intellect. Fischer
     cites *The Description of a Salamander*, *Vanbrug's House*,
     Directions for a Birth-day Song, the *Satirical Elegy*, and
     Epistle to a Lady. A paradigm of Swift's satirical method,
     in prose as well as in verse, would include three things:
     clever jests, bitter indictments, and a sense of the
     process of decay built into the fabric of the world.

68. Fischer, John Irwin. "Introduction: 'All ... Manifestly
     Deduceable.'" *Contemporary Studies of Swift's Poetry*.
     Edited by John Irwin Fischer and Donald C. Mell, Jr.,
     with David M. Vieth, associate editor. Newark: Univer-
     sity of Delaware Press; London and Toronto: Associated
     University Presses, 1980, pp. 11-22.

     Contemporary Studies is reviewed by Richard B. Schwartz
     in *Studies in English Literature* 21 (Summer 1981): 522;
     by John H. Middendorf in *Johnsonian News Letter*, vol.
     41, no. 3 (September 1981): 9; by David Nokes in *London
     Times Literary Supplement*, 23 October 1981, p. 1240.

     Describes the critical milieu that gave rise to this
     volume of sixteen essays by fifteen Swift specialists,
     and outlines the circumstances that led to its publica-
     tion. The essays were largely written for delivery in
     Special Sessions at annual meetings of the Modern Language
     Association in 1976, 1977, and 1978. The three critical
     approaches that they supersede are identified by Fischer
     as the biographical and bibliographical treatment that
     was needed by the earlier twentieth century; the notion

of Swift as a realistic "anti-poet," opposed to Romantic transcendence; and a more recent rhetorical emphasis upon Swift's adjustment of strategic means to intended ends. Collectively, the essays affirm a belief in Swift as the "greatest satirist and second poet of his age."

69. Fischer, John Irwin. *On Swift's Poetry*. Gainesville: University Presses of Florida, 1978. Pp. 207.

Reviewed by Peter J. Schakel in *The Scriblerian*, vol. 10, no. 2 (Spring 1978): 122-24; by Clive T. Probyn in *London Times Literary Supplement*, 17 November 1978, p. 1334; by Kenneth J. Wagner in *University of Toronto Quarterly* 48 (Winter 1978/9): 182-85; by James L. Tyne, S.J., in *Thought: A Review of Culture and Idea* 54 (March 1979): 111-12; by Eric Rothstein in *Studies in English Literature* 19 (Summer 1979): 544-46; by Francis Doherty in *Review of English Studies* n.s. 30 (August 1979): 353-55; by Louise K. Barnett in *Review*, vol. 2, edited by James O. Hoge and James L.W. West III (Charlottesville: University of Virginia Press, 1980): 41-48; by Merritt Eugene Lawlis in *Journal of English and Germanic Philology* 80 (January 1981): 138-40; by Richard Rodino in *The Eighteenth Century: A Current Bibliography* n.s. 4--for 1978 (New York: AMS Press, 1981): 460-62. See also the review essay by John R. Clark, item 50.

Fischer's volume was the second of four book-length critical studies of Swift's poetry to be published during 1977-1980, after Nora Jaffe's book (see item 78) and before Peter Schakel's and A.B. England's (see items 105, 62). Departing from the scatter-gun approaches of Jaffe and also Maurice Johnson (see item 81), Fischer was the first to achieve a comprehensive interpretation of Swift's poems supported by incisive, detailed analyses of a representative range of individual works. Fischer's synthesis, here as in his earlier publications on Swift, centers upon Christian aspects of the poetry. Swift's writings, he feels, enact a lifelong dramatic conflict between Swift's hubristic sense of absolute right and wrong, which demands condemnation of the imperfections of his fellow men, and his sense of personal entanglement with the corruption but also with the chaotic vitality of the human condition. Unfortunately, some readers are offended by Fischer's religious emphasis, which tends to obscure Swift's humor.

Principal poems discussed: Chapter 1: the early odes. Chapter 2: *Verses Wrote in a Lady's Ivory Table-Book*,

Frances Harris's *Petition*, *A Ballad on the Game of
Traffick*, *To the Tune of the Cutpurse*, *Baucis and Phile-
mon*, *Vanbrug's House*, and *A Description of a City Shower*.
Chapter 3: *Cadenus and Vanessa*. Chapter 4: the Stella
poems. Chapter 5: *Verses on the Death of Dr. Swift*.
Chapter 6: *On Poetry: A Rapsody*. Conclusion: *The Legion
Club*.

70. Fricke, Donna G. "Swift, Hogarth, and the Sister Arts."
     Eighteenth-Century Life, vol. 2, no. 2 (December 1975):
     29-33.

     Using a *Zeitgeist* approach derived from Helmut Hatzfeld,
     Fricke places Swift and Hogarth in the same satiric
     pictorial tradition. Hogarth's "A Harlot's Progress"
     provides detailed analogues for *A Beautiful Young Nymph
     Going to Bed* and Swift's "progress" poems. Other "scato-
     logical" poems are elucidated by Hogarth's "Marriage-à-
     la-Mode" series and "The Rake's Progress." *The Bubble* is
     compared with Hogarth's "The South Sea Scheme." Hogarth
     offers pictorial equivalents for *Gulliver's Travels*,
     Baucis and Philemon, *The Lady's Dressing Room*, and two
     or three more poems.

71. Golden, Morris. "Swift." *The Self Observed: Swift,
     Johnson, Wordsworth*. Baltimore and London: Johns
     Hopkins Press, 1972, pp. 33-66.

     Pursuing the dichotomy adumbrated in the title of his
     volume, Golden examines the discrepancy between the
     idiosyncratic, partial personae dramatized in Swift's
     works and the normative, general self Swift implicitly
     shares with the reader. Although it covers Swift's life
     as well as his works, and the prose as well as the
     poetry, Golden's chapter comments upon more than two
     dozen of the poems--without, however, analyzing any of
     them in detail.

72. Hagstrum, Jean H. "Verbal and Visual Caricature in the
     Age of Dryden, Swift, and Pope." *England in the
     Restoration and Early Eighteenth Century: Essays on
     Culture and Society*. Edited by H.T. Swedenberg, Jr.
     Publications of the 17th and 18th Centuries Studies
     Group, UCLA. Berkeley, Los Angeles, London: University
     of California Press, 1972, pp. 173-95.

     Swift's satirical characters belong to emblematic
     rather than portrait caricature, and they represent a
     persistence of the hieroglyphic qualities of the seven-

teenth-century emblem tradition. His animal grotesquer-
ie--droll, savage, cruel, playful--is the most brilliant
in literary history. Hagstrum discusses *The Description
of a Salamander* in detail.

73. Hill, Geoffrey. "Jonathan Swift: The Poetry of 'Reac-
    tion.'" *The World of Jonathan Swift: Essays for the
    Tercentenary.* Edited by Brian Vickers. Cambridge:
    Harvard University Press, 1968, pp. 195-212. Reprint
    (in part). *Jonathan Swift: A Critical Anthology.*
    Edited by Denis Donoghue. Harmondsworth, Eng.: Penguin
    Books, 1971, pp. 273-84.

    Swift's creative intelligence was at once resistant
    and reciprocal--resistant to established patterns of
    human behavior, yet responsive to their residual vitality.
    His sense of tradition and community is constantly chal-
    lenged by a strong feeling for the anarchic and predatory,
    but his finest works display a most sensitive awareness
    of the things being reacted against. Hill's perceptive
    essay touches upon many of Swift's poems, giving special
    attention to the "scatological" pieces. He stresses
    Swift's probable indebtedness to Rochester's satires.

74. Horne, C.J. "'From a Fable form a Truth': A Considera-
    tion of the Fable in Swift's Poetry." *Studies in the
    Eighteenth Century: Papers Presented at the David Nichol
    Smith Memorial Seminar, Canberra 1966.* Edited by R.F.
    Brissenden. Canberra: Australian National University
    Press; Toronto: University of Toronto Press, 1968,
    pp. 193-204.

    Observes that about a score of Swift's poems either are
    fables themselves or employ fable material--not to mention
    prose fables such as the Spider and the Bee in *The Battle
    of the Books*, the three brothers in *A Tale of a Tub*, and
    Gulliver among the Houyhnhnms. Horne emphasizes Swift's
    favorable attitude toward this popular Restoration and
    eighteenth-century genre, which characteristically con-
    sists of a simple tale, patently fabricated, often fan-
    tastic, and intended through allegory to convey a moral.
    Among Swift's verse fables, whose two main sources are
    Aesop and Ovid's *Metamorphoses*, Horne provides illumi-
    nating discussions of *Baucis and Philemon*, *The Fable of
    Midas*, *The Faggot*, *The Bubble* (from which the quotation
    in the title of his essay is taken), and *The Beast's
    Confession to the Priest*.

75. Horne, Colin J. "Swift's Comic Poetry." *Augustan Worlds:*
     New Essays in Eighteenth-Century Literature. Edited by
     J.C. Hilson, M.M.B. Jones, and J.R. Watson. (The Arthur
     Humphreys *Festschrift* volume.) Leicester: Leicester
     University Press; New York: Barnes and Noble, 1978,
     pp. 51-67.

     Objecting that the main defect of Swift criticism has
     been to take him too solemnly, Horne, in this "corrective
     view," directs attention to a series of poems that are
     "truly comic in the more popular sense of that term as
     being funny." Only in the poetry, and intermittently in
     some of his letters, is this lighter, more genial side
     of Swift's nature clearly evident. Horne comments on
     Swift's raillery, his fondness for common, lowly people,
     and his direct link with the tradition of Gaelic humor.

76. Hunting, Robert. "The Left-handed Poet." *Jonathan Swift.*
     Twayne's English Authors Series 42. New York: Twayne
     Publishers, 1967, pp. 61-79.

     A survey of Swift's poetry which makes little claim to
     new insights, although it recognizes the superiority of
     the later poems. As representative samples, Hunting
     singles out *A Description of a City Shower*, *Stella's*
     Birthday, 1721, *Cadenus and Vanessa*, *A Pastoral Dialogue*
     (1729), *A Satirical Elegy*, *A Beautiful Young Nymph Going*
     to Bed, and the dialogue of *Verses on the Death of Dr.*
     Swift. Hunting rates Swift's poetry relatively low,
     reiterating the old question of whether it is poetry at
     all.

77. Irwin, W.R. "Swift the Verse Man." *Philological*
     Quarterly 54 (Winter 1975): 222-38.

     Attempts to establish the qualities of "light verse,"
     especially as written by Swift. For example, light verse
     may be occasional, at least if the occasion is sufficient-
     ly trivial, and it utilizes obtrusive tricks of style
     such as rhyme and rhythm. Most important, in Irwin's
     view, is the pretended detachment of the poet from his
     performance. In *The Day of Judgement*, Swift combines
     this kind of detachment with emotional involvement.

78. Jaffe, Nora Crow. *The Poet Swift.* Hanover, NH: The
     University Press of New England, 1977. Pp. x + 190.

     Reviewed by Claude Rawson in *London Times Literary*
     Supplement, 10 February 1978, p. 165; by Maurice John-
     son in *Eighteenth-Century Studies* 11 (Spring 1978):

410-13; by Peter J. Schakel in *The Scriblerian*, vol. 10, no. 2 (Spring 1978): 122-24; by John M. Aden in *South Atlantic Quarterly* 77 (Summer 1978): 384-85; by Kenneth J. Wagner in *University of Toronto Quarterly* 48 (Winter 1978/9): 182-85; by Colin J. Horne in *Modern Language Review* 75 (October 1980): 852-54; by Louise K. Barnett in *Review*, vol. 2, edited by James O. Hoge and James L.W. West III (Charlottesville: University of Virginia Press, 1980): 41-48; by Merritt Eugene Lawlis in *Journal of English and Germanic Philology* 80 (January 1981): 138-40; by Richard Rodino in *The Eighteenth Century: A Current Bibliography* n.s. 4--for 1978 (New York: AMS Press, 1981): 460-62. See also the review essay by John R. Clark, item 50.

Nora Jaffe's volume was only the second book-length critical study of Swift's poetry ever published, and the first in the twenty-seven years since Maurice Johnson's *The Sin of Wit*, 1950 (see item 81). As such, it is designed for readers who respond to Swift's verse enthusiastically but not analytically. "The difficulty," as Jaffe formulates her task, "lies in finding the right words to describe a poetry that is superficially simple but at its best can be emotionally overpowering." Distrusting extended, systematic analyses of Swift's poems, Jaffe offers a less formal kind of commentary on their salient features. She champions no thematic bias and subscribes to no particular school such as the New Criticism, leaning instead toward a reader-oriented or even author-oriented approach which sometimes entails extraliterary considerations. Nevertheless, although she minimizes the importance of allusions, imagery, and verse techniques in the poetry, she recognizes Swift's control of tone and similar rhetorical complexities.

Principal poems discussed: Chapter 1: *Stella's Birthday, 1721* and *1727*; *On Dreams*; *A Description of the Morning*; *The Author upon Himself*; imitation of Horace, *Satires 2.6*; *Verses on the Death of Dr. Swift*; *An Epistle to a Lady*; *The Day of Judgement*; and *Helter Skelter*. Chapter 2: *On Poetry: A Rapsody*, *Apollo: Or, A Problem Solved*, *Directions for a Birth-day Song*, and *A Love Song in the Modern Taste*. Chapter 3: the early odes, *Baucis and Philemon*. Chapter 4: the two *Description* poems. Chapter 5: the Stella poems. Chapter 6: the "scatological" poems. Chapter 7: *To Mr. Delany*; the poems to Sheridan, including *Mary the Cook-Maid's Letter*; the Market Hill poems, particularly *Death and Daphne*, *On Cutting Down the Old Thorn at Market Hill*, and *The Grand Question Debated*; Frances

Harris's *Petition*; *On the Little House by the Church Yard of Castleknock*; *To Lord Harley, on His Marriage*; *Cadenus and Vanessa*; imitation of Horace, *Epistles* 1.7; *An Apology to the Lady Carteret.* Chapter 8: *The Legion Club.*

79. Jeffares, A. Norman. "The Poetry." *Jonathan Swift.* Writers and their Work. Harlow, Essex: Longman for the British Council, 1976, pp. 36-43. Reprint. *British Writers: Edited under the Auspices of the British Council.* Edited by Ian Scott-Kilvert. Daniel Defoe to the Gothic Novel, vol. 3. New York: Charles Scribner's Sons, 1980, pp. 30-32.

    This brief general essay stresses, along with other familiar features of Swift's poetry, its informality, personal quality, and concern with the difference between truth and illusion.

80. Jefferson, D.W. "The Poetry of Age." *Focus: Swift.* Edited by C.J. Rawson. London: Sphere Books, 1971, pp. 121-37.

    Adopts the thesis that "Swift developed late as a poet"--specifically, that his "latest and greatest period" extends from the verses *To Mr. Delany* (1718) to *The Legion Club* (1736). Instead of developing this important, valid thesis in depth, however, Jefferson offers a rather casual chronological survey of Swift's poetical career, commenting briefly though often perceptively on several dozen poems. Jefferson finds *Cadenus and Vanessa* "awkward and unsatisfying," but *On Poetry: A Rapsody* is Swift's "most memorable comic poem," and *Verses on the Death of Dr. Swift* is "his greatest poem."

81. Johnson, Maurice. *The Sin of Wit: Jonathan Swift as a Poet.* Syracuse: Syracuse University Press, 1950. Pp. xvii + 145. Reprint. New York: Gordian Press, 1966.

    Reviewed by James Clifford in *Johnsonian News Letter*, vol. 10, no. 5 (November 1950): 5; by Harold Williams in *Philological Quarterly* 30 (July 1951): 294-95; by Oliver W. Ferguson in *Journal of English and Germanic Philology* 50 (1951): 425-26; by Bonamy Dobrée in *Review of English Studies* n.s. 3 (January 1952): 89-90; by Clarence L. Kulisheck in *Modern Language Quarterly* 13 (March 1952): 105-06; by James R. Sutherland in *Modern Language Notes* 68 (January 1953): 69-71; by Bernhard Fabian in *Archiv für das Studium der neueren Sprachen* 196 (1960): 210-11.

Johnson's volume is the earliest book-length critical study of Swift's poetry and, as such, is a landmark of mid-twentieth-century Swift criticism. Although Johnson tends to avoid comprehensive analysis of individual works, his discussion is distinguished by witty, incisive remarks on a wide range of the poems. There is an appendix on "Eliot, Hardy, Joyce, Yeats, and the Ghost of Swift."

82. Johnson, Maurice. "Swift's Poetry Reconsidered." *English Writers of the Eighteenth Century*. Edited by John H. Middendorf. New York and London: Columbia University Press, 1971, pp. 233-48.

This influential essay emphasizes the special impact of Swift's "biographical presence" in his poems. Because of what we already know concerning their author, they evoke a response beyond that implicit in the imaginative constructs they represent, making Swift's own identity and his poetry seem inseparable. Johnson identifies three general patterns in the structure of the poems: mutually exclusive opposites; deflating, unmasking, and stripping bare; and incongruities in a seemingly undiscriminating continuum of items. A large number of poems are discussed briefly.

83. Johnston, Oswald. "Swift and the Common Reader." *In Defense of Reading: A Reader's Approach to Literary Criticism*. Edited by Reuben A. Brower and Richard Poirier. New York: E.P. Dutton, 1962, pp. 174-90.

Most neoclassical poetry succeeds by arousing conventional expectations concerning such things as genre and poetic language, and then satisfying those expectations. Swift's poetry, however, succeeds by arousing these conventional expectations and then thwarting them, thereby asserting a less exalted reality than the conventions imply. Taking *A Description of a City Shower* as a paradigm for what he sees as Swift's "anti-poetry," Johnston perceptively discusses *On Poetry: A Rapsody*, *A Love Song in the Modern Taste*, *The Progress of Beauty*, and *On Stella's Birthday, 1719*.

84. Krieger, Murray. "The Human Inadequacy of Gulliver, Strephon, and Walter Shandy—and the Barnyard Alternative." *The Classic Vision: The Retreat from Extremity in Modern Literature*. Baltimore: Johns Hopkins, 1971, pp. 258-68.

Locates Swift's "minimal classic" vision in the spark of human sympathy that animates the "human barnyard" in

A Description of the Morning, The Lady's Dressing Room,
and *A Beautiful Young Nymph Going to Bed.*

85. Lee, Jae Num. *Swift and Scatological Satire.* Albuquerque:
     University of New Mexico Press, 1971. Pp. 158.

     Lee's book develops the rather obvious thesis that
     Swift uses scatology, not for purposes of obscenity, but
     for satire, with an intermingling of humor. Among the
     "scatological" poems, Lee discusses *The Lady's Dressing
     Room, Cassinus and Peter,* and *Strephon and Chloe,* all of
     which he classifies as moral satire (pp. 82-91). Other
     poems discussed include *The Problem, A Panegyrick on the
     Dean, The Legion Club,* and several riddles.

86. Löffler, Arno. *"The Rebel Muse"--Studien zu Swifts
     kritischer Dichtung.* Buchreihe der Anglia, vol. 21.
     Tübingen: Max Niemeyer, 1981. Pp. 270.

     In German. Accepting the now-outmoded notion of
     Swift's verse as "anti-poetry," Löffler attempts to
     relate its various aspects to Swift's theories of litera-
     ture and to the temper of the age.

87. Mell, Donald C., Jr. "Imagination and Satiric Mimesis in
     Swift's Poetry: An Exploratory Discussion." *Contemporary
     Studies of Swift's Poetry.* Edited by John Irwin Fischer
     and Donald C. Mell, Jr., with David M. Vieth, associate
     editor. Newark: University of Delaware Press; London
     and Toronto: Associated University Presses, 1980,
     pp. 123-35.

     The recent "vigorous and sustained interest" in Swift's
     poetry has not yet "dispelled doubt about his full com-
     mitment to the Augustan ideal of the poetic imagination
     as an instrument for transforming the particulars of ex-
     perience and shaping them into moral and aesthetic order,
     about his faith in the mimetic function of art." The
     notion of Swift's verse as "anti-poetry," as an undiffer-
     entiating mirror of actuality, expressed by Ricardo
     Quintana and Herbert Davis, persists in commentaries by
     Martin Battestin, Oswald Johnston, and A.B. England.
     Despite Swift's own self-deprecating remarks, however--
     which can be paralleled in Pope--even the squalidly
     realistic urban scenes depicted in the two *Description*
     poems assert the validity of the classical ideals that
     are tacitly invoked to satirize them, and Swift's ridicule
     of false art indirectly expresses a belief in art's moral
     force. In *On Poetry: A Rapsody,* Swift's enactment of the
     perversions of false art implicitly supports the imagina-
     tive ideals that are being violated.

88. Mercier, Vivian. "Swift's Humour." *Jonathan Swift 1667-1967: A Dublin Tercentenary Tribute.* Edited by Roger McHugh and Philip Edwards. Dublin: Dolmen Press, 1967, pp. 116-36. Reprint (with additions). *Tri-Quarterly*, no. 11 (Winter 1968): 125-43.

    Humor, as Swift describes it, is not "black" humor, satire, or wit. It is natural, spontaneous, benign, and common to human nature at all social levels although it may be unconscious. The exponent of true humor must, like Swift the man, be both a humorist and a humor, a practical joker and a butt, a sane observer and an eccentric, capable of laughing at himself. Mercier's wide-ranging survey illuminates passages from more than a dozen of Swift's poems, concluding with *Cadenus and Vanessa.*

89. Murry, John Middleton. *Jonathan Swift: A Critical Biography.* London: Jonathan Cape, 1954; New York: Noonday Press, 1955. Pp. 508.

    Middleton Murry announces in his Preface, "My aim has been to write a book which should be at once a life of Swift and a critical study of his works." As a critical study, his volume has been regularly cited in more recent discussions of Swift's poems. The passages mentioned most frequently include those on the early odes, *Cadenus and Vanessa,* the "scatological" poems (in the chapter with the notorious title "The Excremental Vision"), and *Verses on the Death of Dr. Swift.*

90. Naumov, Nićifor. "Poezija Dzonatana Swifta" (The Poetry of Jonathan Swift). *Anali Filološkog Fakulteta* (Belgrade University) 7 (1967): 401-32.

    This evaluation of Swift's poems, which have been neglected until the last few decades, justifies the conclusion that they deserve a definite place in the history of English poetry. Naumov analyzes *Verses on the Death of Dr. Swift, Cadenus and Vanessa, On Poetry: A Rapsody,* poems to Stella, *Baucis and Philemon,* and Frances Harris's *Petition.* A summary in English is provided at the end of the article.

91. Nemoianu, Virgil. "Swift si istoria rimei engleze" (Swift and the History of English Rhyme). *Revista de istorie si teorie literara* (Bucharest), vol. 16, no. 3 (1967): 441-48.

    In Rumanian. "The author examines two theories which contributed to the progress of criticism of Swift's work,

those of R. Quintana and Martin Price. He proposes a new
classification of Swift's poetry: the 'Odes,' poetry of
realistic description, and the political polemics as
verses which unveil false forms. The rhyme has a deter-
minant role in Swift's endeavour to impose a rationalistic
simplicity on the chaotic aspects of reality." (Quoted
from *The Scriblerian*, vol. 1, no. 1 [Autumn 1968]: 4.)

91A. Novak, Maximillian E. "Introduction." *The Poetry of
Jonathan Swift*. Papers read at a Clark Library Seminar
20 January 1979. Los Angeles: William Andrews Clark
Library, University of California, 1981, pp. v–ix.

An introduction to the lectures delivered by Robert C.
Elliott and Arthur H. Scouten (see items 61A, 105A).
Implicitly denying that this program by two senior Swiftians was set up to compete with the highly successful
Special Sessions on Swift's poetry by younger scholars
at meetings of the Modern Language Association in 1976,
1977, and 1978 (in which Scouten participated; see item
106), Novak tells of Elliott's death, glosses over the
use in Elliott's lecture of *A Panegyric on the Reverend
Dean Swift* (proved spurious in items 413 and 426), and
praises the Hume-Scouten article of 1973 on *Verses on the
Death of Dr. Swift* (see item 278) to the tacit detriment
of the many essays subsequently published on that poem.

92. Parkin, Rebecca Price. "Neoclassic Defensive Techniques
in the Verse of Swift and Johnson Dealing with the
Theme of *Christianus Perfectus*." *Studies on Voltaire
and the Eighteenth Century* 89 (1972): 1255–75.

Swift's poems, despite their many portrayals of clergy-
men, avoid direct personal advocacy of the ideal of
Christian commitment. His verse abounds in Christian
allusions which reflect his sincere belief in the ideal,
but his presentation is almost always oblique, employing
irony, satire, and even scurrility to demonstrate what
Christian perfection is *not*. Parkin comments briefly on
many poems without analyzing any at length.

93. Paulson, Ronald. "Swift, Stella, and Permanence." *ELH*
27 (1960): 298–314. Reprint (revised). *The Fictions
of Satire*. Baltimore: Johns Hopkins Press, 1967,
pp. 189–206.

Traces the theme of body and soul, flesh and spirit,
through a series of Swift's poems: *Verses on the Death of
Dr. Swift* and *The Life and Genuine Character of Doctor
Swift*, the pindaric odes, the "dressing room" ("scatological") poems, and the Stella and Vanessa poems.

94. Price, Martin. *Swift's Rhetorical Art: A Study in
     Structure and Meaning.* Yale Studies in English, vol.
     123. New Haven: Yale University Press, 1953. Pp. viii
     + 117. Reprint. Arcturus Books. Carbondale and
     Edwardsville: Southern Illinois University Press; London
     and Amsterdam: Feffer and Simons, 1973.

     Briefly discusses *Ode to the Honourable Sir William
     Temple*, *Baucis and Philemon*, *The Description of a Sala-
     mander*, *The Fable of Midas*, and *Cadenus and Vanessa*.
     Cites eleven of Swift's other poems.

95. Probyn, Clive T. "Realism and Raillery: Augustan Conver-
     sation and the Poetry of Swift." *Durham University
     Journal* 70 (December 1977): 1-14.

     As occasional verse, Swift's poetry abounds in conver-
     sational and dramatic qualities that represent its very
     essence although they tend to discourage traditional
     criticism. "The dominant tone of Swift's poetry is not
     rhetorical forms, but human voices." Moreover, "Swift's
     poetry is full of talk at war with the forms and conven-
     tions imposed from without." In poem after poem, the
     ritual strategies of art and society are shown crumbling
     as the attempt is made to apply them to the chaotic par-
     ticularities of life. Probyn discusses many works brief-
     ly; no single poem is analyzed in detail.

96. Rawson, C.J. "The Nightmares of Strephon: Nymphs of the
     City in the Poems of Swift, Baudelaire, Eliot." *English
     Literature in the Age of Disguise*. Edited by Maximil-
     lian E. Novak. Berkeley: University of California
     Press, 1977, pp. 57-99.

     Indulges in wide-ranging comparisons between Swift's
     verse and that of Baudelaire and T.S. Eliot. Rawson's
     essay is essentially three loosely connected discussions
     of (1) Swift's poetic treatment of cities in the two
     Description poems; (2) the "scatological" poems, especially
     The Progress of Beauty, *A Beautiful Young Nymph Going to
     Bed*, *Strephon and Chloe*, *Cassinus and Peter*, and *The Lady's
     Dressing Room*; and (3) the poems to Lady Acheson, espe-
     cially *Epistle to a Lady*, and to Stella. Swift's "city"
     poems differ from Eliot's and Baudelaire's in their banal
     flatness, their sober and deadpan note. The "scatological"
     poems, which are more lighthearted and animated than is
     usually supposed, do not yield the facile middle ways and
     golden means that critics persist in trying to discover.
     In the Stella poems, the conventions of romantic love are
     not so much deflated as revalidated in the context of
     reality.

97. Raymond, John. "The Excremental Vision." *New Statesman*,
     vol. 55, no. 1421 (7 June 1958): 735-36.

     A review essay on Joseph Horrell's edition (see item
     10). Raymond offers an eloquent, provocative commentary
     on various features of the informal kind of verse Swift
     wrote during his later years in Ireland. Singled out
     for quotation are *The Grand Question Debated*, *The Legion
     Club*, and *The First of April*.

98. [Read, Herbert.] "The Poems of Swift." *London Times
     Literary Supplement*, 4 July 1929, pp. 521-22.

     A review essay on Ball's study (item 45) and Roberts's
     edition (item 13). This sympathetic discussion main-
     tains that in breaking existing literary conventions,
     Swift did not lack all convention but instead discovered
     new ones. In contrast to the Romantic notion that good
     poetry should describe beautiful subjects, Swift's poems
     utilize everyday subject matter, whose substance deter-
     mines his form. Read damns the ode to the Athenian
     Society, praises Frances Harris's *Petition*, misses the
     tongue-in-cheek manner of *On Poetry: A Rapsody*, and finds
     A Description of the Morning similar to T.S. Eliot's
     poems. This essay is an extended version of the one in
     Read's *In Defence of Shelley* (see item 99).

99. Read, Herbert. "Swift's Poetry." *In Defence of Shelley
     and Other Essays*. London: Heinemann, 1936, pp. 167-76.
     Reprint. *Collected Essays in Literary Criticism*.
     London: Faber and Faber, 1938, pp. 213-19. 2d ed.
     1954.

     This essay is a truncated version of Read's "The Poems
     of Swift" (see item 98). Read cites *Ode to the Athenian
     Society*, Frances Harris's *Petition*, and *On Poetry: A
     Rapsody*.

100. Roberts, Philip. "Swift's Poetry." *Swift*. Edited by
     W.A. Speck. Arco Literary Critiques. New York:
     Arco Publishing Company, 1970, pp. 49-72.

     Designed for the general reader rather than the
     specialist in Swift's poetry. Roberts repeats most of
     the conventional attitudes, including the tendency to
     ignore the later poems and focus upon the earlier ones.
     Covering a total of thirty-three poems, his chronological
     survey includes sections on the early odes, "Poetry,
     1698-1709," "Political Poems 1710-14," "'Cadenus and
     Vanessa,'" "Poems in Ireland 1715-27," and "Last Poems."

Special attention is given to *Cadenus and Vanessa*, although little of value is said about it. The only earlier discussion cited is Maurice Johnson's *The Sin of Wit* (see item 81).

101. Roberts, R. Ellis. "Jonathan Swift in his Poems and Minor Writings." *Reading for Pleasure and Other Essays*. London: Methuen, 1928, pp. 197-222. The latter half of this essay is identical with the introduction to Roberts's edition of Swift's *Miscellaneous Poems* (see item 13). Although it consists mostly of psycho-biographical speculation, some critical remarks on the poems are included.

102. Rodino, Richard H. "Notes on the Developing Motives and Structures of Swift's Poetry." *Contemporary Studies of Swift's Poetry*. Edited by John Irwin Fischer and Donald C. Mell, Jr., with David M. Vieth, associate editor. Newark: University of Delaware Press; London and Toronto: Associated University Presses, 1980, pp. 87-100.

Rodino's thesis is that in his poems of 1730-1733, Swift turned sharply toward "vexatious," audience-entrapping works without clear norms--a technique foreshadowed in a group of "open," non-judging poems he had written during 1706-1714. The confused disjunction between idealism and satirical honesty in Swift's early odes gave way in 1698-1714 to relatively conventional verses that imply a middle ground between extremes or some other positive, e.g., *Verses Wrote in a Lady's Ivory Table-Book*. Following the non-conclusive poems of 1706-1714, such as the two *Description* pieces and *Cadenus and Vanessa*, and the relatively undistinguished poems of 1714-1730, Swift's "vexatious" poems of 1730-1733 include *Verses on the Death of Dr. Swift*; *The Beast's Confession to the Priest*, a subversion of the conventional animal fable; *The Lady's Dressing Room* and similar "scatological" poems, prefigured in 1719 by *The Progress of Beauty*; *The Day of Judgement*; and *The Place of the Damn'd*. *The Legion Club* rounds off Swift's development.

103. Rowse, A.L. "Jonathan Swift." *The English Spirit: Essays in History and Literature*. London: Macmillan, 1944, pp. 182-92. Reprints, with the title "Swift as Poet." 2d ed. (revised and reset). London: Macmillan, 1966. Rev. ed. New York: Funk and Wagnalls, 1967, pp. 170-78. *Fair Liberty Was All His Cry: A*

Tercentenary Tribute to Jonathan Swift 1667-1745.
Edited by A. Norman Jeffares. London: Macmillan;
New York: St. Martin's Press, 1967, pp. 98-106.
Swift: Modern Judgements. Edited by A. Norman Jeffares.
London: Macmillan, 1969; Nashville, TN: Aurora, 1970,
pp. 135-42.

Except for its opening section, this essay is identical
with Rowse's review of Sir Harold Williams's edition of
the poems (see item 16). Rowse pleads for more sympa-
thetic appreciation now that the Williams edition has
made Swift's verse more readily accessible. Conceding
that because Swift tended to repress his emotions, his
poetry lacks variety in tone, Rowse urges that Swift
expressed himself more fully in his verse than in his
prose, said nothing in prose that he did not say as well
in verse, and found verse a perfect vehicle for his
chief emotion, intellectual passion.

104. San Juan, E., Jr. "The Anti-Poetry of Jonathan Swift."
     Philological Quarterly 44 (July 1965): 387-96.

     The "anti-poetic" element in Swift's poetry (the con-
     cept is here credited to Wallace Stevens) involves a
     two-step process. It starts with the extraordinary mass
     of concrete details in the poems, rendered with sensual
     immediacy and the pungency of everyday actuality. These
     discordant particulars are, in turn, harmonized through
     idealizing aesthetic patterns and the establishment of
     meaningful relationships--although "as a rule the resolu-
     tion of attitudes remains manifold, inexhaustible, and
     susceptible of limitless interpretations." The many
     poems discussed include *The Progress of Beauty*, *The
     Lady's Dressing Room*, *A Beautiful Young Nymph Going to
     Bed*, *On Dreams*, *The Author upon Himself*, *Verses Wrote
     in a Lady's Ivory Table-Book*, and Frances Harris's
     Petition.

105. Schakel, Peter J. *The Poetry of Jonathan Swift: Allusion
     and the Development of a Poetic Style.* Madison: Uni-
     versity of Wisconsin Press, 1978. Pp. x + 218.

     Reviewed by Eric Rothstein in *Studies in English
     Literature* 19 (Summer 1979): 546-47; by Richard H.
     Rodino in *The Scriblerian*, vol. 12, no. 1 (Autumn
     1979): 42-44; by Dustin Griffin in *Journal of English
     and Germanic Philology* 78 (October 1979): 554-56; by
     Pat Rogers in *London Times Literary Supplement*, 21
     December 1979, p. 165; by Patricia Meyer Spacks in

Modern Language Quarterly 40 (December 1979): 403-11;
by Francis Doherty in *Review of English Studies* n.s.
31 (November 1981): 469-70; by Carmela Perri in *Style*
15 (Winter 1981): 40-42. See also the review essay
by John R. Clark, item 50.

Peter Schakel's volume, which concentrates upon Swift's
use of classical, biblical, and contemporary allusions,
was the third of four book-length critical studies of
Swift's poetry to be published during 1977-1980, after
the books by Nora Jaffe and John Irwin Fischer (see items
78, 69) and before that of A.B. England (see item 62).
"The characteristic trait of his best poetry," Schakel
claims, is Swift's "use of allusions or of an external
source to expand an initially local or personal situation or incident into a significant statement on art and
morality." Schakel "traces Swift's development as a
poetic craftsman from the early odes, where allusions
are scattered and mostly decorative, through the early
verse satires and classical imitations, where Swift
learned that conventions or structures borrowed from
others could free him to give attention to descriptive
and satiric detail, to the later satires, where such
borrowings become integral to the poems, unifying structure, tone, and theme." Although this emphasis on allusions invites a skewed treatment and may initially
seem to yield disappointing results, later chapters ex-
ploit it to produce well-rounded, illuminating analyses
of many individual works.

Principal poems discussed: Chapter 1: the early odes.
Chapter 2: *Vanbrug's House*, *The Description of a Sala-
mander*, *Baucis and Philemon*, *Verses Wrote in a Lady's
Ivory Table-Book*, and *A Description of a City Shower*.
Chapter 3: imitations of Horace, *Epistles* 1.5 (*Toland's
Invitation to Dismal*), *Odes* 2.1 (*to Richard Steele*),
Epistles 1.7 and *Satires* 2.6 (both to Harley), and
The Author upon Himself; *Cadenus and Vanessa*. Chapter
4: the three *Progress* poems (of love, beauty, and mar-
riage) and the Stella poems; *To Lord Harley, on His
Marriage*; *The Lady's Dressing Room*, *A Beautiful Young
Nymph Going to Bed*, and *Strephon and Chloe*. Chapter 5:
Verses on the Death of Dr. Swift; *A Libel on Doctor De-
lany*, *A Panegyric on the Reverend Dean Swift*, and *To
Doctor Delany on the Libels*; *An Epistle to a Lady*; and
On Poetry: A Rapsody. Chapter 6: imitation of Horace,
Odes 1.14 (*inscribed to Ireland*), *Traulus. The First
Part*, *On the Words--Brother Protestant and Fellow Chris-
tian*, and *The Legion Club*.

105A. Scouten, Arthur H. "Jonathan Swift's Progress from
      Prose to Poetry." *The Poetry of Jonathan Swift.*
      Papers read at a Clark Library Seminar 20 January 1979.
      Los Angeles: William Andrews Clark Memorial Library,
      University of California, 1981, pp. 25-52.

      Accounts biographically for Swift's brilliant burst of
      poetry in the years 1729-1731, which recent books on the
      poems have neglected to explain. This development is
      signaled by a shift from prose pamphlets on the plight
      of Ireland (such as *A Modest Proposal*, 1729) to verse
      on public affairs in England designed to bolster Swift's
      public image; by abortive attempts to write Popean heroic
      couplets to establish himself as a serious poet (e.g.
      To Mr. Gay and *On Mr. Pulteney*); and by a rift in Swift's
      friendship with Pope. The poems produced include *Traulus*,
      A Libel on Doctor Delany, most of the "scatological"
      poems (*The Lady's Dressing Room*, *A Beautiful Young Nymph*,
      Strephon and Chloe, *Cassinus and Peter*), *Verses on the
      Death of Dr. Swift*, *The Day of Judgement*, *An Epistle to
      a Lady*, *On Poetry: A Rapsody*, and *The Legion Club*.
      Scouten also discusses *A Panegyrick on the Dean*, *Direc-
      tions for a Birth-day Song*, and *A Love Song in the Modern
      Taste*. He concludes with a review of critical attitudes
      toward Swift's poetry over the past two centuries.

106. Scouten, Arthur H. "Swift's Poetry and the Gentle Read-
      er." *Contemporary Studies of Swift's Poetry.* Edited
      by John Irwin Fischer and Donald C. Mell, Jr., with
      David M. Vieth, associate editor. Newark: University
      of Delaware Press; London and Toronto: Associated Uni-
      versity Presses, 1980, pp. 46-55.

      Writing before the Romantic notion of literature as
      self-expression, Swift displays an opposite tendency
      toward intense audience-consciousness, drawing a sharp
      line between poems designed for publication and occasion-
      al verse aimed at a specific private audience. Even in
      his public poems he distinguishes several categories of
      readers, and with the private poems there is extreme
      danger of misinterpretation unless one knows exactly what
      audience is being addressed. Thus students of Swift
      have missed the characteristic playfulness of his mind
      either by ignoring his poetic bagatelles or by taking
      them too seriously, as has happened recently with *Stella's
      Birth-day, a Great Bottle of Wine Being That Day Dug up*
      and *The Journal*. By way of analogue, Scouten cites a
      letter to Swift whose raillery cannot be appreciated un-
      less its highly private allusions are explicated.

107. Scruggs, Charles. "Swift's Views on Language: The Basis of His Attack on Poetic Diction." *Texas Studies in Literature and Language* 13 (Winter 1972): 581-92.

    Central to Swift's concern for "correctness" in language is his emphasis on "simplicity," whose two main attributes are force or energy and "compass," i.e. the cosmopolitan awareness of the gentleman-scholar. Scruggs discusses *Cassinus and Peter*, *On Poetry: A Rapsody*, *The Progress of Beauty*, *The Lady's Dressing Room*, *Strephon and Chloe*, *Phillis, Or, the Progress of Love*, and *A Satirical Elegy*.

108. Selden, Raman. *English Verse Satire 1590-1765.* London: George Allen and Unwin, 1978, pp. 144-52.

    Discusses Swift's verse in terms of the polarity between "Horatian" and "Juvenalian" satire that provides the thesis of Selden's volume. Swift's "Horatian" qualities include his "laughing," anti-romantic, low style, his fondness for mock poems, and above all the autobiographical immediacy of his poetry. On the "Juvenalian" side is his *saeva indignatio*, often expressed in scatology and obscenity, which makes him the only Augustan satirist to doubt the moral efficacy of satire. Among the poems briefly discussed are *Horace, Part of the Sixth Satire of the Second Book Imitated* (1714) and *An Apology to Lady Carteret.*

109. Stavrou, C.N. "The Love Songs of J. Swift, G. Bernard Shaw and J.A.A. Joyce." *Midwest Quarterly* (Pittsburgh, KS) 6 (1964): 135-62.

    Belletristic. There is no extended discussion of any single poem.

110. Suddard, Sarah Julie Mary. "Swift's Poetry." *Keats, Shelley, and Shakespeare Studies and Essays in English Literature.* Cambridge: Cambridge University Press, 1912, pp. 231-51.

    The characteristic pattern in Swift's verse is the portrayal of a romantic illusion, followed by debunking of that illusion in accordance with his pessimistic philosophy of human nature. His dedication to reality is directed against the idealism and the very forms of poetry itself. Yet Swift's narrow conception of poetry includes, in practice, such poetic qualities as a sharp sense of concrete detail, imagination, an understanding of human psychology, careful poetic structuring, an un-

pretentious but efficacious style, and an instinct for
the dramatic. Suddard's distinguished but little-known
essay sensitively registers the general feeling about
Swift's poetry at the time--February 1906--when it was
written.

111. Taylor, W.D. "Poems." *Jonathan Swift, A Critical
      Essay.* London: Peter Davies, 1933, pp. 234-52.

      In most of Swift's poetry, according to this old-
      fashioned essay, "Swift is Mephistopheles, his mission
      being to drag men's high aspirations down to the dust
      and worms whence they sprung." But Swift "is also
      Faust," and Taylor can praise three poems extravagantly
      for their "passion": *Verses on the Death of Dr. Swift,
      Cadenus and Vanessa,* and *The Day of Judgement. Baucis
      and Philemon* is discussed favorably, as are Swift's
      verses written for the amusement of his Irish friends.
      Nevertheless, the "scatological" poems turn all to
      "excrement and venom."

112. Trickett, Rachel. *The Honest Muse: A Study in Augustan
      Verse.* Oxford: Clarendon Press, 1967, pp. 121-26.

      Traces the influence of Restoration Court poetry, or
      the obverse of it, in the two *Description* poems, *Cadenus
      and Vanessa, Stella's Birthday, 1721, The Description
      of an Irish Feast,* and *Baucis and Philemon.*

113. Tyne, James L., S.J. "Gulliver's Maker and Gullibility."
      Criticism 7 (1965): 151-67.

      In contrast to the romanticizing illusions of the poets
      who preceded him, Swift in his anti-romantic poems ex-
      poses the gullibility of those who accept such pleasant
      lies. Tyne gives special attention to *Cassinus and
      Peter, The Lady's Dressing Room,* and *Strephon and Chloe.*
      In these "scatological" poems, but more conspicuously in
      Verses on the Death of Dr. Swift, Swift advocates a
      balanced, open-eyed acknowledgement of human limitations.

114. Uphaus, Robert W. "Swift's Irony Reconsidered."
      Contemporary Studies of Swift's Poetry. Edited by
      John Irwin Fischer and Donald C. Mell, Jr., with
      David M. Vieth, associate editor. Newark: University
      of Delaware Press; London and Toronto: Associated
      University Presses, 1980, pp. 169-77.

      Uphaus cites F.R. Leavis's essay on "The Irony of Swift"
      to distinguish between the "philosophical" satire of

Pope and Gibbon and Swift's "vexatious" satirical prose,
in which any themes or positives tend to be separated
from the disorienting effect this prose produces on a
reader. In Swift's later poems, however--those written
after 1726--the missing positives of his earlier prose
are replaced by what Maurice Johnson has called his
"biographical presence" (see item 82). Brushing aside
the complexities of irony and satire, persona techniques,
and affective or intentional fallacies, Swift straight-
forwardly projects his own identity as he understood it
in a poem like *Verses on the Death of Dr. Swift*, asserts
his distinction as a freeman among slaves in a poem like
Holyhead. Sept. 25, 1727, and bluntly denounces evil
in poems like *The Place of the Damn'd*, *The Day of Judgement*, *The Beast's Confession*, and *The Legion Club*. For
poetic artifice he substitutes personal animus. These
later poems deserve more critical attention than they
generally receive.

115. Uphaus, Robert W. "Swift's Poetry: The Making of
     Meaning." *Eighteenth-Century Studies* 5 (Summer 1972):
     569-86.

     Disputing the view of Swift's verse as "anti-poetry,"
     Uphaus tries to show how Swift makes poetry by projecting
     his own vision of reality--a simultaneous opposition to
     the visionary imagination and a firm commitment to the
     material world as the primary source of human knowledge--
     within certain traditional literary conventions. Swift
     alters or reshapes these poetic conventions, as is the
     traditional prerogative and responsibility of poets,
     and in the process makes meaning. Uphaus discusses
     Verses Wrote in a Lady's Ivory Table-Book, *The Descrip-
     tion of a Salamander*, *A Satirical Elegy*, *Stella's Birth-
     day, 1727*, *A Beautiful Young Nymph Going to Bed*, and
     On Poetry: A Rapsody.

116. Vickers, Brian. "Introduction." *The World of Jonathan
     Swift: Essays for the Tercentenary*. Cambridge:
     Harvard University Press, 1968, pp. 15-18.

     Editor's comments on the two essays on Swift's poetry
     in Vickers's volume, by Roger Savage and Geoffrey Hill
     (see items 163, 73).

117. Vieth, David M. "Metaphors and Metamorphoses: Basic
     Techniques in the Middle Period of Swift's Poetry,
     1698-1719." *Contemporary Studies of Swift's Poetry*.
     Edited by John Irwin Fischer and Donald C. Mell, Jr.,

with David M. Vieth, associate editor. Newark: University of Delaware Press; London and Toronto: Associated
University Presses, 1980, pp. 56-68.

Calls attention to the similarity between poems in
which a mock-Ovidian metamorphosis (or mock-Christian
miracle) transforms little or nothing and poems in
which the vehicle of a metaphor transforms the tenor
almost beyond recognition. In either case, the skewed
relationship between the two terms being compared projects an absurd universe in which seemingly meaningful
connections are at best dubious. The "metamorphosis"
poems discussed are the two *Description* pieces, *Verses
on the Death of Dr. Swift*, *The Day of Judgement*, *Vanbrug's House*, and *Baucis and Philemon*. The "metaphor"
poems are *The Description of a Salamander*, *The Fable of
Midas*, *The Virtues of Sid Hamet the Magician's Rod*, and
The Progress of Beauty. Also discussed are *Verses Wrote
in a Lady's Ivory Table-Book*, *An Elegy on Mr. Patrige*,
Apollo Outwitted, and *Cadenus and Vanessa*.

118. Vieth, David M. "A Symposium on Women in Swift's Poems:
      Vanessa, Stella, Lady Acheson, and Celia: Introduction."
      Papers on Language and Literature 14 (Spring 1978):
      115-16.

      An introduction to a series of five papers (see items
      170, 181, 191, 211, and 241) which were delivered in a
      Special Session on Swift's poetry at the annual meeting
      of the Modern Language Association of America in New
      York City in December 1976. Vieth concludes that the
      papers collectively shed more light on the nature of
      Jonathan Swift, as a poet and a man, than on the nature
      of women.

119. Vurgaft, E. *Satiricheskaia Poeziia Svifta*. Mosk.
      ordena Lenina gos. un-t im. M.V. Lomonosova. Trudy
      Nauch. studencheskovo o-va. Filol. fak. Kafedra
      vseobshchei literaturi, Vyp. 2. Moscow: Izd-vo Mosk.
      gos. un-ta, tip. M-va tiazh. mash., 1948. Pp. 59.

      A study of Swift's satiric poetry in Russian.

120. Ward, David. "Swift's Verse." *Jonathan Swift: An
      Introductory Essay*. London: Methuen, 1973, pp. 184-204.

      A general essay with no single thesis or special point
      of view. Ward discusses Frances Harris's *Petition*, the
      two *Description* poems, *Cadenus and Vanessa*, *An Apology to
      the Lady Carteret*, *Directions for a Birth-day Song*, *The
      Legion Club*, *On Poetry: A Rapsody*, and *Verses on the
      Death of Dr. Swift*.

121. Watson, Sheila. "Swift and Ovid: The Development of
     Metasatire." *Humanities Association Bulletin*,
     vol. 18, no. 1 (Spring 1967): 5-13.

     Discusses the prevalence of Ovidian allusions and
     metamorphoses in Swift's poetry and prose. Numerous
     poems are cited, with special attention given to *The
     Bubble*, *The Description of a Salamander*, and *On the
     Little House by the Church Yard of Castleknock*. These
     examples "suggest that for Swift the Ovidian technique
     had become a probe for exploring the temper of the age
     in which he lived."

122. White, H.O. "The Art of Swift." *Hermathena* 69 (May
     1947): 1-8.

     Extracts from a lecture delivered in November 1945
     at Trinity College, Dublin. White's comments on Swift's
     poetry, though brief, are incisive as well as apprecia-
     tive.

123. Williams, Kathleen M. "'Animal Rationis Capax.' A
     Study of Certain Aspects of Swift's Imagery." *ELH* 21
     (September 1954): 193-207. Reprint. *Fair Liberty Was
     All His Cry: A Tercentenary Tribute to Jonathan Swift
     1667-1745*. Edited by A. Norman Jeffares. London:
     Macmillan; New York: St. Martin's Press, 1967, pp.
     131-45.

     The vast quantity of imagery of the physical in Swift's
     works, often so unpleasant as to disgust his readers,
     serves to convey a dazzling variety of meanings. In
     "scatological" poems like *The Progress of Beauty* and
     Strephon and Chloe, disagreeable imagery of the human
     body is used to ridicule the unreal elegance of con-
     temporary poetry of compliment and love. Williams com-
     ments in passing on *A Panegyric on the Reverend Dean
     Swift*, *On Poetry: A Rapsody*, *Ode to the Athenian Society*,
     and *Ode to Dr. William Sancroft*.

124. Williams, Kathleen. *Jonathan Swift and the Age of
     Compromise*. Lawrence: University of Kansas Press,
     1958; London: Constable, 1959, pp. 38-41, 146-53, and
     passim. Reprint (paperback). Lawrence: University
     of Kansas Press, 1968.

     Discusses Swift's early odes and his use of physical
     imagery in a variety of the poems.

125. Wilson, Edmund. "Cousin Swift, You Will Never Be a
     Poet." *The Shores of Light: A Literary Chronicle of
     the Twenties and Thirties.* New York: Farrar, Straus
     and Young, 1952, pp. 696-700.

     A review article prompted by the publication of Sir
     Harold Williams's edition of the poems in 1937 (see
     item 16). Praising Swift's "strong sensuous side,"
     Wilson finds the poetry remarkable for its vivid descrip-
     tions of eighteenth-century city life and similar uses
     of concrete detail. Also noteworthy are Swift's flights
     of macabre fantasy and his gift for self-dramatization,
     which created a new kind of lyric out of curses and
     sneers.

126. Wolfe, Humbert. *Notes on English Verse Satire.* London:
     Hogarth Press, 1929, pp. 33, 85-91.

     Barely allowing Swift to be a poet, Wolfe divides his
     verse satires into three types: political, anti-feminist,
     and ("what alone has merit") the more general attack on
     human frailties. On the negative side are *Traulus* (an
     "almost maniac onslaught"), *A Beautiful Young Nymph Going
     to Bed* ("It is doubtful whether in the history of verse
     there exists anything so wantonly brutal"), and *The
     Furniture of a Woman's Mind*; on the positive side, *The
     Beast's Confession to the Priest, Verses on the Death
     of Dr. Swift,* and four lines from *On Poetry: A Rapsody*
     (which, "because of their compression," can be "favour-
     ably compared with the effect even of his great prose
     satires").

127. Wyld, Henry Cecil. *Studies in English Rhymes from
     Surrey to Pope: A Chapter in the History of English.*
     London: John Murray, 1923. Pp. xiii + 140. Reprint.
     New York: Russell and Russell, 1965.

     Swift is one of eighteen poets from whom Wyld draws
     his examples.

IV. SPECIALIZED STUDIES

A. Swift's Verse Style

128. Bond, Richmond P. *English Burlesque Poetry 1700-1750*.
Harvard Studies in English, vol. 6. Cambridge:
Harvard University Press, 1932. Pp. xi + 483.
Reprint. New York: Russell and Russell, 1964.

Generally relevant to Swift's use of parody and the
"burlesque style," but provides surprisingly little
specific information.

129. Bullitt, John M. "Swift's 'Rules of Raillery.'" *Veins
of Humor*. Edited by Harry Levin. Harvard English
Studies 3. Cambridge: Harvard University Press, 1972,
pp. 93-108.

Drawing upon statements in several of the poems including *To Mr. Delany*, Bullitt focuses Swift's conception
of raillery as good-humored ridicule which does not
offend its subject, in contrast to railing or ridicule
designed to hurt. Swift's model was Voiture, who provided the formula of the seeming complaint that turns
into a graceful compliment. In his correspondence,
Swift much improved Voiture's rhetorical model. See
the articles on Swift's raillery by Eugene F. Timpe and
David Sheehan, items 136 and 185.

130. England, A.B. "Byron, Swift, Butler, and Burlesque."
*Byron's "Don Juan" and Eighteenth-Century Literature:
A Study of Some Rhetorical Continuities and Disconti-
nuities*. Lewisburg, PA: Bucknell University Press;
London: Associated University Presses, 1975, pp. 80-147.

Defining and illustrating what was known technically,
in the late seventeenth and early eighteenth centuries,
as the "burlesque style," England employs it as a context
for stylistic analysis of Butler's *Hudibras*, a range of

poems by Swift, and Byron's *The Vision of Judgement* and
Don Juan. In contrast to Pope's verse style, which
implies a hierarchy of values, the burlesque style tends
to undercut and disrupt the Popeian kind of coherence.
Its verbal texture projects a special view of external
reality through polysyllabic Hudibrastic rhymes, incon-
gruous diction, absurd juxtaposing of opposites (including zeugma), heterogeneous accumulation of concrete details, abrupt shifts in tone, and other forms of discon-
tinuity. In addition to the poems also cited in his short-
er essay "The Style of *Don Juan* and Augustan Poetry" (see
item 131), England offers illuminating comments on passages
in *An Epistle upon an Epistle*, *Apollo Outwitted*, *Death
and Daphne*, *Directions for a Birth-day Song*, *The Day of
Judgement*, *Cadenus and Vanessa*, *The Journal of a Modern
Lady*, and *A Description of the Morning*.

131. England, A.B. "The Style of *Don Juan* and Augustan
      Poetry." *Byron: A Symposium*. Edited by John D. Jump.
      London: Macmillan, 1975, pp. 94-112.

      Utilizes the verse styles of Pope and Swift to illus-
      trate the eighteenth-century antecedents of Byron's
      style in *Don Juan*. Whereas Pope's style implies a
      hierarchy of values, Swift's "burlesque style," descended
      from Butler's *Hudibras*, tends to undermine rather than
      to affirm hierarchical structures. England analyzes
      the juxtaposition of apparent opposites in passages from
      The Dean's Reasons for Not Building at Drapier's Hill,
      On Poetry: A Rapsody, *Verses Wrote in a Lady's Ivory
      Table-Book*, *A Description of a City Shower*, and *The
      Journal*. Some of the points made in this illuminating
      essay duplicate those in England's book *Byron's "Don
      Juan" and Eighteenth-Century Literature* (see item 130).

132. Fricke, Donna G. "Swift and the Tradition of Informal
      Satiric Poetry." *Contemporary Studies of Swift's
      Poetry*. Edited by John Irwin Fischer and Donald C.
      Mell, Jr., with David M. Vieth, associate editor.
      Newark: University of Delaware Press; London and
      Toronto: Associated University Presses, 1980, pp. 36-
      45.

      Swift's preference for writing satirical verse in the
      informal or colloquial mode, rather than the classical
      formal mode championed by Dryden and Pope, was not an
      aberration but has roots that run deep in English litera-
      ture. Deriving from the octosyllabic couplets of ac-
      centual Latin hymns and medieval French poetry, but also

from four-stress Old English verse, the informal style
was more truly indigenous than the heroic couplet.
Swift refines upon the earlier satiric use of colloquial
verse by Chaucer and especially Skelton and Butler;
Lodge, Jonson, Herrick, Lovelace, and Marvell adapted
octosyllabic couplets to love lyrics that foreshadow
Swift's verses to Stella. In his broad satiric range,
Swift's immediate poetic predecessor is not so much
Butler as Rochester or perhaps Marvell. See also the
essays by Dona Munker and William K. Wimsatt, items
134 and 138.

133. Kulisheck, Clarence L. "Swift's Octosyllabics and the
      Hudibrastic Tradition." *Journal of English and
      Germanic Philology* 53 (1954): 361-68.

      Examines the ways in which Swift's verse style may
      have been indebted to that of Samuel Butler in *Hudibras*.

134. Munker, Dona F. "That Paultry Burlesque Stile:
      Seventeenth-Century Poetry and Augustan 'Low Serious-
      ness.'" *Seventeenth-Century News*, vol. 33, nos. 1-2
      (Spring-Summer 1975): 14-22.

      Traces the development of the "burlesque style" from
      early classical times to its post-Restoration culmina-
      tion in Rochester, Prior, and Swift. This style is
      characterized by down-to-earth (even grotesque) realism,
      a complex satirical speaker (persona or *eirōn*), banter-
      ing colloquial language, the four-foot burlesque line,
      and the mocking irreverence of the late medieval "bour-
      geois tradition." Special attention is given to *The
      Lady's Dressing Room*. See also the essays by Donna
      Fricke and William K. Wimsatt, items 132 and 138.

135. Piper, William Bowman. *The Heroic Couplet.* Cleveland
      and London: Case Western Reserve University Press,
      1969, pp. 361-63.

      Illustrates ways in which Swift exploits the devices
      of the pentameter couplet "to reduce, to humble, to
      deflate the objects of his satiric address."

136. Timpe, Eugene F. "Swift as Railleur." *Journal of
      English and Germanic Philology* 69 (January 1970): 41-49.

      Clarifies what Swift intended by raillery, which had
      been referred to by Quintillian and practiced in France
      by Voiture. "Raillery," wrote Swift in his best descrip-
      tion, "was to say something that at first appeared a

Reproach, or Reflection; but, by some Turn of Wit un-
expected and surprising, ended always in a Compliment,
and to the Advantage of the Person it was addressed to."
Although Timpe's illustrations are drawn mostly from the
prose writings, there is discussion of Swift's definition of raillery in *To Mr. Delany* and his early attempt
to practice it in *Ode to the Athenian Society*. See the
later essays by John M. Bullitt and David Sheehan, items
129 and 185.

137. Tyne, James L., S.J. "'Only A Man of Rhimes': Swift's
      Bridled Pegasus." *Papers on Language and Literature*
      14 (Spring 1978): 189-204.

      "Sense" and "rhyme" were, for Swift, the two essentials
      in which anyone claiming to be a poet must prove himself
      expert. The poet must strive for clear sense and employ
      only the vocabulary of common life—conforming to ele-
      mentary grammatical rules and principles of syntax, avoid-
      ing fatuous tautologies and abbreviations, and giving
      full attention to denotations. Rhymes must be exact
      without distorting the natural pronunciation of words.
      Although his verse exhibits the lean, bare look of good
      prose, Swift's revisions show him also working to maxi-
      mize connotations and associations. His rhymes sustain
      the tone and appearance of prose while achieving complex
      poetic effects.

138. Wimsatt, William K. "Rhetoric and Poems: The Example
      of Swift." *The Author in His Work: Essays on a Problem
      in Criticism*. Edited by Louis L. Martz and Aubrey
      Williams; introduction by Patricia Meyer Spacks. New
      Haven and London: Yale University Press, 1978, pp.
      229-44.

      Analyzes Swift's fortunate preference for the short,
      four-stress couplet instead of the long, pentameter
      couplet of Dryden and Pope. Vernacular and anti-classical
      rather than classical in its late medieval origins, the
      short couplet came down to Swift from the Goliardic poets
      through Skelton, Scarron, and Butler. As used by Swift,
      it is characterized by asymmetrical rhetorical structures,
      ready-made phrases, an orientation toward *things*, ex-
      travagant rhymes, and a sense of speed, energy, and ex-
      uberance. "Rhyme is the most brilliantly attractive
      feature of Swift's verse," remarks Wimsatt in this essay
      which possesses special value as the only extended treat-
      ment of Swift's poetry by one of the foremost critics of

the twentieth century. See also the essays by Donna
Fricke and Dona Munker, items 132 and 134.

See also items 511, 521, 542.

B. The Early Odes

139. Ehrenpreis, Irvin. "Swift's First Poem." *Modern
      Language Review* 49 (April 1954): 210-11.

      Argues that *Ode to King William, on His Successes in
      Ireland*, which Sir Harold Williams virtually rejects in
      his edition (see item 16), is spurious, whereas *Ode to
      the King on His Irish Expedition* is genuine Swift.
      Ehrenpreis notes that the satire on Louis XIV at the
      end of the latter poem, including the reference to his
      fistula in ano, is matched by a paragraph in *A Tale of
      a Tub*.

140. French, David P. "Swift, the Non-Jurors, and Jacobitism."
      Modern Language Notes 72 (April 1957): 258-64.

      A careful reading of *Ode to Dr. William Sancroft*
      (1692) reveals that Swift was closer at this time to the
      opinions of the Non-jurors and Jacobites than has been
      noticed. The poem contains two sets of ideas, somewhat
      opposed: enthusiasm for the Non-juring position and
      reluctant acceptance of the necessity for *Realpolitik*
      under William III. See item 146.

141. Fricke, Donna G. "Jonathan Swift's Early Odes and the
      Conversion to Satire." *Enlightenment Essays*, vol. 5,
      no. 2 (Summer 1974): 3-17.

      Attempts to strike a compromise between two popular
      critical positions on Swift's early odes: Irvin Ehren-
      preis's view that they are straightforward panegyrics
      which dissolve into anticlimax and therefore bathos
      (see item 61), and Kathryn Harris's view that they use
      the context of panegyric to effect satire (see item
      143). Fricke maintains that the early odes reveal Swift
      in the process of altering his emphasis from sincere
      Cowleian panegyric toward satire and an independent
      moral voice.

142. Garrison, James D. *Dryden and the Tradition of Pane-
     gyric.* Berkeley, etc.: University of California
     Press, 1975, pp. 243-57.

     Comparing *Ode to the King on His Irish Expedition*
     with Cowley's *Ode upon His Majesties Restoration and
     Return*, Garrison uses Swift's poem to illustrate the
     attrition of the tradition of panegyric by the end of
     the seventeenth century.

143. Harris, Kathryn Montgomery. "'Occasions So Few':
     Satire as a Strategy of Praise in Swift's Early Odes."
     Modern Language Quarterly 31 (March 1970): 22-37.

     Cowley, in his odes, typically praises his heroes with
     accounts of their successful achievements. Swift, on
     the other hand, shifts the emphasis of the ode from
     panegyric to satire, celebrating his ideal by castigating
     the hostile world that surrounds and threatens it. His
     heroes are praised, not so much for their possession of
     an ideal or for deeds in its service, but rather for
     their holding action against hostile opponents. Such a
     strategy of compliment is fundamentally satiric and
     derives from a vision of reality that becomes clearer
     and more strident in Swift's later poems--which Harris
     briefly surveys at the end of her discussion.

144. Jarrell, Mackie Langham. "'Ode to the King': Some
     Contests, Dissensions, and Exchanges among Jonathan
     Swift, John Dunton, and Henry Jones." *Texas Studies
     in Literature and Language* 7 (Summer 1965): 145-59.

     Observing that the case for Swift's authorship of *Ode
     to the King on His Irish Expedition* is not so strong as
     had been assumed (see, for example, item 139), Jarrell
     presents additional internal evidence that the poem is
     probably genuine. Her argument, involving plagiarisms
     by John Dunton from the *Ode* and echoes of Dryden's *All
     for Love* both in the *Ode* and in other early works attrib-
     uted to Swift, seems overly elaborate.

145. Johnson, Maurice. "Swift's Renunciation of the Muse."
     Notes and Queries 197 (24 May 1952): 235-36.

     Swift's well-known couplet in *Occasioned by Sir William
     Temple's Late Illness and Recovery*, in which he renounces
     the Muse's "visionary pow'r," may have been suggested by
     Temple's essay *Of Popular Discontents*.

146. Rosenheim, Edward W., Jr. "Swift's *Ode to Sancroft*: Another Look." *Modern Philology* 73 (Supplement to honor Arthur Friedman, May 1976): 24-39.

Confessing "a somewhat untraditional respect" for the *Ode to Sancroft*, Rosenheim stresses its close tie to contemporary politics--specifically, the Non-juring controversy, to which it relates in ways that differ only in degree, not in kind, from later works of Swift the satirist and controversialist. Not merely "a poetic act of piety," it is addressed to a figure who was "embattled in a controversy that was as passionate as it was consequential." Perhaps the young poet saw his lines, which remained unpublished until 1789, as "a dangerous and illegal act." Structurally, the *Ode* dramatizes a struggle between praise of Sancroft and the irrepressible instinct to attack those who had made a martyr of him. Although usually considered unfinished, the poem ends appropriately with an allusion to a well-known passage in Lucan's *Civil War*. See item 140.

147. Sheehan, David. "Swift on High Pindaric Stilts." *Contemporary Studies of Swift's Poetry*. Edited by John Irwin Fischer and Donald C. Mell, Jr., with David M. Vieth, associate editor. Newark: University of Delaware Press; London and Toronto: Associated University Presses, 1980, pp. 25-35.

Critics of Swift's poetry have attempted to explain his early odes as aesthetic failures, as anticipations of his later satires, or as expressions of a personal conflict between panegyric and satirical impulses. Sheehan calls attention to a circumstance that should have been noted long ago, namely that these odes belong to a minor tradition of seventeenth-century poetry which utilized the Pindaric form for purposes of satire. Among the practitioners of the satiric ode were Ben Jonson, Charles Cotton, Samuel Butler, John Oldham, Thomas Otway, and even Abraham Cowley and John Dryden. To illustrate the value of his perspective, Sheehan analyzes the least-often discussed of Swift's early odes, *Ode to the King on His Irish Expedition*.

148. Sisson, C.H. "The Early Poems of Jonathan Swift." *Books and Bookmen*, vol. 18, no. 8 (May 1973): 54-56.

A rather superficial review of the early odes, whose most characteristic quality is said to be their truthfulness. Portions of this brief essay appear also in Sisson's introduction to his edition of Swift's *Selected Poems* (see item 14).

149. Uphaus, Robert W. "From Panegyric to Satire: Swift's Early Odes and *A Tale of a Tub*." *Texas Studies in*

Literature and Language 13 (Spring 1971): 55-70.

Examines the close relationship between the pervasive
disunity of Swift's early odes and his use of satire in
the *Tale*. Swift's frustrated attempt at writing Pindar-
ics—his "sublime" desire to panegyrize "heroic" figures
even at the expense of his own ironic awareness of human
imposture—becomes one of the models for the persona's
eccentric inventiveness in the *Tale*. Thus the shift
from panegyric to satire in Swift's early literary career
is not so abrupt as it appears.

See also items 47A, 48A, 49, 51, 56, 61, 62, 66, 69, 78, 89,
91, 93, 94, 98, 99, 100, 102, 105, 123, 124, 136, 227, 245,
322, 402, 405, 454, 502, 505, 509, 510, 512, 529, 537, 547,
551, 553, 560, 571.

C. The *Description* Poems
(*A Description of the Morning* and
A Description of a City Shower)

150. Bateson, F.W. "Swift's 'Description of the Morning.'"
      English Poetry: A Critical Introduction. London and
      New York: Longmans, Green, 1950, pp. 175-80. Reprints.
      New York: Barnes and Noble, 1966, pp. 123-26. *Jonathan
      Swift: A Critical Anthology*. Edited by Denis Donoghue.
      Harmondsworth, Eng.: Penguin Books, 1971, pp. 269-73.

      Noting its realism, Bateson finds that "the clue to
      the poem's peculiar flavour" is its juxtaposition of
      what is morally neutral (or at most venial) behavior
      with real social evils, especially those resulting from
      modern *laissez-faire* capitalism. The human beings in
      the poem behave like independent automata, in contrast
      to the Christian dictum that we are members of one an-
      other. Yet the poem's "sense of fact," its "conviction
      of actuality," makes it refreshing instead of depressing.

151. Brooks, Cleanth, and Robert Penn Warren. "A City Shower."
      Understanding Poetry. 3d ed. New York: Holt, Rine-
      hart and Winston, 1960, pp. 200-04. Reprint (revised).
      4th ed. New York: Holt, Rinehart and Winston', 1976,
      pp. 211-13.

      Brooks and Warren's questions provide a helpful intro-
      duction to *A Description of a City Shower*, especially
      for students approaching Swift's poetry for the first
      time.

152. Carnochan, W.B. *Confinement and Flight: An Essay on
      English Literature of the Eighteenth Century.*
      Berkeley, Los Angeles, London: University of California
      Press, 1977, pp. 67-71.

      Brief but suggestive. *A Description of the Morning*
      "is a study in arrested motion," whereas the *City Shower*
      "comes to a crescendo of movement" which "turns out to
      be a recycling, not a purgation, and the storm brings
      the normal life of the city to a standstill."

153. Chalker, John. *The English Georgic: A Study in the
      Development of a Form.* London: Routledge and Kegan
      Paul; Baltimore: Johns Hopkins Press, 1969, pp. 167-69.

      Background on *A Description of a City Shower.* "Swift
      calls his poem a Georgic because it imitates the section
      on the signs of the weather in Book I of Virgil's poem,
      but his style is distinctly Juvenalian."

154. Clark, William Ross. "Poems for Teaching." *The Clearing
      House* 35 (February 1961): 381-82.

      Emphasizes the realism of *A Description of the Morning*,
      which seems merely to set down a list of details about a
      morning in a large city but is actually "a vivid socio-
      logical report on a whole urban civilization, magnifi-
      cently pictorial and atmospheric."

155. Ehrenpreis, Irvin. "Four of Swift's Sources." *Modern
      Language Notes* 70 (February 1955): 95-100.

      Two lines in *A Description of a City Shower*, "Here
      various Kinds by various Fortunes led, / Commence Ac-
      quaintance underneath a Shed," reflect a couplet in
      Dryden's *Aeneid* (I, 519), in which Aeneas addresses the
      disguised Venus: "On various Seas by various Tempests
      tost, / At length we landed on your *Lybian* Coast."

156. Fischer, John I. "Apparent Contraries: A Reading of
      Swift's 'A Description of a City Shower.'" *Tennessee
      Studies in Literature* 19 (1974): 21-34.

      Attempts to reconcile Ehrenpreis's relatively cheerful
      interpretation of the *Shower* (item 61, 2:386) with the
      gloomier interpretations of O Hehir and Savage (see items
      159 and 163). Insisting that these two seemingly oppo-
      site responses to the poem must be simultaneously true,
      Fischer explores the complex, self-contradictory implica-
      tions of Swift's allusions to Noah's Flood. The approach
      is rather ponderously Christianized.

157. Haas, Rudolf. "Swifts *Description of a City Shower* als
      satirische Sozialkritik." *Theorie und Praxis der
      Interpretation: Modellanalysen englischer und ameri-
      kanischer Texte.* Berlin: Erich Schmidt, 1977,
      pp. 164-68.

      In German. Citing the value of Swift's poem for
      social criticism and cultural history, Haas interprets
      its details as satirical analysis of human behavior
      during a shower.

158. Motto, Anna Lydia, and John R. Clark. "Idyllic Slumming
      'midst Urban Hordes: The Satiric *Epos* in Theocritus
      and Swift." *The Classical Bulletin* 47 (January 1971):
      39-44.

      Juxtaposes *A Description of a City Shower* with Theo-
      critus's *Idyll* 15 in order to bring out the similar
      parody of heroic matter in Swift's poem. Unlike the
      Trojan War, the *Description* has no central characters
      or actors. Minor figures mostly pretend to act, while
      the poem's dominant action is performed by the natural
      elements themselves. "Indeed, parodying a Second Deluge
      or Flood, ... this sad and filthy modern Troy ... is
      controverted, in the best wretched metaphorical manner,
      into Ocean."

159. O Hehir, Brendan. "Meaning of Swift's 'Description of
      a City Shower.'" *ELH* 27 (September 1960): 194-207.

      The poem's "meaning," argues O Hehir, is "an oblique
      denunciation of cathartic doom upon the corruption of
      the city." While concrete details in the poem convey
      a cumulative sense of moral and physical corruption, its
      literary allusions focus upon divinely ordained floods
      and the falls of cities such as Troy. Besides the all-
      important allusions to Noah's Flood, Swift's sources for
      allusion and burlesque include Virgil's first *Georgic*
      and second and fourth books of the *Aeneid*, Dryden's
      addiction to the triplet and alexandrine, and Garth's
      Dispensary.

160. Östman, Hans. *Realistiska drag i engelsk 1700-talspoesi:
      Eklog, lärodikt och topografisk poesi.* Acta Universi-
      tatis Stockholmiensis; Stockholm Studies in History of
      Literature 23. Stockholm: Almqvist & Wiksell Interna-
      tional, 1980, pp. 87-89.

      In Swedish. Östman discusses both *A Description of
      the Morning* and *A Description of a City Shower*.

161. Price, Martin. *To the Palace of Wisdom: Studies in Order and Energy from Dryden to Blake.* Garden City, NY: Doubleday, 1964, pp. 257-58. Reprint. Arcturus Books. Carbondale and Edwardsville: Southern Illinois University Press; London and Amsterdam: Feffer and Simons, 1970, pp. 258-59.

     Discusses both of the *Description* poems.

162. Real, H.J. "'A Description of the Morning,' Ll. 3-4." *Notes and Queries* 223 (February 1978): 37.

     Lines 3-4 of Swift's poem, "Now *Betty* from her Masters Bed had flown, / And softly stole to discompose her own," may owe something to a passage in Richard Blackmore's *Prince Arthur*, which Swift is known to have read in 1697-1698.

163. Savage, Roger. "Swift's Fallen City: *A Description of the Morning.*" *The World of Jonathan Swift: Essays for the Tercentenary.* Edited by Brian Vickers. Cambridge: Harvard University Press, 1968, pp. 171-94.

     Places Swift's poem in relation to the classicist tradition of the *descriptio*, specifically the subsidiary tradition of the "dawn-scene," examples of which are cited from Homer down to Swift's own day. In Swift's burlesque treatment, the ideal nature or *la belle nature* of the classical dawn-scene is implicitly set in balance with the sordidly realistic nature of contemporary London, each being accorded exactly the same validity. As elsewhere in Swift, there is no resolution of the conflicting claims of ideal and real. Savage's important essay extends his insights to *A Description of a City Shower* and includes comments on *Apollo's Edict*, *The Day of Judgement*, *To Lord Harley, on His Marriage*, and three "scatological" poems: *Cassinus and Peter*, *Strephon and Chloe*, and *The Lady's Dressing Room*.

164. Vieth, David M. "*Fiat Lux*: Logos versus Chaos in Swift's 'A Description of the Morning.'" *Papers on Language and Literature* 8 (Summer 1972): 302-07.

     Literally, *A Description of the Morning* catalogues random details from an urban dawn scene. At a second level, it implicitly contrasts this sordid environment with the ideal nature of classical pastoral. Further, the poem parodies the divine fiat of Creation, "Let there be light," by which God imposed Logos upon Chaos. In a fallen world, this daily reenactment of Creation is necessarily parodic, producing only a little light and order.

See also items 47A, 48, 48A, 51A, 56, 61, 62, 64, 69, 76, 78, 83, 84, 87, 96, 98, 102, 105, 112, 117, 120, 130, 131, 393, 464, 468, 527, 559.

D. *Baucis and Philemon*

165. Hirai, Takashi. "Philemon to Baucis no henbō" (The Metamorphosis of Philemon and Baucis). *English and English-American Literature, Yamaguchi University* 12 (1977): 17-32. Abstracted in *The Scriblerian*, vol. 11, no. 2 (Spring 1979): 79.

In Japanese. Hirai compares Dryden's Christian paraphrase and Swift's realistic and cynical imitation of the Ovidian story. Swift describes the metamorphosis more vividly; his method is not magnifying but reductive. Ironically, Baucis and Philemon are transformed into yew trees, which symbolize both immortality and death.

166. Parkin, Rebecca Price. "Swift's *Baucis and Philemon*: A Sermon in the Burlesque Mode." *Satire Newsletter* 7 (Spring 1970): 109-14.

Swift's poem, besides mocking the conventional saint's legend, burlesques a concept present both in the Ovidian original and in Dryden's translation in the *Fables*: metamorphosis as an instance of the power of the gods. The various items transformed in the poem obey a humorous "principle of minimal metamorphosis consistent with decorum"--that is, the least possible change from their original form, nature, and function. Parkin usefully emphasizes the anti-Puritan satire in Swift's depiction of the two visiting "saints."

167. Rothstein, Eric. "Jonathan Swift as Jupiter: 'Baucis and Philemon.'" *The Augustan Milieu: Essays Presented to Louis A. Landa*. Edited by Henry Knight Miller, Eric Rothstein, and G.S. Rousseau. Oxford: Clarendon Press, 1970, pp. 205-24.

A study of the relationship between Swift's two versions of *Baucis and Philemon*. Challenging the usual

view, Rothstein concludes that Swift's revisions,
undertaken partly at Addison's instigation, have the
beneficial effect of sharpening the poem's thematic
focus upon an unthinking materiality that renders any
spiritual transfiguration unlikely. Swift's revisions
are considered against the background of Dryden's version
of Ovid's story, Ovid's original in the context of
classical culture, and attempts to Christianize Ovid.
If Rothstein's analysis seems at times overly elaborate
and detailed, it is nevertheless packed with perceptive
suggestions for interpreting Swift's poem.

168. Webster, C.M. "*Hudibras* and Swift." *Modern Language
     Notes* 47 (April 1932): 245-46.

     Lines 93-94 of *Baucis and Philemon*, "The Ballads
     pasted on the Wall, / Of *Joan* of *France*, and *English
     Moll*," echo *Hudibras*, I. ii. 367-68: "A bold *Virago*,
     stout and tall / as *Joan* of *France*, or *English Mall*."
     See also Clarence L. Kulischek, item 192.

See also items 26, 34, 47A, 61, 62, 69, 70, 74, 78, 90, 94,
105, 111, 112, 117, 553, 579.

                    E. *Cadenus and Vanessa*

169. Borkat, Roberta Sarfatt. "The Cage of Custom."
     University of Dayton Review, vol. 10, no. 3 (Summer
     1974): 47-57.

     A feminist treatment that gives Swift surprisingly
     high grades for asking women to "develop an intellect
     and a moral character, courage, substance" instead of
     "filling their time with trifles--cosmetics, clothes,
     and vacuous conversations with equally shallow men."
     Cadenus and Vanessa presents Esther Vanhomrigh as an
     ideal while ridiculing the stereotypical expectations
     of contemporary society. *Stella's Birthday, 1727* also
     celebrates in a real woman the qualities of mind and
     heart that Swift admired.

170. England, A.B. "Rhetorical Order and Emotional Turbulence
     in *Cadenus and Vanessa*." *Papers on Language and
     Literature* 14 (Spring 1978): 116-23. Reprint. *Con-
     temporary Studies of Swift's Poetry*. Edited by John
     Irwin Fischer and Donald C. Mell, Jr., with David M.

Vieth, associate editor. Newark: University of Delaware Press; London and Toronto: Associated University Presses, 1980, pp. 69-78.

Cadenus and Vanessa consists of a multiplicity of rationalistic, stylized structures and frameworks that ludicrously fail to contain the intense, disorderly emotional experiences at the center of Swift's poem. These frameworks range from the legal forms of the opening debate about love's decline to the methodical process of selection and organization used to form Vanessa's personality, to Vanessa's rationalizations of her infatuation for Cadenus, to Cadenus's attempt to formulate the resulting situation as friendship based on rational esteem. At the poem's end, Swift leaves the major characters in a state of impasse, while Venus has been forced to recognize that human nature is not amenable to the type of ordering arrangement that she thought she could impose on it.

171. Freeman, A. Martin, ed. *Vanessa and Her Correspondence with Jonathan Swift. The Letters Edited for the First Time from the Originals.* London: Selwyn and Blount; Boston: Houghton Mifflin, 1921. Pp. 216. Reprints. Folcroft, PA: Folcroft Library Editions, 1969, 1974. Norwood, PA: Norwood Editions, 1976.

Prints, from the original manuscripts, all of the surviving correspondence between Swift and Vanessa, which forms an essential part of the background of *Cadenus and Vanessa.* Explanatory notes are provided, as well as an introduction recounting the facts of the Swift-Vanessa relationship and describing the manuscript volume in which the letters are preserved.

172. Jones, Gareth. "Swift's *Cadenus and Vanessa*: A Question of 'Positives.'" *Essays in Criticism* 20 (October 1970): 424-40.

Answering F.R. Leavis and especially Peter Ohlin (see item 174), Jones insists that *Cadenus and Vanessa* is to be understood, not through simplistic "positives" or generalizing abstractions, but in terms of the actualities of living, the chaos of "its banal and irreducible particularities." Ideals, clichés, legal fictions, and notions derived from books are exposed in Swift's poem as an evasion of the concrete realities of human experience. Swift is concerned with "is" before "ought," and the former qualifies as well as justifies the latter.

As a disconcertingly autonomous structure of words whose counterpointed ironies are not reducible to thesis or easy resolution, *Cadenus and Vanessa* must be explored, experienced, and enacted—not paraphrased. Concluding Jones's brilliant discussion are some important observations concerning *Verses on the Death of Dr. Swift*.

173. Le Brocquy, Sybil. *Cadenus: A Reassessment in the Light of New Evidence of the Relationships between Swift, Stella and Vanessa*. Dublin: Dolmen Press; Oxford University Press; Chester Springs, PA: Dufour Editions, 1962. Pp. 160.

An amateurish, casually documented, but wide-ranging account of the relationship between Swift and Esther Vanhomrigh. One of its less responsible speculations concerns a son allegedly born to them. The correspondence is quoted at length.

174. Ohlin, Peter. "'Cadenus and Vanessa': Reason and Passion." *Studies in English Literature* 4 (Summer 1964): 485-96.

In Swift's poem, Ohlin maintains, "the basic conflict is that between reason and passion, more specifically as it appears in the relationship between men and women." This conflict figures in the mock trial between the shepherds and the nymphs, in the contrast in characterization of Venus and Pallas, in the characterizations of Vanessa and Cadenus and the shifting relationship between them, and in the discomfiture of Venus at the poem's conclusion. Vanessa's virtues when she is first created reflect Swift's understanding of what is admirable in a woman and conform to his concept of Christian marriage as described by St. Paul. The same rational and spiritual ideal pervades the poems to Stella, several of which Ohlin cites. When Vanessa falls in love with Cadenus, allowing passion to sway reason, it is in effect her fall from grace.

175. Rodino, Richard Hodge. "The Private Sense of *Cadenus and Vanessa*." *Concerning Poetry* 11 (Fall 1978): 41-47.

Adopts the premise that though some of his apparently similar poems were public events, designed to instruct or "vex" his friends or the "common reader," *Cadenus and Vanessa* was not intended for publication and was written only for Swift and Esther Vanhomrigh. Critics, failing to recognize that the poem represents a "private assess-

ment of an intimate situation," have been troubled by
the "deceptive *impasse*" it creates between generalizing
extremes--between shepherds and nymphs, Pallas and Venus,
reason and the passions, and so forth. The balance of
opposition offers no viable alternative. Moreover, as
a "serial process" of ironic reversals or oscillations
between these extremes, the poem has "a suspended, open-
ended structure" that moves toward possible future de-
velopments beyond its formal limits, in real life.
"There is more than a hint of hopefulness for Vanessa
to have seized."

176. Schakel, Peter J. "Swift's 'dapper Clerk' and the
     Matrix of Allusions in 'Cadenus and Vanessa.'"
     Criticism 17 (Summer 1975): 246-61.

     Maintains that in *Cadenus and Vanessa*, "Swift achieves
     control, complexity, and comprehensiveness by his use
     of a matrix of allusions" to Ovid's *Art of Love* and
     Virgil's *Aeneid*. Ovid's work provided a source for
     Swift's mythological framework, with shepherds, nymphs,
     Venus, Cupid, darts, and fires of love; additional
     suggestions may have come from the pseudo-Chaucerian
     prosecution of lovers in *The Court of Love*, which was
     published with a translation of *The Art of Love* in 1709.
     The contrast between Ovid's prescriptions for love and
     Cadenus's feelings about Vanessa becomes the poem's most
     powerful and lasting irony. In juxtaposition with
     Virgil's story of Dido and Aeneas, perpetuated and ex-
     tended by the sentimentalizing effect of Courtly Love
     conventions based upon Ovid's *Heroides*, Vanessa emerges
     as a Dido-figure who, though partially comic, loves
     deeply and understandably. By making Cadenus loosely
     and comically analogous to Aeneas, Swift gives him the
     principal responsibility for allowing his relationship
     with Vanessa to develop into an impossible situation.

177. Teerink, Herman. "Swift's *Cadenus and Vanessa*."
     Harvard Library Bulletin 2 (Spring 1948): 254-57.

     Two of the initial editions of *Cadenus and Vanessa* in
     1726 were printed from the same setting of type.
     Teerink attempts to determine the order of these two
     printings and other aspects of the complicated publishing
     history of the poem during that year. See item 178.

178. Teerink, Herman. "Swift's *Cadenus and Vanessa* Again."
     Harvard Library Bulletin 3 (Autumn 1949): 435-36.

     Discusses another instance, like that in item 177,
     in which two editions of *Cadenus and Vanessa* were

printed from the same setting of type. This discovery
requires a small correction in the time-scheme Teerink
had proposed for the editions of the poem published in
1726.

179. Tyne, James L., S.J. "Vanessa and the Houyhnhnms: A
Reading of 'Cadenus and Vanessa.'" *Studies in English
Literature* 11 (Summer 1971): 517-34.

Responding to Peter Ohlin (see item 174), Tyne finds
the focus of *Cadenus and Vanessa* in the disparity between two quite different worlds, the mythological and
the real. On one hand is the ideal, prelapsarian,
transcendently virtuous and completely rational realm
which Vanessa represents; on the other, the imperfect,
fallen, real world of eighteenth-century polite society
in which Vanessa lives and acts. The superhuman ideal
of moral integrity embodied in the mythological world
of the goddesses, Venus and Pallas, in which Vanessa is
created and raised, links her with the Houyhnhnms and
Molière's Alceste. If the highly idealized Vanessa is
clearly a standard by which the Dean exposes the foolish-
ness of the fops, she is also ridiculed for her uncompro-
mising either/or mentality, which refuses to accept the
"common Forms" of society--that is, the familiar Swiftian
"outside" as well as "inside."

See also items 6, 15, 34, 44, 47A, 49, 52, 54, 61, 62, 64, 69,
76, 78, 80, 88, 89, 90, 93, 94, 100, 102, 105, 111, 112, 117,
120, 130, 180, 216, 239, 329, 345, 361, 434, 436, 443, 451,
468, 484, 490, 491, 512, 544, 553, 556, 571.

F. The Stella Poems

180. Davis, Herbert. *Stella: A Gentlewoman of the Eighteenth
Century*. The Alexander Lectures at the University of
Toronto, 1942. New York: Macmillan, 1942. Pp. ix +
103. Reprint. *Jonathan Swift: Essays on His Satire
and Other Studies by Herbert Davis*. Galaxy Books.
New York: Oxford University Press, 1964, pp. 29-97.

Consists of four lectures titled "Swift and Stella,"
"Satire," "Comedy," and "Sentiment." In the process of
bringing Stella's role into focus through Swift's writings, Davis cites eight of the Stella poems and also
A Beautiful Young Nymph Going to Bed, *Verses Wrote in a*

Lady's Ivory Table-Book, The Furniture of a Woman's Mind, The Journal of a Modern Lady, An Epistle to a Lady, and *Cadenus and Vanessa.*

181. Fischer, John Irwin. "Faith, Hope, and Charity in Swift's Poems to Stella." *Papers on Language and Literature* 14 (Spring 1978): 123-29. Reprint. *Contemporary Studies of Swift's Poetry.* Edited by John Irwin Fischer and Donald C. Mell, Jr., with David M. Vieth, associate editor. Newark: University of Delaware Press; London and Toronto: Associated University Presses, 1980, pp. 79-86.

Although several critics have remarked that neither the Stella poems nor the Swift-Stella relationship exhibit much evidence of Christian sensibilities, the poems gain in coherence and power when they are examined within the context of Christian thought. This is true even though stoic elements occur consistently in these poems, which are consolations; they are comic and imaginative attempts to reconcile Stella to mortality. Relevant Christian doctrines include the inseparability of body and spirit, as in the resurrection, and (along with hope and charity) religious faith which transcends "the nightmare of death-in-matter."

182. Fischer, John I. "The Uses of Virtue: Swift's Last Poem to Stella." *Essays in Honor of Esmond Linworth Marilla.* Edited by Thomas Austin Kirby and William John Olive. Louisiana State University Studies, Humanities Series, no. 19. Baton Rouge: Louisiana State University Press, 1970, pp. 201-09.

Stella's Birthday, 1727, which has been praised for its "graceful sentiments" and dismissed, is also a discussion of the advantages, nature, and purposes of a virtuous life. Besides overtly advising Stella that virtue is its own reward, the poem covertly assures her of a future state--of the existence of providence, judgment, hell, and heaven.

183. Le Brocquy, Sybil, ed. *Stella's Birth-Days: Poems by Jonathan Swift.* Dublin: Dolmen Press; London: Oxford University Press; Chester Springs, PA: Dufour Editions, 1967. Pp. 40. (Edition limited to 750 copies).

Seven poems that Swift addressed to Stella on her birthdays are rather carelessly reprinted, with explanatory notes, presumably from the Sir Harold Williams edition. The lengthy introduction maintains that Stella was a natural daughter of Sir William Temple.

184. Le Brocquy, Sybil. *Swift's Most Valuable Friend.* Dublin: Dolmen Press; London: Oxford University Press;

Chester Springs, PA: Dufour Editions, 1968. Pp. 128.

An account of the Swift-Stella relationship that makes
some use of the poems. It is derivative and lacks scholarly integrity—maintaining, among other heresies, that
Stella was a natural daughter of Sir William Temple.

185. Sheehan, David. "Swift, Voiture, and the Spectrum of
     Raillery." *Papers on Language and Literature* 14
     (Spring 1978): 171–88.

Critical efforts to assess Voiture's influence upon
Swift's raillery have underestimated Voiture's achievement. Both Swift and Voiture were masters of a spectrum
of rallying modes, ranging from simple praise-by-blame
to a sharp raillery in which praise and blame coexist
in a delicate balance. Sheehan examines Swift's practice
in several Stella poems: *Stella at Wood-Park*; the birth-
day poems for 1719, 1721, and 1725; *A Receipt to Restore
Stella's Youth*; and *To Stella, Who Collected and Transcribed His Poems*. For this last poem, Sheehan provides
an indispensable explanation of Swift's "absurd" ending.
See the earlier articles on Swift's raillery by Eugene
Timpe and John M. Bullitt (items 136 and 129).

186. Tyne, James L. "Swift and Stella: The Love Poems."
     Tennessee Studies in Literature 19 (1974): 35–47.

Swift's poems addressed to Stella, despite his ridicule
of conventional amatory verse, are love poems of considerable power. If the physical Stella is vaguely
sketched, her psychological profile is a clear delinea-
tion of a reasonable and agreeable companion, fully
endowed with good sense and good humor. Her virtues are
not only masculine but also specifically feminine and,
finally, Christian.

187. Uphaus, Robert W. "Swift's Stella and Fidelity to
     Experience." *The Dublin Magazine*, vol. 8, no. 3
     (Spring 1970): 31–42. Also (revised) in *Eire-Ireland*
     5 (Autumn 1970): 40–52.

The Stella poems contrast and combine a sharp awareness
of the facts of experience with an assertion of the
permanent values of the Swift-Stella relationship.
These contrasting movements reflect manifold discordances
between reason and passion, mind and body, virtue and
beauty, constancy and change; yet "All accidents of life
conspire / To raise up Stella's virtue higher." The
technique of Swift's witty verses enacts a reconciliation
of these opposites.

On the curious double publication of this article,
"Mr. Uphaus explains that the shoddy editorial practices
of *The Dublin Magazine* are responsible for the duplica-

tion as well as for the printing errors" (*The Scriblerian*, vol. 3, no. 1 [Autumn 1970]: 18). The *Eire-Ireland* version should be treated as authoritative.

188. Vance, John A. "As Much for Swift as They are for Stella." *The Gypsy Scholar: A Graduate Forum for Literary Criticism* 5 (Summer 1978): 87-95.

An account of Swift's birthday poems for Stella designed to bring out what Vance sees as their dominant theme, man's concern with his own advancing age and inevitable demise. In terms of this theme, the poems are as much about Swift himself as about Stella.

189. Williams, Harold, ed. Jonathan Swift, *Journal to Stella*. 2 vols. Oxford: Clarendon Press, 1948. Pp. lxii + 801. Reprint (reduced page size). Vols. 15-16 of *The Prose Writings of Jonathan Swift*, edited by Herbert Davis. Oxford: Basil Blackwell and Mott, 1974; New York: Barnes and Noble, 1975.

This is the standard edition of the *Journal to Stella*, which, besides providing background for the Swift-Stella relationship and the poems that emerged from it, contains references to poems Swift was composing during the years 1710-1713.

See also items 26, 47A, 50, 51A, 53, 56, 62, 69, 76, 78, 83, 90, 93, 96, 105, 106, 112, 115, 169, 174, 209, 216, 237, 239, 329, 345, 361, 404, 436, 451, 484, 486, 491, 500, 505, 530, 544, 553, 554, 560, 571.

G. The Market Hill Poems
(The Lady Acheson poems,
including *An Epistle to a Lady*)

190. Cronin, Edward R. "A Panegyric on the Dean." *Revue des Langues Vivantes* (Bruxelles) 37 (1971): 524-34.

A critical analysis and interpretation of the *Panegyrick*, focused upon Swift's ironic use of the persona of Lady Acheson and his burlesquing of literary conventions.

191. Jaffe, Nora Crow. "Swift and the Agreeable Young Lady, but Extremely Lean." *Papers on Language and Literature* 14 (Spring 1978): 129-37. Reprint. *Contemporary Studies of Swift's Poetry*. Edited by John Irwin Fischer and Donald C. Mell, Jr., with David M. Vieth, associate editor. Newark: University of Delaware

Press; London and Toronto: Associated University
Presses, 1980, pp. 149-58.

An interpretation of *Death and Daphne*. Jaffe suggests
that Death is a stand-in for Swift himself and that the
poem is about the tutorial relationship he cultivated
with Lady Acheson, which was similar to his relationships
with Stella and Vanessa. Death, the frightened "old
Batchelor" of the poem, makes advances that his real-
life counterpart would never have dared. The scene ex-
aggerates the unnatural picture of a sixty-three-year-
old man courting a woman very much his junior.

192. Kulischeck, Clarence L. "Hudibrastic Echoes in Swift."
     Notes and Queries 196 (4 August 1951): 339.

     Lines 95-96 of *An Epistle to a Lady*, which are rhymed
     "Philosopher/Gloss over," echo two couplets with similar
     rhymes in *Hudibras*, I.i.127-28 and I.ii.1-2. See
     also C.M. Webster, item 168.

193. Waller, Charles T. "Swift's *Apologia pro Satura Sua*."
     Satire Newsletter, vol. 10, no. 1 (Fall 1972): 19-25.

     Examines *An Epistle to a Lady* in light of the conven-
     tions of the classical *apologia pro satura sua*.

194. Williams, Harold, and Lord Rothschild. "The Grand
     Question Debated." *Review of English Studies* 15
     (July 1939): 328-30.

     When *The Grand Question Debated* was published in
     January 1732, it appeared simultaneously in London and
     Dublin editions under differing titles and with differing
     texts. The London text was followed, with changes and
     corrections, in the Pope-Swift *Miscellanies* volume of
     1732; the Dublin text, published by George Faulkner, was
     followed in Faulkner's edition of Swift's *Works* with the
     addition of four lines authorized by Swift himself. An
     autograph manuscript of the poem, formerly in the William
     Randolph Hearst collection and now in Lord Rothschild's
     Library, follows the Dublin text of 1732 and indicates
     2 September 1729 as the date of composition.

See also items 46, 47, 47A, 49, 52, 53, 54, 56, 58, 61A, 67, 73,
76, 78, 85, 96, 97, 105, 105A, 130, 131, 180, 204, 210, 227,
239, 255, 257, 354, 438, 530, 560, 576.

H. The "Scatological" Poems
(*The Progress of Beauty*, *The Lady's Dressing Room*,
A Beautiful Young Nymph Going to Bed, *Strephon
and Chloe*, *Cassinus and Peter*)

195. Aden, John M. "Corinna and the Sterner Muse of Swift."
English Language Notes 4 (September 1966): 23-31.

Disagrees with earlier critics who felt that the tone
of *A Beautiful Young Nymph Going to Bed* is relentlessly
grim. Instead, Aden maintains, the plight of the whore
Corinna, though admittedly ugly and sordid, is portrayed
with a measure of human sympathy. In an effect of
double perspective, the comic vision is balanced by the
tragic, the ridiculous by the pathetic and pitiful.
More than any of Swift's other poems, in Aden's judgment,
A Beautiful Young Nymph has, because of failure to
understand its tone, blocked an adequate appraisal of
his verse.

196. Aden, John M. "Those Gaudy Tulips: Swift's 'Unprint-
ables.'" *Quick Springs of Sense: Studies in the
Eighteenth Century.* Edited by Larry S. Champion.
Athens: University of Georgia Press, 1974, pp. 15-32.

Too much impressed, perhaps, by Donald Greene's
article on the "scatological" poems (see item 213),
Aden rejoices that it is no longer necessary to apologize
for these works on moral grounds. Now, he continues,
we must "begin assessing them more attentively for their
poetical properties." To this end, he examines *The
Progress of Beauty*, *The Lady's Dressing Room*, *A Beautiful
Young Nymph Going to Bed*, *Strephon and Chloe*, and
Cassinus and Peter. Aden's thesis, pursued with uneven
success through these five poems, is that they "all
undertake to strip down, in one way or another, some
delusion to the reality it masquerades for."

197. Barnett, Louise K. "The Mysterious Narrator: Another
Look at 'The Lady's Dressing Room.'" *Concerning
Poetry*, vol. 9, no. 2 (December 1976): 29-32.

Argues persuasively that Swift's seemingly objective
and reliable narrator must be considered untrustworthy,
for at least two reasons: (1) Far from cataloguing the
contents of the dressing room objectively, he revels in
unsavory details, exhibiting an extravagant relish which
contrasts with Strephon's extravagant disgust. (2) The

advice he offers is ludicrous, namely that when Celia
is present, Strephon must hold his nose and by this
recover a good opinion of women. *The Lady's Dressing
Room* infers that the body must not be celebrated (the
narrator), nor loathed (Strephon), nor covered with
misleading adornment (Celia). Swift's view is that
"the body must be accepted as a reality of the human
condition, but its potential for bringing down the
spirit must equally be recognized."

198. Bleich, David. *Subjective Criticism*. Baltimore and
     London: Johns Hopkins University Press, 1978,
     pp. 284-93.

     Analyzes problems of reader response to *A Beautiful
     Young Nymph Going to Bed* both in twentieth-century
     cultural contexts and in twentieth-century notions of
     eighteenth-century cultural contexts. Little attempt
     is made to analyze the poem itself.

199. Blesch, Edwin J., Jr. "'A Species Hardly a Degree
     Above a Monkey': Jonathan Swift's Concept of Woman."
     *The Nassau Review: The Journal of Nassau Community
     College Devoted to Arts, Letters, and Sciences*,
     vol. 3, no. 3 (1977): 74-84.

     Asserts that from his earliest works, as well as in
     his later "scatological" poems, Swift reveals a deep
     psychological fear and hatred not only of the foibles of
     women but of their very bodies. Blesch focuses upon
     The Lady's Dressing Room, *A Beautiful Young Nymph Going
     to Bed*, *Strephon and Chloe*, and *Cassinus and Peter*, but
     gives attention also to *The Problem*, *Phillis, Or, the
     Progress of Love*, *The Progress of Beauty*, and several
     of Swift's prose works. This essay is essentially a
     denunciation, by a self-declared male feminist, of
     Swift as anti-feminist.

200. Borkat, Roberta F.S. "Swift, Shaw, and the Idealistic
     Swain." *English Studies: A Journal of English
     Language and Literature* 61 (December 1980): 498-506.

     Both Shaw in *Arms and the Man* and Swift in *Cassinus
     and Peter*, *The Lady's Dressing Room*, and *Strephon and
     Chloe* portray the crisis of the romantic idealist.
     When his romantic notions are destroyed, the idealist
     tends to swing to the opposite extreme of complete
     disillusionment. The truth for both authors, Borkat
     believes (in a somewhat old-fashioned view of Swift),
     lies in a mediation between the extremes.

201.   Briggs, Peter M. "Notes toward a Teachable Definition
       of Satire." Eighteenth-Century Life, vol. 5, no. 3
       (Spring 1979): 28-39.

       An article on pedagogy which demonstrates how Lockean
       epistemology can contribute to the interpretation of
       The Lady's Dressing Room. "This is not a poem about
       Celia who is absent, nor even about her dressing room,
       but really about Strephon's perception of that dressing
       room and the inferences which he draws from his per-
       ceptions."

202.   Brilli, Attilio. "Il vaso di Pandora. Sulle poesie
       escrementali di Swift." La materialità del testo.
       Ricerca interdisciplinare sulle pratiche significanti.
       Il lavoro critico/semiotica 11. Verona: Bertani,
       1977, pp. 156-79.

       In Italian. The presentation is informational, with
       attention limited to The Lady's Dressing Room, Strephon
       and Chloe, and Cassinus and Peter. The milieu is that
       of Middleton Murry and Norman O. Brown (see items 89,
       204), with no reference to Donald Greene's influential
       article (see item 213) or more recent significant dis-
       cussions of the "scatological" poems.

203.   Brown, Daniel Russell. "Swiftian Scatology." Books
       and Bookmen, vol. 17, no. 1 (October 1971): 18-23.

       In a journalistic tour de force, this essay leads the
       reader on a wild-goose chase through a variety of
       secondary sources with scarcely any discussion of Swift's
       scatology or his "scatological" poems. There is a single
       reference to The Lady's Dressing Room, Strephon and
       Chloe, Cassinus and Peter, and A Beautiful Young Nymph
       Going to Bed.

204.   Brown, Norman O. "The Excremental Vision." Life
       Against Death: The Psychoanalytical Meaning of History.
       Middletown, CT: Wesleyan University Press; London:
       Routledge and Kegan Paul, 1959, pp. 179-201. Reprints.
       New York: Modern Library, 1960; Vintage Books, 1961,
       pp. 179-201. Discussions of Jonathan Swift. Edited
       by John Traugott. Boston: D.C. Heath, 1962, pp. 92-
       104. Swift: A Collection of Critical Essays. Edited
       by Ernest Tuveson. Twentieth Century Views; A Spectrum
       Book. Englewood Cliffs, NJ: Prentice-Hall, 1964,
       pp. 31-54. Jonathan Swift: A Critical Anthology.
       Edited by Denis Donoghue. Harmondsworth, Eng.: Penguin
       Books, 1971, pp. 189-205.

Credits such predecessors as Aldous Huxley and
Middleton Murry for perceiving, even if unfavorably,
Swift's "excremental vision" in the "scatological" poems,
but criticizes them for not recognizing the positive
Freudian principle of sublimation in these works, whose
real theme is "the conflict between our animal body,
appropriately epitomized in the anal function, and our
pretentious sublimations, more specifically the preten-
sions of sublimated or romantic-Platonic love." Swift's
ultimate horror in these poems is said to be the thought
that sublimation—that is to say, all civilized behavior—
is a lie and cannot survive confrontation with the truth.
In *The Lady's Dressing Room*, we are told, Swift "reasons
with Strephon that sublimation is still possible." In
Strephon and Chloe, "sublimation must be cultivated at
all costs, even at the cost of repression." In *Cassinus
and Peter*, however, "even this solution is exploded."
Also discussed is *A Panegyrick on the Dean*.

205. Calhoun, Douglas. "Swift's 'The Lady's Dressing Room.'"
      Discourse 13 (Autumn 1970): 493-99.

      Maintains that in *The Lady's Dressing Room*, the seem-
      ingly excessive physical description is used to counter-
      act appearance or idealism, suggesting a solution in a
      middle way or "balance which is the proper function of
      the imagination." These two extremes resemble Yahoo
      physicality as opposed to Houyhnhnm rationality. Calhoun
      regards the narrator's conclusion as Swift's own, although
      he wonders provocatively if Swift is really convinced of
      this solution, since the device of the narrator seems
      "a little too mechanical and emotionally detached for
      complete acceptance."

206. Cartwright, Faith Wotton. "Jonathan Swift and the
      Psychoanalysts." *Revista de la Universidad de Costa
      Rica*, no. 39 (October 1974): 47-53.

      Rejecting the views of Huxley, Middleton Murry, and
      the psychoanalysts (see items 220, 89), Cartwright
      insists that Swift's scatology is sensationalism devised
      to dispel romantic illusions about human nature and
      bring the reader back to common sense. She cites Norman
      O. Brown with approval (see item 204) but is uninfluenced
      by discussions later than 1964 such as that of Donald
      Greene (see item 213). There is brief, superficial
      attention to *The Lady's Dressing Room*, *Strephon and
      Chloe*, and *A Beautiful Young Nymph Going to Bed*.

207. Davis, Herbert. "A Modest Defence of 'The Lady's Dressing Room.'" *Restoration and Eighteenth-Century Literature: Essays in Honor of Alan 'Dugald McKillop.* Edited by Carroll Camden. Chicago: Published for William Marsh Rice University by the University of Chicago Press, 1963, pp. 39-48.

   Claims for Swift's authorship the humorously parodic Horatian imitation contained in *A Modest Defence of a Late Poem By an unknown Author, call'd, The Lady's Dressing-Room,* Dublin, 1732. Both the verse and prose portions of this pamphlet are reprinted in Davis's edition of the prose works (V, Appendix C, pp. 337-40). Davis provides brief discussions of other parodic poems by Swift, including several of the "scatological" poems and the "progress" pieces (of love, poetry, beauty, and marriage). See David Woolley, item 252.

208. Dobrée, Bonamy. "'A Beautiful Young Nymph Going to Bed.'" *Johnsonian News Letter,* vol. 10, no. 1 (February 1950): 7-8.

   Suggests that in writing *A Beautiful Young Nymph,* Swift is following a tradition of anti-feminist "undressing" literature. Examples cited include Thomas Killigrew the elder, *The Parson's Wedding* (ca. 1639), act 4, scene 1; Prior, Dorset, and Rochester; and Evelyn's *Mundus Muliebris: or the Ladies Dressing-Room Unlock'd, and Her Toilette Spread. In Burlesque* (1690).

209. Fox, Jeffrey R. "Swift's 'Scatological' Poems: The Hidden Norm." *Thoth,* vol. 15, no. 3 (Fall 1975): 3-13.

   Swift's norm, presented directly in the Stella poems, comprises virtue, wisdom, and an awareness of the transience of youthful beauty and bodily prowess. In the "scatological" poems, all the characters are satirized for the total absence of these positive qualities on which true love can alone be founded. Fox deals briefly with *The Progress of Beauty* and *A Beautiful Young Nymph Going to Bed* and more fully with *The Lady's Dressing Room, Strephon and Chloe,* and *Cassinus and Peter.*

210. Gilmore, Thomas B., Jr. "The Comedy of Swift's Scatological Poems." *PMLA* 91 (January 1976): 33-43.

   Recent criticism, though registering a real gain in its concentration on Swift's moral purposes, scants or ignores the comic aspects of the "scatological" poems.

In *A Beautiful Young Nymph Going to Bed*, the comic
incongruities embrace not only the grimness of Corinna's
plight but a sense of her suffering humanity. In *The
Lady's Dressing Room*, *Strephon and Chloe*, and *Cassinus
and Peter*, the basic incongruities are between fantasy
and fact, sublimation and reality, the standards of
pastoral romance or polite society and the need to
evacuate waste. In *Cassinus and Peter*, the comic incongruities dissolve hilariously with scarcely a moral.
For the more enigmatic conclusions of *The Lady's Dressing
Room* and *Strephon and Chloe*, a middle way may be pointed
by the fable of the two outhouses in *A Panegyrick on
the Dean in the Person of a Lady in the North* (Lady
Acheson). The "Forum" section in a later issue of *PMLA*
provides further comments by Donald Greene, Peter J.
Schakel, and Gilmore; see items 214, 242, and 212.

211. Gilmore, Thomas B., Jr. "Freud and Swift: A Psychologi-
      cal Reading of *Strephon and Chloe*." *Papers on Language
      and Literature* 14 (Spring 1978): 147-51. Reprint.
      Contemporary Studies of Swift's Poetry. Edited by
      John Irwin Fischer and Donald C. Mell, Jr., with David
      M. Vieth, associate editor. Newark: University of
      Delaware Press; London and Toronto: Associated Univer-
      sity Presses, 1980, pp. 159-68.

      In defense of his earlier views (see items 210 and
      212), and in reply to Peter Schakel (see item 241;
      also 242), Gilmore asserts the value of psychoanalytic
      criticism of Swift's poems. Such criticism may, for
      example, reveal an unsuspected degree of unity in
      Strephon and Chloe, where the shocked disillusionment of
      the newlyweds can represent part of the process of
      maturing ("from polymorphous perversity to anal fixa-
      tion--from the innocence of children to the neurosis
      of immature adults"). Complete maturity would require
      sublimation of the sex drive to produce culture or
      civilization, the Freudian communal bond based on friend-
      ship (of which the couple's "great Society in Stinking"
      is the unsublimated travesty).

212. Gilmore, Thomas B., Jr. "Swift's Scatological Poems."
      PMLA 91 (May 1976): 466-67 (Forum).

      Gilmore rejects the criticisms of his earlier *PMLA*
      article offered by Donald Greene and Peter J. Schakel;
      see items 210, 214, and 242.

213. Greene, Donald. "On Swift's 'Scatological' Poems."
      Sewanee Review 75 (Autumn 1967): 672-89.

      Greene's influential article proposes a thoroughgoing
      Christian interpretation of *The Lady's Dressing Room*,
      Strephon and Chloe, and *Cassinus and Peter*--poems which
      inspired Norman O. Brown with Freudian admiration for
      Swift's "excremental vision" (see item 204) and shocked
      Middleton Murry and Aldous Huxley with Swift's perverse
      obsession with excrement and sex (see items 89 and 220).
      In *Cassinus and Peter*, retorts Greene, the horror at the
      discovery that "*Caelia, Caelia, Caelia* sh---" is con-
      demned by Swift as a product of the human sin of pride,
      which permits Cassinus to live in squalor while enter-
      taining an unrealistically romantic image of himself and
      Caelia. Similarly, in *The Lady's Dressing Room*, Strephon
      should not merely reconcile himself to the "Order from
      Confusion sprung" but bless it as an expression of God's
      own creativity. The conclusion of *Strephon and Chloe*
      gives a serious and straightforward sermon such as a
      Christian clergyman like Swift might offer a young
      couple asking him to marry them.

214. Greene, Donald. "Swift's Scatological Poems." *PMLA* 91
      (May 1976): 464-65 (Forum).

      Greene avers, in answer to Thomas B. Gilmore's *PMLA*
      article (see item 210), that the didactic Christian
      interpretation put forward in his own earlier article
      (see item 213) did not minimize the comic qualities of
      the "scatological" poems. Greene's objection, not
      entirely justified, seems to stem from Gilmore's dis-
      tinction between aesthetics and morality.

215. Griffith, Philip Mahone. "Middleton Murry on Swift:
      'The *Nec Plus Ultra* of Objectivity'?" *The D.H.*
      Lawrence Review, vol. 2, no. 1 (Spring 1969): 60-67.

      "Both Lawrence's and Murry's responses [to Swift's
      'scatological' poems] are symptomatic, I believe, of
      their own inability to reconcile flesh and spirit and
      of that peculiar atmosphere of lower or lower-middle
      class prudery that somehow, difficult as it is to
      define or document, pervades the work of both men."
      See items 224, 225, 89.

216. Gubar, Susan. "The Female Monster in Augustan Satire."
      Signs: Journal of Women in Culture and Society 3
      (Winter 1977): 380-94.

Maintains that in his "scatological" and other poems
relating to women, Swift projects his own, and other
men's, anxiety and ambivalence about female sexuality
and power, imaged in repeated portrayals of an archetypal
"female monster." These poems are not spoken by a persona; the filthiness of Chloe and Caelia horrifies not
only Strephon and Cassinus, but Swift himself. Gubar
discusses mainly *The Lady's Dressing Room, Strephon and
Chloe*, and *Cassinus and Peter*, but comments also on the
Stella poems, *Cadenus and Vanessa, A Beautiful Young
Nymph Going to Bed*, and *The Progress of Beauty*. (See
items 217 and 231).

217. Gubar, Susan. "Reply to Pollak." *Signs: Journal of
Women in Culture and Society* 3 (Spring 1978): 732-33.

Accepting Ellen Pollak's distinction between Swift
and such contemporaries as Pope and Gay (see item 231),
Gubar nevertheless asserts the validity of her "archetypal" use of "female monsters."

218. Halsband, Robert. "'The Lady's Dressing Room' Explicated
by a Contemporary." *The Augustan Milieu: Essays
Presented to Louis A. Landa*. Edited by Henry Knight
Miller, Eric Rothstein, and G.S. Rousseau. Oxford:
Clarendon Press, 1970, pp. 225-31.

Swift's poem was "explicated" by Lady Mary Wortley
Montagu, who in 1734 published her verse reply in the
anonymous eight-page pamphlet *The Dean's Provocation
For Writing the Lady's Dressing-Room*. Halsband prints
her verses in full.

219. Heidenhain, Adolf. "Koprophilie und Reinlichkeit."
*Über den Menschenhass: Eine Pathographische Unter-
suchung über Jonathan Swift*. Stuttgart: Ferdinand
Enke, 1934, pp. 69-74.

Paraphrases *Strephon and Chloe* and *The Lady's Dressing
Room* in connection with Swift's alleged coprophilia,
impotence, and mania for cleanliness.

220. Huxley, Aldous. "Swift." *Do What You Will*. New York:
Doubleday, Doran, 1929, pp. 97-112. Reprint. London:
Chatto and Windus, 1949, pp. 93-106.

On Swift's "hatred of bowels." In such poems as *The
Lady's Dressing Room, Cassinus and Peter*, and *A Beautiful
Young Nymph Going to Bed*, Swift displays a compulsion to
remind himself of the coarse bodily functions that so
disgusted him.

221. Johnston, Denis. "Swift of Dublin." *Eire-Ireland*,
     vol. 3, no. 3 (Autumn 1968): 38-50.

     In the "cloacal poems," "Swift's deliberate intention
     was to offend and shock young lovers out of what he
     considered to be the romantic illusions that they might
     cherish about courtship and marriage." Swift's feelings
     of revulsion over bodily functions, Johnston avers, are
     characteristically Irish.

222. Kendle, Burton S. "D.H. Lawrence: The Man Who Misunder-
     stood Gulliver." *English Language Notes* 2 (September
     1964): 42-46.

     Analyzes Lawrence's misunderstanding of *The Lady's
     Dressing Room* (see items 224, 225). Lawrence failed
     to grasp the poem's comic focus, its implicit distinction
     between Swift, the author and the character, Strephon,
     and its acceptance of the totality of human nature.

223. Kulisheck, Clarence L. "Swift's Poems about Women."
     Johnsonian News Letter, vol. 10, no. 3 (May 1950):
     11-12.

     Suggests that Book IV of Lucretius's *De Rerum Natura*
     is good evidence that Swift is following a recognizable
     literary convention in his scatological poems about
     women such as *The Lady's Dressing Room*.

224. Lawrence, D.H. "À Propos of Lady Chatterley's Lover."
     (First published by Mandrake Press, 1929). Reprints.
     Sex, Literature, and Censorship. By D.H. Lawrence.
     Edited by Harry T. Moore. Compass Books. New York:
     Viking Press, 1959, pp. 82-111. *À Propos of Lady
     Chatterley's Lover and Other Essays.* Harmondsworth,
     Eng.: Penguin Books, 1961, pp. 85-126.

     A briefer version of Lawrence's remarks in his essay
     "Introduction to Pansies" (see item 225). Commenting
     on the line "But—Celia, Celia, Celia shits!" (*sic*),
     Lawrence thinks that Swift's "insanity" is at least
     partly traceable to the mind's terror of the body.

225. Lawrence, D.H. "Introduction to Pansies." (First
     published in private edition by P.R. Stephenson, 1929.
     Published by Martin Secker, 1929). Reprints. *Phoenix:
     The Posthumous Papers of D.H. Lawrence.* Edited by
     Edward D. McDonald. London: Heinemann, 1936, pp. 279-
     82. *À Propos of Lady Chatterley's Lover and Other
     Essays.* Harmondsworth, Eng.: Penguin Books, 1961,
     pp. 7-12.

The mad, maddened refrain "But--Celia, Celia, Celia, shits!" (*sic*) and similar thoughts reduced the great mind of Swift to "gnashing insanity," poisoning him "like some terrible constipation." It was the *thought* that Celia shits, not the *fact*, that horrified his "insolent and sicklily squeamish mind."

226. Loffredo, Irene. *"Minus amant qui acute vident.* Elementi rinascimentali negli 'unprintable poems' di Jonathan Swift." *La materialità del testo. Ricerca interdisciplinare sulle pratiche significanti.* Il lavoro critico/semiotica 11. Verona: Bertani, 1977, pp. 196-205.

In Italian. Calls attention to Renaissance elements in *The Lady's Dressing Room*, specifically "love-melancholy" as described by Robert Burton in *The Anatomy of Melancholy* and by John Marston in his poems.

227. Manousos, Anthony. "Swiftian Scatology and Lockian Psychology." *The Gypsy Scholar*, vol. 7, no. 1 (Winter 1980): 15-25.

From *A Tale of a Tub* to the Strephon poems, Swift portrays a series of madmen whose condition amounts to a Lockian coupling of unrelated ideas. Besides the doctrine of association, Swift's poetry reflects Locke's concept of the mind as a *tabula rasa* at birth and as the warehouse, treasury, or repository for mental pictures. Typical of Swift's empirical psychology is his equation of mental and alimentary functions and his use of the eighteenth-century device of the "survey." Manousos focuses upon *The Lady's Dressing Room* and discusses also *Cassinus and Peter, Strephon and Chloe, My Lady's Lamentation and Complaint against the Dean, A Panegyrick on the Dean, Verses Wrote in a Lady's Ivory Table-Book*, and *Ode to the Honourable Sir William Temple*.

228. Murtuza, Athar. "Twentieth-Century Critical Response to Swift's 'Scatological Verse': A Checklist." *Bulletin of Bibliography* 30 (January-March 1973): 18-19.

This checklist continues to be useful but is misleading and disappointing. Although it claims to supplement the bibliographical information in Landa and Tobin (see item 38), Stathis (see item 42), and *The Scriblerian*, the majority of its items are in fact listed in those sources, Murtuza's contribution consisting mostly of recording new editions or reprints. Moreover, nine of his entries are books having only a subsidiary concern with Swift's poetry in general or with the "scatological" poems in particular, six are Ph.D. dissertations, one is an M.A. thesis, and still others are marginal at best.

229. Nussbaum, Felicity. "Juvenal, Swift, and *The Folly of Love*." *Eighteenth-Century Studies* 9 (Summer 1976): 540-52.

    Seventeenth-century interpretations of Juvenal's Sixth Satire, especially Dryden's rather free translation, provided a context of commonplaces and set scenes for Swift's intimate revelation of a woman's dressing room in *A Beautiful Young Nymph Going to Bed*. His antifeminist antecedents include two hitherto ignored items: Richard Ames's *The Folly of Love*, 1691, and Ovid's *Remedia Amoris*, which supplies the motto "Pars minima est ipsa Puella sui" on Swift's title page. Like Ovid, Swift warns not so much against marriage as against the folly of love, and as John Aden has pointed out (see items 195, 196), he allows unusual sympathy for Corinna's plight. Some of Nussbaum's observations apply also to *The Lady's Dressing Room* and *Strephon and Chloe*.

230. Orwell, George. "Politics vs. Literature: An Examination of *Gulliver's Travels*." (First published in *Shooting an Elephant and Other Essays*, 1946). Reprints. *Discussions of Jonathan Swift*. Edited by John Traugott. Boston: D.C. Heath, 1962, pp. 80-91. *Fair Liberty Was All His Cry: A Tercentenary Tribute to Jonathan Swift 1667-1745*. Edited by A. Norman Jeffares. London: Macmillan; New York: St. Martin's Press, 1967, pp. 166-85. *The Collected Essays, Journalism and Letters of George Orwell*. Edited by Sonia Orwell and Ian Angus. 4 vols. London: Secker and Warburg, 1968, 4:205-23. *Swift: Modern Judgements*. Edited by A. Norman Jeffares. London: Macmillan, 1969; Nashville, TN: Aurora, 1970, pp. 192-209. *Jonathan Swift: A Critical Anthology*. Edited by Denis Donoghue. Harmondsworth, Eng.: Penguin Books, 1971, pp. 342-61.

    Cites *The Lady's Dressing Room* and *A Beautiful Young Nymph Going to Bed* as examples of Swift's "diseased" view of human nature and human life.

231. Pollak, Ellen. "Comment on Susan Gubar's 'The Female Monster in Augustan Satire.'" *Signs: Journal of Women in Culture and Society* 3 (Spring 1978): 728-32.

An answer to Gubar's article (see item 216). Pollak
objects that Gubar's archetypal "female monsters" danger-
ously confuse myth, art, and neurosis. Recommending
more attention to contemporary social and economic condi-
tions, Pollak observes that these contexts were more
congenial to Pope, Gay, Addison, and Steele than they
were to Swift. See Gubar's reply, item 217.

232. Probyn, Clive T. "A Poem by Swift and Pope's Revision
     of 'The Dunciad.'" *Notes and Queries* 216 (September
     1971): 331.

     The opening quatrain of *Cassinus and Peter* ("Two
     College Sophs of *Cambridge* Growth ...") is clearly based
     on lines 4-5 of Virgil's *Eclogue 7* ("Ambo florentes
     aetatibus, Arcades ambo ...") as rendered by Pope in the
     1728 *Dunciad*, II, 347-50 ("Three Cambridge Sophs and
     three pert Templars came ..."). In the later four-book
     version of the *Dunciad*, Pope altered "Three Cambridge
     Sophs" to "Three College Sophs" (II, 379).

233. Rawson, Claude. "Order and Cruelty: A Reading of Swift
     (with some comments on Pope and Johnson)." *Essays in
     Criticism* 20 (January 1970): 24-56. Reprint. *Gulliver
     and the Gentle Reader: Studies in Swift and our Time.*
     London and Boston: Routledge and Kegan Paul, 1973,
     pp. 33-59. Reprint (in part). *Swift: Gulliver's
     Travels, A Casebook.* Edited by Richard Gravil. Lon-
     don: Macmillan, 1974, pp. 223-47.

     Briefly compares the undressing of Corinna in *A Beauti-
     ful Young Nymph Going to Bed* with the flayed woman of
     the "Digression on Madness."

234. Rawson, C.J. "A Phrase of John Gay in Swift's *Modest
     Defence of The Lady's Dressing-Room*?" *Review of
     English Studies* n.s. 16 (November 1965): 406-07.

     A phrase in the verse portion of *A Modest Defence of
     ... The Lady's Dressing Room* (1732), "voids out Worms
     of monst'rous Size," unaccountably echoes a letter
     written sixteen years earlier by John Gay but not pub-
     lished until 1959.

235. Real, Hermann J. [No title]. *The Scriblerian*, vol. 11,
     no. 2 (Spring 1979): 145.

     A response to Arthur Sherbo, item 245. Real notes
     that the term "puppy water" (*The Lady's Dressing Room*,

1. 31) is found also in Sir Charles Sedley's *Bellamira,
or the Mistress:* "Merry. You spend it him in Coach-
hire, Puppy-water and Paint, every day of your Life"
(I.i.153-54). The term is glossed incorrectly by
Sedley's editor, V. de Sola Pinto. See item 236.

236. Real, Hermann. "A Recipe for Puppy Water." *The
Scriblerian*, vol. 7, no. 2 (Spring 1975): 121-122.

Among the items Strephon discovers in *The Lady's
Dressing Room* is "Puppy Water, Beauty's Help / Distill'd
from *Tripsy*'s darling Whelp" (11. 31-32). Real quotes
a recipe for puppy water from the anonymous pamphlet
Mundus Muliebris: Or, the Ladies Dressing-Room Unlock'd
(London, 1690), to which is appended a "Fop-Dictionary;
or, an Alphabetical Catalogue of the Hard and Foreign
Names, and Terms of the Art Cosmetick." See items 235
and 245.

237. Rees, Christine. "Gay, Swift, and the Nymphs of Drury-
Lane." *Essays in Criticism* 23 (January 1973): 1-21.

Examines the fiction, employed by both Gay and Swift,
of the "Nymph" whose beauty is satirically defined by
the conflicting principles of art and nature. Two
literary antecedents for these nymphs are conventionally
grotesque satire directed against women's use of cosmetic
arts and, more important, pastoral, in which the relation
between nature and art is a fundamental issue. In *The
Lady's Dressing Room*, the speaker condemns Strephon's
original illusion (art) and his subsequent disillusion
(nature) as ferments of a diseased imagination, but his
own answer in the concluding lines is equally ironic and
untenable. In *The Progress of Beauty*, though the poetic
equation of whore to moon disintegrates as Celia's
cosmetic arts prove futile against natural decay, Swift's
art prevails because his comparison has the makings of
myth. Conversely, in *A Beautiful Young Nymph Going to
Bed*, Swift ruthlessly dismantles Corinna's artifice in
the going-to-bed sequence but cannot as poet assist her
in the process of reassembling her image; hence the
poem is more than the sum of its parts. Rees's illuminating analysis includes comments on *To Stella, Who
Collected and Transcribed His Poems*.

238. Rodino, Richard H. "Blasphemy or Blessing? Swift's
      'Scatological' Poems." *Papers on Language and Litera-*
      ture 14 (Spring 1978): 152-70.

      Most of Swift's "scatological" poems, composed from
      1730 to 1733, are "vexatious" works which force the
      reader into an urgent, but seemingly impossible, choice
      between fraudulent alternatives. Potential middle ways
      or golden means are discredited by being embodied in
      unreliable narrators. "Vexatious" writing is "moral"
      only by the extent to which it allows the reader some
      motive, however tenuous, to resist its own extreme in-
      difference to moral reform and to seek a way out of the
      impasse. Examples are *The Progress of Beauty* (although
      written earlier, in 1719), *The Lady's Dressing Room*,
      and *A Beautiful Young Nymph Going to Bed*. In *Strephon*
      and Chloe, however, a middle way is at least promised
      in abstract terms, while in *Cassinus and Peter* the
      vexatious extremes dissolve into a "shared experience
      of comic discrimination."

239. Rogers, Katharine M. "'My Female Friends': The Misogyny
      of Jonathan Swift." *Texas Studies in Literature and*
      Language 1 (Autumn 1959): 366-79.

      An egregiously slanted argument that Swift's attacks
      on women reveal a deeper misogyny than is apparent in
      conventional contemporary anti-feminist literature, an
      unconscious misogyny covering their physical aspects.
      Swift degrades the romantic ideal, disparages mother-
      hood, and indulges in remarkably nauseating descriptions
      of the female body and sexual relations. Rogers focuses
      upon the "scatological" poems but refers to many other
      poems (including *Cadenus and Vanessa* and poems relating
      to Stella and Lady Acheson) as well as prose works
      (chiefly *Gulliver's Travels*). See also item 240.

240. Rogers, Katharine M. *The Troublesome Helpmate: A History*
      of Misogyny in Literature. Seattle: University of
      Washington Press, 1966, pp. 166-74.

      A much-revised version of Rogers's article "'My Female
      Friends'" (see item 239). Although some material is
      condensed, a passage is added on *The Journal of a Modern*
      Lady.

241. Schakel, Peter J. "Swift's Remedy for Love: The 'Scato-
      logical' Poems." *Papers on Language and Literature*
      14 (Spring 1978): 137-47. Reprint. *Contemporary*

Studies of Swift's Poetry. Edited by John Irwin
Fischer and Donald C. Mell, Jr., with David M. Vieth,
associate editor. Newark: University of Delaware
Press; London and Toronto: Associated University
Presses, 1980, pp. 136-48.

Although presumably intended, like Ovid's *Remedia
Amoris*, to be comic poems with an underlying seriousness,
Swift's "scatological" poems are less effective because
Swift could not maintain a light, dispassionate attitude
toward his subject matter. *The Lady's Dressing Room*
as a whole is not successful comedy, mostly because
Swift was unable to dissociate himself from the harsh-
ness of his material. In *A Beautiful Young Nymph Going
to Bed*, despite the successful comic elements and the
apparent comic intent of the whole, much of the poem is
not comic at all because many lines invite sympathy for
Corinna. The comic intent of *Strephon and Chloe* is un-
mistakable, and the first 218 lines are good comedy,
but the final ninety-six lines of heavy-handed sermon-
izing destroy the unity and effectiveness of the poem.
There is an apparent inconsistency in the "scatological"
poems: Swift wants to *know* but not *get too near* the
realities in question.

242. Schakel, Peter J. "Swift's Scatological Poems." *PMLA*
      91 (May 1976): 465-66 (Forum).

      Expresses two reservations concerning Thomas B. Gil-
      more's earlier *PMLA* article (see item 210): (1) Swift's
      personal involvement in the "scatological" poems is
      greater than Gilmore recognizes; and (2) though these
      poems have comic elements, they do not (except for
      Cassinus and Peter) have a pervasive comic tone. Swift,
      Schakel feels, was not entirely at ease with his sub-
      ject. See Gilmore's reply, item 212.

243. Sena, John F. "Swift as Moral Physician: Scatology and
      the Tradition of Love Melancholy." *Journal of English
      and Germanic Philology* 76 (July 1977): 346-62.

      Conceding to such predecessors as Donald Greene and
      Jae Num Lee (see items 213 and 85) that Swift's language,
      tone, and rhetorical techniques were undoubtedly in-
      fluenced by earlier satires of women and by a scatologi-
      cal tradition in literature, Sena urges that *The Lady's
      Dressing Room* and *A Beautiful Young Nymph Going to Bed*
      may reflect also the tradition of medical works written
      to cure "love melancholy." This tradition, whose history

Sena traces, began with Ovid's *Remedia Amoris* and
extended through the eighteenth century. Swift, however,
altered and enlarged a tradition which was essentially
medical and secular into an effective vehicle for the
satiric, moral, and philosophical reflections of a
Christian humanist.

244. Sheehan, David. "The Ironist in Rochester's 'A letter
      from Artemisia in the Town to Chloe in the Country.'"
      Tennessee Studies in Literature 25 (1980): 72-83.

      Addressing the controversial question of whether any
      normative point of view can be found in Rochester's
      poem, Sheehan devotes several suggestive paragraphs to
      the analogous problem posed by *The Lady's Dressing Room.*

245. Sherbo, Arthur. "Mundus Muliebris." *The Scriblerian,*
      vol. 11, no. 1 (Autumn 1978): 45-46.

      Calls attention to *Mundus Muliebris: or, The Ladies
      Dressing-Room Unlock'd, And her Toilette Spread,* 1690,
      and a reprinting of it, *The Ladies Dressing-Room Un-
      lock'd,* 1700. Appended to *Mundus Muliebris* is a *Fop-
      Dictionary,* of unknown authorship, which defines many
      unfamiliar terms having to do with feminine dress or
      cosmetics, including "puppy water" (*The Lady's Dressing
      Room,* 1. 31), "plumpers" (*A Beautiful Young Nymph Going
      to Bed,* 1. 62), and "commode" (*Ode to the Athenian
      Society,* 1. 233). See Hermann Real, items 235 and 236.

246. Solomon, Harry M. "'Difficult Beauty': Tom D'Urfey and
      the Context of Swift's 'The Lady's Dressing Room.'"
      Studies in English Literature 19 (Summer 1979): 431-44.

      Taking Christine Rees's article as his point of de-
      parture (see item 237), Solomon asserts that *The Lady's
      Dressing Room* must be read in the context of early
      eighteenth-century pastoral conventions. He suggests
      that the poem is a mock variation of a poem by Tom
      D'Urfey which may be hinted at in Swift's text. Swift's
      poem must also be read in the context of the scatological
      feminist satire of the Restoration.

247. Solomon, Miller. "'To Steal a Hint Was Never Known':
      The Sodom Apple Motif and Swift's 'A Beautiful Young
      Nymph Going to Bed.'" *Tennessee Studies in Litera-
      ture* 22 (1977): 105-16.

      Although often praised for its originality, *A Beauti-
      ful Young Nymph* draws upon a particular strain in

Restoration antifeminist satire--the "Sodom apple motif" --which portrays the dangerous disparity between a woman's rich outward appearance and her reality beneath the paint and the petticoat. In Swift's verse, the traditional roughness of the antifeminist satires is modified by the influence of Matthew Prior's "easy" style.

248. Tyne, James L., S.J. "Terrestrial and Transcendental Man as Viewed by Swift and Byron." *Enlightenment Essays*, vol. 8, no. 1/2/3/4 (Spring-Summer, Winter-Fall 1977): 22-37.

   Although Byron and Swift both satirize the fantasies of idealizing poetry, Byron utilizes realistic norms such as eating, whereas Swift prefers the grotesque distortions of scatology, as illustrated by quotations from *Strephon and Chloe*. Swift's parody of pastoral conventions, however, prevents his portrayal from being totally one-sided. Tyne also briefly compares Byron's *The Vision of Judgement* and Swift's *The Day of Judgement*.

249. Vieth, David M. "Swift: Poetical Works." *Notes and Queries* 220 (1975): 562-63.

   Lines 133-34 of *The Lady's Dressing Room* read, in the Sir Harold Williams edition (item 16), "To him that looks behind the Scene, / *Satira*'s [sic] but some pocky Quean." "*Satira*'s" is a misprint for the obviously correct reading "*Statira*'s," an allusion to one of the two leading female roles in Nathaniel Lee's popular tragedy *The Rival Queens*.

250. Watanabe, Koji. "*The Lady's Dressing Room*." *English Quarterly* (Kyoto) 11 (October 1974): 229-45.

   In Japanese. Watanabe contends that *The Lady's Dressing Room* is not only a parody of romantic love, but an ironically allusive poem to Caroline, Queen of George II. See the abstract in *The Scriblerian*, vol. 8, no. 2 (Spring 1976): 83-84.

251. Wendt, Allan. "Who's a Yahoo!" *College English* 33 (December 1971): 317-23.

   Description of a pedagogical experiment utilizing Pope's *The Rape of the Lock* and Swift's *The Lady's Dressing Room*, *A Beautiful Young Nymph Going to Bed*, *The Progress of Beauty*, and *Gulliver's Travels*.

252. Woolley, David. "The Canon of Swift." *Johnsonian News Letter*, vol. 20, no. 2 (June 1960): 8.

Argues briefly for Swift's authorship of the prose tract *A Modest Defence of a Late Poem By an unknown Author, call'd, The Lady's Dressing-Room.* See Herbert Davis, item 207.

See also items 6, 40, 47, 47A, 48A, 50, 52, 53, 54, 59, 62, 64, 70, 73, 76, 78, 83, 84, 85, 89, 93, 96, 102, 104, 105, 105A, 107, 111, 113, 115, 117, 123, 126, 134, 163, 180, 257, 315, 322, 329, 345, 356, 361, 448, 478, 490, 497, 505, 517, 529, 531, 535, 536, 541, 546, 553, 554, 556, 560, 561, 571.

I. On Poetry: A Rapsody

253. Davis, Herbert. "Some Free Thoughts of a Tory Dean." *Virginia Quarterly Review* 28 (Spring 1952): 258-72. Reprint (slightly condensed). *Jonathan Swift: Essays on His Satire and Other Studies by Herbert Davis.* Galaxy Books. New York: Oxford University Press, 1964, pp. 236-48.

Cites a letter of 27 May 1742 from William Livingston, later governor of New Jersey, to Noah Wells, then at Yale, illustrating the response in the American colonies to *On Poetry: A Rapsody.* The response was enthusiastic; Livingston "comments with great satisfaction on Swift's satire upon the King and the Prince of Wales."

254. Mahony, Robert, ed. *Different Styles of Poetry: Verses by Wentworth Dillon, Fourth Earl of Roscommon, Thomas Parnell, & Jonathan Swift.* Irish Writings from the Age of Swift, vol. 8. Dublin: The Cadenus Press, 1978. Pp. 143. (Edition limited to 250 copies).

This seemingly out-of-the-way publication should be consulted by anyone writing on *On Poetry: A Rapsody.* It consists of an extended critical essay on the poem by way of introduction, a text of the poem with explanatory notes (pp. 82-123), and, in Appendix III, a detailed textual note (pp. 135-42). The introduction offers a variety of perceptive comments focused upon what is said to be the poem's subject: "the degrading perversity that poetic ambition spawns," especially

when it interacts with politics. The text of the poem
is that of Faulkner's 1735 edition into which lines
have been inserted that were omitted in the early editions.

255. Mayhew, George P. "'Rage or Raillery': Swift's *Epistle
      to a Lady* and *On Poetry: A Rapsody*." *Huntington
      Library Quarterly* 23 (February 1960): 159-80. Reprint
      (slightly revised). "'Rage or Raillery': Transcrip-
      tions of *An Epistle to a Lady* and *On Poetry: A Rap-
      sody*." *Rage or Raillery: The Swift Manuscripts at
      the Huntington Library*. San Marino, CA: Huntington
      Library, 1967, pp. 94-114.

      A manuscript in the Huntington Library, bound as an
      additional gathering into a copy of Faulkner's edition
      of Swift's *Works*, 1735, preserves several passages that
      were suppressed when the *Epistle* and the *Rapsody* were
      published in separate pamphlets in 1733. Mayhew's
      valuable article prints (1) six passages of political
      satire omitted from the *Rapsody*, (2) the complete
      variant version of the *Epistle* as it appears in the
      manuscript, including four couplets omitted in 1733,
      and (3) two hitherto unpublished passages of Anglo-
      Latin by Swift and Sheridan that are preserved in
      Forster MS. 530 in the Victoria and Albert Museum.
      Mayhew also gives an account of the colorful circum-
      stances surrounding the initial publication of the
      Epistle and the *Rapsody* late in 1733.

256. Probyn, Clive T. "Swift's Borrowing from Gay." *Notes
      and Queries* 214 (May 1969): 184.

      In *On Poetry: A Rapsody*, Swift's reference to a shoe-
      shine boy and would-be poet (ll. 33, 35-36) may allude
      to an incident in John Gay's *Trivia* (ll. 140-42).

257. Rawson, C.J. *Gulliver and the Gentle Reader: Studies
      in Swift and Our Time*. London and Boston: Routledge
      and Kegan Paul, 1973. Pp. x + 190.

      Comments briefly on *A Beautiful Young Nymph Going to
      Bed* and *An Epistle to a Lady* and more extensively on
      On Poetry: A Rapsody. See item 258.

258. Rawson, C.J. "''Tis only infinite below': Speculations
      on Swift, Wallace Stevens, R.D. Laing and Others."
      Essays in Criticism 22 (April 1972): 161-81.

      Discusses figures of infinity and circularity in
      On Poetry: A Rapsody. This article appears, in

slightly different form, as Chapter 3 in Rawson's
book *Gulliver and the Gentle Reader* (see item 257).

259. Tyne, James L., S.J. "Swift's Mock Panegyrics in
      'On Poetry: A Rapsody.'" *Papers on Language and
      Literature* 10 (Summer 1974): 279-86.

      Illustrates how two passages in *A Rapsody*, on George
      II and Walpole, parody the ways in which the Augustan
      myth was debased in serious panegyrics by dunces like
      Cibber and Eusden. Swift's passages carry four levels
      of meaning: what is stated, what is meant, what the
      laureates regularly predicated of George, and what
      Virgil and Horace say of their Augustus.

See also items 6, 15, 47A, 48, 50, 56, 62, 64, 69, 78, 80,
83, 87, 90, 98, 99, 105, 105A, 107, 115, 120, 123, 126, 130,
131, 275, 393, 452, 469, 512, 530, 544, 546, 553, 576, 580.

                J. *Verses on the Death of Dr. Swift*

260. Anderson, Phillip B. "Transformations of 'Swift' and
      the Development of Swift's Satiric Vision in *Verses
      on the Death of Dr. Swift.*" *Publications of the
      Arkansas Philological Association*, vol. 6, no. 1
      (Spring 1980): 19-32.

      Complaining that *Verses* has not been read adequately
      as a whole poem, Anderson interprets it as the inter-
      action of two concurrent developments: Swift's "satiric
      intention," drawn out from La Rochefoucauld's maxim,
      and a series of "transformations" of Swift's "fictive
      self." As the civilized raillery of the "proem" modu-
      lates to a satirical indictment more severe than any-
      thing in La Rochefoucauld's worldy wisdom, the speaker
      is transformed from a friendly conversationalist, much
      like the "real" Swift, to an ailing man, to a dead man,
      then to a man represented by his literary works, and
      even those only in memory. "Swift" in the concluding
      panegyric is both myth and truth, a juxtaposition of
      incredibly idealized virtue with a *Dunciad*-like vision
      of universal corruption, each qualifying the other.

261. Booth, Wayne C. *A Rhetoric of Irony*. Chicago and
     London: University of Chicago Press, 1974, pp. 120-22.

     On the difficulty of determining the exact degree of
     irony in the concluding self-portrait in *Verses on the
     Death of Dr. Swift*. It is difficult to distinguish the
     internal context from the external—that is, from our
     impressions of Swift the man.

262. Davis, Herbert. "Swift's Character." *Jonathan Swift
     1667-1967: A Dublin Tercentenary Tribute*. Edited by
     Roger McHugh and Philip Edwards. Dublin: Dolmen
     Press, 1967, pp. 1-23.

     Davis proposes "to try and discover what we can
     gather from some of those self-portraits which Swift
     drew at different times, where at least he was pretending
     to tell us something about himself, or to give us a
     sketch of his life and character." *Verses on the Death
     of Dr. Swift* receives the most attention, but there are
     comments on other poems including *The Author upon Him-
     self*, *A Panegyric on the Reverend Dean Swift*, and *The
     Life and Character of Dean Swift*.

263. Davis, Herbert. "Verses on the Death of Dr. Swift."
     The Book-Collector's Quarterly, no. 2 (March-May
     1931): 57-73.

     Examines the circumstances surrounding the publication
     of Swift's *Verses* in 1739, the authenticity of *The Life
     and Genuine Character of Doctor Swift* (1731), and the
     relationship of these two poems to each other.

264. Ehrenpreis, Irvin. *Literary Meaning and Augustan Values*.
     Charlottesville: University Press of Virginia, 1974,
     pp. 33-37.

     This "anti-persona" approach insists that there is no
     irony in the concluding eulogy in the *Verses*. Ehren-
     preis finds Swift's self-praise gross and disgusting.

265. Elkin, P.K. *The Augustan Defence of Satire*. Oxford:
     Clarendon Press, 1973, pp. 111-14.

     Examines the *Verses* as a traditional satirist's
     apologia. The poem is a good eighteenth-century example
     of the type, largely conventional in content and form
     but distinguished by a personal slant and strong per-
     sonal feeling. Elsewhere in the volume, Elkin briefly

cites Swift's poems for statements about the nature of
satire, concluding that alone among the major writers
of the period, Swift basically had no faith in satire's
ability to reform.

266. Fetting, Hans F. "Swift's *Verses on the Death of Dr.
      Swift*, 189-192." *The Explicator*, vol. 26, no. 9
      (May 1968): item 75.

      "Walpole's" inquiry in line 191, "Why, is he dead
      without his shoes?", is an ironic reference to the more
      common English proverb "to die in one's shoes," meaning
      a sudden death or hanging--what Walpole would wish for
      Swift.

267. Fischer, John Irwin. "How to Die: *Verses on the Death
      of Dr. Swift*." *Review of English Studies* n.s. 21
      (November 1970): 422-41.

      In what is essentially a long footnote to Waingrow
      (item 285), Fischer Christianizes the notion that the
      subject of Swift's concluding panegyric is a model of
      altruistic behavior. This exemplary figure is refined
      into a charitable man who is aware of death and trusts
      in God, while the poem as a whole is seen as a seven-
      teenth-century traditional meditation on death. Fischer
      is the first to explore the significance of the biblical
      allusions in the *Verses*.

268. Higgins, T.F. "More Swiftiana." *London Times Literary
      Supplement*, 13 December 1934, p. 895.

      Prints several advertisements relating to works by
      Swift, including *Verses on the Death of Dr. Swift*, *The
      Life and Genuine Character of Doctor Swift*, and Faulk-
      ner's edition of 1735, the second volume of which
      contains the poems.

269. Johnson, Maurice. "'Verses on the Death of Dr. Swift.'"
      Notes and Queries 199 (1954): 473-74.

      Answers objections that Swift's concluding encomium
      of himself is incongruous with the rest of the *Verses*.
      Johnson suggests that this exaggerated praise of the
      "dead" Dean, in the latter part of the poem, has the
      structural function of balancing the exaggerated weak-
      ness of character Swift imputes to himself in early
      lines.

270. Kernan, Alvin B. *The Plot of Satire.* New Haven and
     London: Yale University Press, 1965, pp. 14, 51,
     87-89.

     Discusses irony in *Verses on the Death of Dr. Swift*,
     especially in the scene of the ladies playing cards
     (11. 225-42).

271. Klein, Julie Thompson. "The Art of Apology: 'An
     Epistle to Dr. Arbuthnot' and 'Verses on the Death
     of Dr. Swift.'" *Costerus* 8 (1973): 77-87.

     Examines the *Verses* for occurrences of various features
     of the traditional Roman *apologia pro satura sua*.
     Klein concludes that Swift drastically alters the
     structure of the apologetic formula even while retaining
     its spirit. Apart from developing the maxim from La
     Rochefoucauld into the conventional contrast between a
     vice and its opposite virtue, Swift's only direct use
     of apology is reserved for the eulogist in the latter
     portion of the poem.

272. Maguire, Conor A., ed. *The Legacy of Swift: A Bi-Cen-
     tenary Record of St. Patrick's Hospital, Dublin.*
     Dublin: Printed for the Governors, At the Sign of
     the Three Candles, 1948. Pp. xii + 70.

     Information on the "House for Fools and Mad," mentioned
     in the conclusion of *Verses on the Death of Dr. Swift*,
     which was subsequently established under the terms of
     Swift's will.

273. Mell, Donald C. "Elegiac Design and Satiric Intention
     in *Verses on the Death of Dr. Swift.*" *Concerning
     Poetry*, vol. 6, no. 2 (Fall 1973): 15-24. Reprint.
     *A Poetics of Augustan Elegy: Studies of Poems by
     Dryden, Pope, Prior, Swift, Gray, and Johnson.*
     Amsterdam: Rodopi, 1974, pp. 53-62.

     To the conventions of satire, Swift in the *Verses*
     adds those of formal elegy--which, like satire, portrays
     the loss of something valuable. Out of the interplay
     of these two traditional genres Swift develops the theme
     of the imagination as a defense against time and mortali-
     ty, and the more fundamental opposition between art
     and time. Mell's enumeration of elegiac features in
     the *Verses* is illuminating.

274. Reichard, Hugo M. "The Self-Praise Abounding in Swift's
      Verses." *Tennessee Studies in Literature* 18 (1973):
      105-12.

      Argues unconvincingly that in the *Verses*, Swift
      praises himself in particular, and human nature in
      general, more than most readers have thought.

275. Said, Edward W. "Swift's Tory Anarchy." *Eighteenth-
      Century Studies* 3 (Fall 1969): 48-66.

      An approach to Swift's works as highly dramatic en-
      counters between the explosive resistance of his identity
      and any form of fixed boundaries and categories. Most
      of Swift's writing was occasional--that is, stimulated
      by specific events and planned in some way to change them.
      Verses on the Death of Dr. Swift was his endeavor to
      project his own presence onto the future as an event in
      history. Dealing also with *On Poetry: A Rapsody*, Said's
      essay is a brilliant, comprehensive application of
      current critical methodology to the full range of Swift's
      life and works.

276. Schakel, Peter J. "The Politics of Opposition in
      'Verses on the Death of Dr. Swift.'" *Modern Language
      Quarterly* 35 (September 1974): 246-56.

      Suggests that the various themes in the *Verses* come
      to focus in a political purpose, the opposition to
      Walpole, but also in the ethical principle on which
      Swift feels such opposition must be grounded. This
      conclusion is drawn from three considerations: the
      politically biased speaker of the concluding eulogy,
      Swift's selectivity in emphasizing or omitting certain
      aspects of his career, and the relationship of the eulogy
      to the earlier portion of the poem. Schakel observes
      that the Rose Tavern, where the eulogy is spoken, was
      consistently used throughout the Restoration and early
      eighteenth century as a symbol of disrepute.

277. Scouten, A.H. "The Earliest London Printings of 'Verses
      on the Death of Doctor Swift.'" *Studies in Bibli-
      ography* 15 (1962): 243-47.

      Scouten demolishes Teerink's theory that the Bathurst
      text of the *Verses*, published in January 1739, was
      printed from a hitherto unknown piracy of 1736 (see
      items 281 and 282). On the contrary, as the textual
      variants show, Teerink's "1736" edition was printed
      from a later descendant of the Bathurst editions. The
      title page of the piracy must therefore be misdated.

278. Scouten, Arthur H., and Robert D. Hume. "Pope and
      Swift: Text and Interpretation of Swift's Verses on
      His Death." *Philological Quarterly* 52 (April 1973):
      205-31.

      This important article stitches together what are
      really two separate discussions: an account of the
      early textual history of the *Verses*, and an interpreta-
      tion of its meaning. The first half traces the poem's
      textual history step by step, from its composition and
      first publication, in 1739, through successive attempts
      to conflate it with *The Life and Genuine Character of
      Doctor Swift*, down to the recovery of a satisfactory
      text in the Williams edition of 1937 (see item 16). The
      second half of the article, after assessing the critical
      tradition represented by Middleton Murry, Slepian, Wain-
      grow, and John Irwin Fischer (items 89, 279, 285, 267),
      proposes a bifurcated interpretation combining a theme--
      the folly of such forms of vanity as "Self-love, Ambi-
      tion, Envy, Pride"--with a sense of Swift's personal
      presence in his work. Useful interpretive comments are
      provided on *The Life and Genuine Character* and on the
      hybrid poem formed by conflating it with the *Verses*.

279. Slepian, Barry. "The Ironic Intention of Swift's
      Verses on His Own Death." *Review of English Studies*
      n.s. 14 (1963): 249-56.

      Slepian's important article maintains that the con-
      cluding panegyric in the *Verses*, which Middleton Murry
      criticized as "an extravagance of self-laudation" (see
      item 89), is Swift's ironical satire on his own vanity.
      Slepian divides the poem into three parts. The first
      part (ll. 1-72) says that people are vain; the second
      part (ll. 73-298) that other men are vain; the third
      part (ll. 299-484) that Swift is vain.

280. Steensma, Robert C. "Swift's Apologia: 'Verses on the
      Death of Dr. Swift.'" *Proceedings of the Utah Academy
      of Sciences, Arts, and Letters* 42 (1965): 23-28.

      Explores ways in which the *Verses* may be considered
      Swift's *apologia pro sua vita*. Although in the first
      part of the poem Swift is not defending himself except
      by implication, the "Character impartial" drawn by the
      member of the club at the Rose Tavern serves as his
      apologia, justifying his personality, his career, and
      his satire. The concluding lines afford "the most lucid
      explanation of the purpose and method of his satire
      that Swift was ever to make."

281. Teerink, H. "Swift's *Verses on the Death of Doctor Swift*." *Studies in Bibliography* 4 (1951): 183-88.

Presents evidence that the first printing of Swift's *Verses* occurred, not in the Bathurst edition of January 1739, as is usually supposed, but as early as 1736. The principal evidence is a pirated edition of Pope's *Essay on Man*, dated 1736 on its title page, which includes a text of the *Verses*. Textual variants are offered to support Teerink's theory that the Bathurst edition was printed from the one dated 1736. See also item 282 and Arthur Scouten's answer, item 277.

282. Teerink, H. "'*Verses On the Death of Doctor Swift*' Again." *Studies in Bibliography* 7 (1955): 238-39.

Calls attention to still another "1736" edition of Swift's *Verses*; see item 281 and Arthur Scouten's answer, item 277.

283. Uphaus, Robert W. "Swift's 'whole character': The Delany Poems and '*Verses on the Death of Dr. Swift*.'" *Modern Language Quarterly* 34 (December 1973): 406-16.

Three poems written in 1730, ostensibly to satirize Patrick Delany and his verse *Epistle to Lord Carteret*, anticipate the radically new stance Swift was to adopt in *Verses on the Death of Dr. Swift*. In *An Epistle upon an Epistle*, *A Libel on Doctor Delany*, and *A Panegyric on the Reverend Dean Swift*, he departs from the kind of irony we normally expect from him and instead projects his own personality; in place of a poetic convention like the *vir bonus*, the norm he offers is Swift the man. Similarly, in the *Verses*, which are not a conventional *apologia*, Swift "affirms his own identity and convictions, his own sense of self, as the model from which he and the reader are to make judgments." Any irony is subservient to Swift's "biographical presence," in Maurice Johnson's phrase (see item 82); La Rochefoucauld's maxim is not an accusation of selfishness, as Uphaus's predecessors have thought, but "a morally neutral fact of human nature."

284. Vieth, David M. "The Mystery of Personal Identity: Swift's Verses on His Own Death." *The Author in His Work: Essays on a Problem in Criticism.* Edited by Louis L. Martz and Aubrey Williams; introduction by Patricia Meyer Spacks. New Haven and London: Yale University Press, 1978, pp. 245-62.

Maintains that the *Verses* must be read *affectively*.
Part of the poem's affective structuring is its multiplication of identities which can each be called "Jonathan Swift." The most "real" of these multiple identities is the idealized portrait of Swift in the half-
sincere, half-fictitious encomium that concludes the
poem. The poem's general purpose is to probe the para-
doxes of personal identity, while its specific purpose
is to project the identity of "Swift" into the future
as a historical "fact."

285. Waingrow, Marshall. "'Verses on the Death of Dr. Swift.'"
     Studies in English Literature 5 (Summer 1965): 513-18.

     Takes a middle position between Middleton Murry's
     view that Swift's conluding panegyric in the *Verses*
     displays an objectionable degree of vanity and Slepian's
     view that these lines are intended ironically (see items
     89 and 279). Waingrow regards the principal speaker in
     the poem as a qualified but praiseworthy model of moral
     perception and behavior.

286. Woolley, James. "Autobiography in Swift's Verses on
     His Death." *Contemporary Studies of Swift's Poetry*.
     Edited by John Irwin Fischer and Donald C. Mell, Jr.,
     with David M. Vieth, associate editor. Newark: Uni-
     versity of Delaware Press; London and Toronto: Asso-
     ciated University Presses, 1980, pp. 112-22.

     Maintains that in the *Verses*, the concluding eulogy
     is not as inaccurate or ironic as a number of recent
     interpretations have assumed. Even where there appear
     to be factual inaccuracies, Swift may be expressing
     what he sincerely believed about himself, as Woolley
     demonstrates by ample quotations from the correspondence.
     Points at issue include how well Swift was received at
     Court, how far he sought wealth and power, whether he
     granted favors disinterestedly, what he really thought
     of Queen Anne, and whether he had any social friendships
     with members of the Irish House of Lords. If "in the
     eulogy Swift puts forward a myth about himself," Woolley
     concludes, "it is a myth he himself took seriously."

287. Woolley, James. "Friends and Enemies in *Verses on the
     Death of Dr. Swift*." *Studies in Eighteenth-Century
     Culture* 8, edited by Roseann Runte (Madison: Univer-
     sity of Wisconsin Press, 1979): 205-32.

     Woolley argues three related points: first, that
     Swift thought of the *Verses* as a poem about friendship

and enmity, not so much exalted *amicitia* as useful
friendship; second, that a crucial context of the poem
is Swift's actual friendship and enmity with Queen
Caroline and Mrs. Howard between 1726 and the composition of the poem in 1731; and third, that the concluding
eulogy is largely praise that Swift thought he deserved.

288. Yamaguchi, Katsumasa. *"Verses on the Death of Dr.
Swift* ni tsuite" ["An Essay on *Verses* ..."]. *Annual
Reports of English and American Literature, Osaka
Shōin Women's College* 14 (March 1977): 1-15.

In answer to Middleton Murry, who took the concluding
panegyric in the *Verses* as evidence of Swift's mental
deterioration (see item 89), Yamaguchi argues that it
should be read as a satirical elegy in which Swift
consciously dramatizes and eulogizes himself in accord-
ance with the elegiac panegyric convention. He also
finds an ironic use of the diction of pastoral elegy,
as "Where's now this Fav'rite of *Apollo*? / Departed;
and his Works must follow" (11. 249-50). (Information
excerpted from *The Scriblerian*, vol. 11, no. 1 [Autumn
1978]: 12).

See also items 6, 15, 40, 46, 47A, 49, 50, 52, 53, 54, 56,
58, 61A, 62, 69, 76, 78, 80, 89, 90, 91A, 93, 102, 105, 105A,
111, 113, 114, 117, 120, 126, 172, 297, 376, 390, 405, 475,
479, 501, 512, 517, 529, 553, 565, 571, 580.

K. *The Day of Judgement*

289. Carnochan, W.B. "The Occasion of Swift's 'Day of
Judgement.'" *PMLA* 87 (May 1972): 518-20.

Notes the contradiction implicit in Maurice Johnson's
contention that *The Day of Judgement*, which most readers
take as a general "satire on mankind, Jove's joke on
everybody," may have been occasioned specifically by
agitation for repeal of the Test Act in Ireland in
1732-1733 (see item 294). Less plausibly, Carnochan
suggests that Swift's poem is directed against eighteenth-
century doctrines of "universal restoration," associated
in their beginnings with Origen and holding that everybody will be saved. Swift's specific target was possibly
the chiliastic group calling itself the Philadelphian
Society, founded in the late seventeenth century by
Mrs. Jane Lead and carried on by the Reverend Richard
Roach.

290. Cunningham, J.S. "On Earth as it Laughs in Heaven:
     Mirth and the 'Frigorifick Wisdom.'" Augustan Worlds:
     New Essays in Eighteenth-Century Literature. Edited
     by J.C. Hilson, M.M.B. Jones, and J.R. Watson. Leices-
     ter, Eng.: Leicester University Press; New York:
     Barnes and Noble, 1978, p. 137.

     On laughter as the appropriate reader response to
     The Day of Judgement. An illuminationg analogue is the
     divine laughter at human expense described by Stultitia
     in Erasmus's Moriae Encomium.

291. Fischer, John Irwin. "The Dean Contra Heathens:
     Swift's The Day of Judgement. Revue des Langues
     Vivantes (Bruxelles) 43 (1977): 592-97.

     Attempts to reconcile the poem's "felt strength" and
     its "purposive absurdity" by suggesting that "Jove" is
     a persona who does not represent Swift's most inclusive
     vision.

292. Gulick, Sidney L., Jr. "Jonathan Swift's 'The Day of
     Judgement.'" PMLA 48 (1933): 850-55.

     Gulick's pioneer article reviews the known facts
     concerning eighteenth-century appearances of The Day of
     Judgement. The data include Lord Chesterfield's apparent
     reference to the poem in his letter to Voltaire, printed
     in Letters to His Son (7 April 1774); the publication
     of the text of the poem in the St. James's Chronicle
     (12 April 1774); and the subsequent reprinting of the
     poem in the Monthly Review (July 1774), in the fourth
     edition of Chesterfield's Letters (29 October 1774),
     and in John Nichols's collection of Swift's works (1775).
     Recognizing that the poem had been accepted as Swift's
     on insufficient grounds, especially since Chesterfield's
     letter to Voltaire does not quote any portion of its
     text, Gulick offers two arguments for its authenticity:
     the probability that the letter paraphrases part of its
     content, and the presence of a similar paraphrase, with
     ascription to Swift, in one of Chesterfield's later
     letters.

293. Gulick, Sidney L. "No 'Spectral Hand' in Swift's 'Day
     of Judgement.'" Papers of the Bibliographical Society
     of America 71 (Third Quarter 1977): 333-36.

     Points out the weakness of Leland Peterson's argu-
     ments (see item 296).

294. Johnson, Maurice. "Text and Possible Occasion for
      Swift's 'Day of Judgement.'" *PMLA* 86 (March 1971):
      210-17.

      Augments Sidney Gulick's account of the early texts
      and authenticity of the poem (see item 292) by analyzing
      two manuscript versions, transcribed by William Collins
      and William Shenstone, as well as the earliest printed
      version, in *The Friends* (1773). All three versions
      attribute the poem to Swift. Johnson adduces evidence
      that the eighteenth-century audience read the poem as a
      satire on divisive religious sects. He suggests that
      it may have been occasioned by agitation for the repeal
      of the Test Act in Ireland during 1732-33.

295. Mayhew, George. "Swift's 'On the Day of Judgement' and
      Theophilus Swift.'" *Philological Quarterly* 54
      (Winter 1975): 213-21.

      Presents virtually conclusive evidence that the version
      of *The Day of Judgement* printed in the *St. James's
      Chronicle*, 1774, and accepted into the Williams edition
      (see item 16) is indeed the most nearly authentic sur-
      viving text. The principal new evidence is a substan-
      tively identical version of the poem preserved in a
      clipping from a contemporary Dublin newspaper which is
      found, together with other notes from Theophilus Swift,
      among the papers of Sir Walter Scott in the National
      Library of Scotland. Theophilus Swift may be the "Mer-
      cutio" who, in the headnote in the Dublin and *St. James*
      versions, vouches for the poem's authenticity. Mayhew
      argues persuasively that the poem's title should be
      worded *On the Day of Judgement*, the form used in these
      two sources.

296. Peterson, Leland D. "The Spectral Hand in Swift's
      'Day of Judgement.'" *Papers of the Bibliographical
      Society of America* 70 (Third Quarter 1976): 189-219.

      This is a highly speculative attempt to determine
      which of five surviving eighteenth-century versions of
      The Day of Judgement, two in manuscript and three in
      print, is most nearly authentic. Instead of the version
      printed in the *St. James's Chronicle*, 1774, which was
      selected for the Williams edition (see item 16), Peter-
      son prefers the earlier, shorter version printed in
      The Friends, 1773. The textual variants are then ex-
      plained as later revisions, not by Swift, but by at
      least one "ghost" or "spectral hand" who may have been
      Lord Chesterfield. Peterson usefully reproduces all
      five versions in full.

297.   Rodino, Richard H.   "Robert Gould and Swift's 'The Day
       of Judgement.'"   *Notes and Queries* 224 (December
       1979): 549.

       The "likely source" of the most controversial lines in
       The Day of Judgement, "You who in different Sects have
       shamm'd / And come to see each other damn'd," is a
       couplet in Robert Gould's *A Satyr against Man*: "What
       Species of 'em have so far been shamm'd / To think their
       other Brethren all are damn'd." Gould's reputation as
       a strenuous defender of Anglicanism, reflected in the
       context from which his couplet is quoted, may lend
       weight to the interpretation of Swift's poem as a satire
       on dissenting sects rather than a categorical dismissal
       of mankind. Also, the famous pronouncement in *Verses on
       the Death of Dr. Swift*, "He lash'd the Vice but spar'd
       the Name," appears in almost identical form in the
       "Advertisement" to Gould's poem: "Tho' I shall lash the
       Vice I'll spare the *Name*."

298.   Sleeth, Charles R.   "Swift's 'Day of Judgement.'"   *PMLA*
       88 (January 1973): 144-45 (Forum).

       Responding to W.B. Carnochan's *PMLA* article on *The
       Day of Judgement* (see item 289), Sleeth observes that
       Jove's concluding words, "Go, go, you're bit," echo
       "Depart from me, ye cursed" in the account of the Last
       Judgment in Matthew 25:41. As such, they undermine any
       hint of forgiveness and pronounce "a sentence of banish-
       ment from the presence of God which is indistinguishable
       from damnation."

299.   Smith, T. Henry.   "Swift's 'The Day of Judgement.'"
       The Explicator, vol. 22, no. 1 (September 1963):
       item 6.

       A line-by-line interpretation of the poem, turning
       on its rhetorical organization as a "bite." The reader,
       representative of the human race, is led to expect
       damnation from Jove--who, however, dismisses "the World's
       mad Business" as too trivial for such grand treatment.

See also items 48A, 51-54, 77, 78, 102, 105A, 111, 114, 117,
130, 163, 248, 322.

V. MISCELLANEOUS

300. Anonymous. "The Osborn Collection at Yale." *The*
      Scriblerian, vol. 3, no. 1 (Autumn 1970): 33-34.

      The James Marshall and Marie-Louise Osborn Collection
      contains three poems in manuscript attributed to Swift
      but apparently not mentioned in the edition by Sir
      Harold Williams (see item 16). They are "The function
      of a Viceroy (or L^d. Lieut. of Ireland)," "B^p Atterbury's
      Character of himself after his Exile," and "Eulogium
      of A. Pope." The text of the "Eulogium," beginning
      "Hail! happy Pope, whose gen'rous mind," is printed in
      full. For correction of some of the information in
      this article, see James D. Woolley and James M. Osborn,
      items 427 and 376.

301. Anonymous. "The Swift Canon." *London Times Literary*
      Supplement, 10 July 1943, p. 331.

      An editorial, prompted by E. St. John Brooks's "A
      Poem of Swift's" (see item 320), offering caveats con-
      cerning the difficulties of establishing the text of
      Swift's poetry.

302. Anonymous. "Swift's Life and Writings." *London Times*
      Literary Supplement, 16 April 1954, p. 248.

      This review of John Middleton Murry's *Jonathan Swift:*
      A Critical Biography (see item 89) offers evidence and
      arguments against Murry's contention that Swift wrote
      A Description of Mother Ludwell's Cave. See also items
      355, 373.

303. Aden, John M. "Swift, Pope, and 'the Sin of Wit.'"
      Papers of the Bibliographical Society of America
      62 (First Quarter 1968): 80-86.

      Swift's well-known phrase "the sin of wit" occurs in
      The Author upon Himself, written between the end of May

and the middle of August 1714, while Swift was at Let-
combe. About a year later, apparently, Pope used the
identical phrase in a lesser-known epigram. Aden
speculates on the probability that Pope derived the
phrase from Swift's poem, which was not published until
1735.

304. Aitken, George A. "Jonathan Swift." *The Athenaeum*,
     no. 3850 (10 August 1901): 189-90.

     Writing to Stella on 7 August 1712, Swift mentions
     "at least 7 penny Papers of my own" that he published
     during "the last Fortnight" before the Stamp Tax went
     into effect on the first of the month. Somewhat over-
     optimistically, perhaps, Aitken claims that five of the
     seven titles, including the poems *Toland's Invitation
     to Dismal* and *Peace and Dunkirk*, can be ascertained from
     earlier entries in the *Journal to Stella*, while two
     more can be conjecturally identified from advertisements
     in *The Examiner* by Swift's bookseller, Morphew. See
     the response by H. Lavers-Smith, item 456; also items
     330, 425, 482, and 489.

305. Allhusen, E.L. "A Swift Epitaph?" *London Times Liter-
     ary Supplement*, 2 May 1935, p. 288.

     Allhusen prints the text of a satirical epitaph on
     Gilbert Burnet, Bishop of Salisbury, beginning "Here
     Sarum lies who was as wise," which he found ascribed
     to Swift in "an old manuscript book, dated 1809."
     See the reply by Harold Williams, item 420.

306. Alspach, Russell K. "Molyneux, Swift, and MacCurtin."
     Irish Poetry from the English Invasion to 1798.
     Philadelphia: University of Pennsylvania Press;
     London: Humphry Milford, Oxford University Press,
     1943, pp. 75-80. 2d ed., rev. 1959.

     Places Swift in the context of Irish literature and
     the development of Irish nationalism. One poem is
     discussed, *The Description of an Irish Feast*.

307. Anderson, G.L. "A Reply to Swift's 'Excellent New
     Song' (1711)." *Papers of the Bibliographical Society
     of America* 69 (Second Quarter 1975): 237-40.

     Prints and discusses briefly *The Nottingham Ballad.
     An Excellent New Song, Being the Intended Speech of a
     Famous Orator*, an anonymous Whig broadside written in
     1711 in answer to Swift's attack on the Earl of Notting-

ham in *An Excellent New Song, Being the Intended Speech of a Famous Orator against Peace.* Anderson thinks the Whig ballad could be the work of John Oldmixon.

308. Ault, Norman. "Pope and His Dogs." *New Light on Pope, with Some Additions to His Poetry Hitherto Unknown.* London: Methuen, 1949, pp. 337-50. Reprint. Hamden, CT.: Archon, 1967.

Attributes *Bounce to Fop* to Pope, rather than Swift or Gay. See items 358 and 359.

309. Bà, Paolo. "A Character, Panegiric [*sic*], and Description of the Legion Club di Jonathan Swift." *Studi Urbinati di Storia, Filosofia e Letteratura*, series B, vol. 44, nos. 1-2 (1970): 54-75.

In Italian. Dividing *The Legion Club* into two parts, a panoramic vision and an analysis of particulars, Bà comments on the poem almost line by line.

310. Bà, Paolo. "Il Posto dei Dannati di Jonathan Swift." *Lettore di Provincia* 2 (1971): 35-41.

A detailed discussion, in Italian, of Swift's *The Place of the Damn'd.* The poem is mistakenly identified as *The Legion Club* in the abstract in *The Scriblerian*, vol. 8, no. 2 (Spring 1976): 83.

311. Ball, F. Elrington. "Congreve as a Ballad-Writer." *Notes and Queries* 12 s. 8 (16 April 1921): 301-03.

Claims *Jack Frenchman's Lamentation* for Congreve's authorship on the strength of Lady Cowper's ascription in her diary. See items 338, 415, 417.

312. Ball, F. Elrington. "Gay's Works." *Notes and Queries* 12 s. 12 (3 March 1923): 174. See also 12 s. 12 (17 February 1923): 130-31.

Responding to G.C. Faber, Ball supplies bibliographical information concerning *Blue-Skin's Ballad* (*Newgate's Garland*) and *A Poem Address'd to the Quidnunc's* (*The Quidnuncki's*). Ball thinks both poems were written by Swift. See items 316, 317, 335.

313. Ball, F. Elrington. "Swift's Verse." *Notes and Queries* 12 s. 8 (1 January 1921): 1-3.

An impassioned plea for a new edition of Swift's poetry. The existing collections are arranged neither according to subject nor according to chronology, they lack the most elementary annotation, and they include many doubtful or spurious poems.

314. Barnett, George L. "Gay, Swift, and 'Tristram Shandy.'" *Notes and Queries* 185 (4 December 1943): 346-47.

A versified "Receipt for Stewing Veal," sent by Gay to Swift in a letter of 22 October 1726, was attributed in print to Swift in 1727 as "An excellent Receipt to make good Soup" and printed in 1760 as "A Receipt for a Soup for Tristram Shandy."

315. Battestin, Martin C. *The Providence of Wit: Aspects of Form in Augustan Literature and the Arts.* Oxford: Clarendon Press, 1974, pp. 216-26.

A brief but vigorous expression of the old-fashioned conception of Swift as an "anti-poet," an anomaly in his age who repudiated the Augustan premise that art should imitate *la belle nature* and even the notion that there is a meaningful analogy between macrocosm and microcosm in the universe. *The Lady's Dressing Room* is a "paradigmatic example" of Swift's sardonic world-view.

316. Beattie, Lester M. "The Authorship of *The Quidnuncki's.*" *Modern Philology* 30 (February 1933): 317-20.

Arbuthnot's authorship of *A Poem Address'd to the Quidnunc's* (*The Quidnuncki's*) is established by references in two letters from Dr. William Stratford, canon of Christ Church, Oxford, to Edward Harley, soon to become Earl of Oxford. See items 312, 317, and 335.

317. Beattie, Lester M. *John Arbuthnot: Mathematician and Satirist.* Harvard Studies in English, vol. 16. Cambridge: Harvard University Press, 1935, pp. 285-87.

Claims *A Poem Address'd to the Quidnunc's* (*The Quidnuncki's*) for Arbuthnot's authorship. See also items 312, 316, 335.

318. Bensly, Edward. "Swift: 'An Ass's Hoof.'" *Notes and Queries* 168 (23 March 1935): 210. See also 168 (9 March 1935): 172.

In the initial couplet of *On Burning a Dull Poem* (1729), "An Ass's Hoof alone can hold / That pois'nous Juice which kills by Cold," the "pois'nous Juice" is the water of the river Styx, which was believed to be a deadly poison destructive of every kind of vessel except those made of a horse's or ass's hoof. According to legend, Alexander the Great was poisoned by it.

319. Breslar, M.L.R. "Lines on Swift." *Notes and Queries* 9 s. 6 (11 August 1900): 107.

Asks who wrote the famous verses said to have been affixed to the door of St. Patrick's Cathedral when Swift was installed as Dean in 1713. See the responses by George Marshall, item 362, and John Pickford, item 379, who identifies the author as Jonathan Smedley.

320. Brooks, E. St. John. "A Poem of Swift's." *London Times Literary Supplement*, 10 July 1943, p. 331.

Prints a variant version of *On the Little House by the Church Yard of Castleknock* which is some ten lines longer than the one reproduced by Sir Harold Williams from Faulkner's edition of 1746 (see item 16). The variant text appears in Volume II of *Brett's Miscellany*, Dublin, 1752, a rare collection assembled by Peter Brett, parish clerk and schoolmaster of Castleknock.

321. Brooks, Harold F. "The 'Imitation' in English Poetry, Especially in Formal Satire, before the Age of Pope." *Review of English Studies* 25 (April 1949): 124-40.

In all the greatest Augustan imitations, including the two, from Horace's *Epistles* 1.7 and *Satires* 2.6, that Swift addressed to Harley in 1713 and 1714, the method is essentially that of Rochester's *An Allusion to Horace, the Tenth Satyr of the First Book*. The poet gives a modern equivalent for each paragraph of the original: a procedure midway between Oldham's practice of translating almost sentence by sentence and the freer adaptations by Cowley and in Rochester's other imitations such as *A Satyr against Mankind*. See also Leonard A. Moskovit and Eric Rothstein, items 374, 393A.

322. Byrd, Max. "Swift." *Visits to Bedlam: Madness and Literature in the Eighteenth Century*. Columbia: University of South Carolina Press, 1975, pp. 58-87.

The angry, cheerless vision in *The Legion Club* typifies the Augustan response to madness. Byrd also comments briefly on Swift's vision of madness in the early odes, especially the *Ode to Dr. William Sancroft* and *Occasioned by Sir William Temple's Late Illness and Recovery*, the "scatological" poems, and several other poems including *The Day of Judgement*.

323. Carnochan, W.B. *Lemuel Gulliver's Mirror for Man.*
      Berkeley and Los Angeles: University of California
      Press, 1968. Pp. 226.

      Includes brief discussions of a number of Swift's
      poems.

324. Case, Arthur E. "Philips or Carey?" *London Times
      Literary Supplement*, 22 May 1930, p. 434.

      Reviewing the exchange between Frederick T. Wood and
      Mary G. Segar (see items 397, 398, 422, 423, 424), Case
      presents evidence and arguments that *A Christmas Box
      for Namby Pamby* satirizes Ambrose Philips--not, as Wood
      maintained, Henry Carey.

325. Clarke, Austin. "Swift's Verse." *London Times Literary
      Supplement*, 8 August 1968, p. 857. See also *TLS*,
      4 July 1968, p. 707, and 22 August 1968, p. 897.

      Clarke objects to the *TLS* reviewer's comment on his
      essay "The Poetry of Swift" in McHugh and Edwards,
      Jonathan Swift 1667-1967: A Dublin Tercentenary Tribute
      (see item 51). The anonymous reviewer responds.

326. De Bhaldraithe, Tomás. "Fonóta do lucht Swiftiana"
      [A Footnote for Those Interested in Swiftiana].
      Studia Hibernica, no. 14 (1974): 140-42.

      In Gaelic. De Bhaldraithe's note concerns the epi-
      grams against Charles Carthy, specifically *Irish Epigram
      English'd*. He identifies Tom Mac Lobe, who is mentioned
      in line 4 and in a footnote in the original printing,
      and speculates about the authorship of this epigram.
      The Irish version, headed *An Irish Ode on Carthy's
      Horace*, is implausibly ascribed to "Mr. Patrick Murphy,
      Porter of Trinity College." See the abstract in *The
      Scriblerian*, vol. 10, no. 1 (Autumn 1977): 7.

327. Doughty, Oswald. *English Lyric in the Age of Reason.*
      London: O'Connor, 1922, pp. 67-71. Reprint. New
      York: Russell and Russell, 1971.

      Recognizing Swift's claim to excellence in satire and
      realistic narrative, whether in verse or prose, Doughty
      denies him any genius as a lyric poet. "In Swift there
      was almost no impulse to sing." None of the poems is
      discussed in detail.

328. Downie, J.A. "Swift's Dismal." *Notes and Queries* 223
(February 1978): 43.

Disputes A.J. Varney's contention that Antonio in
Venice Preserved may have been a model for Swift's
travesty of Nottingham as "Dismal" in *An Excellent New
Song, Being the Intended Speech of a Famous Orator
against Peace* (see item 409). Downie objects--too
strenuously, perhaps, since *Venice Preserved* was widely
known--that Varney has not demonstrated a connection
between Antonio and Dismal, or even that Swift was ac-
quainted with Otway's works.

329. Ehrenpreis, Irvin. *The Personality of Jonathan Swift.*
Cambridge: Harvard University Press, 1958. Pp. 158.

Chapter 1, "Women," discusses Swift's relationships
with Vanessa and Stella (pp. 11-28). Chapter 2, "Ob-
scenity," defends the "scatological" poems using *A
Beautiful Young Nymph Going to Bed* as an illustration
(pp. 29-49). Answering such critics as Huxley, Orwell,
and Middleton Murry (see items 220, 230, 89), Ehrenpreis
claims that in these poems Swift writes as a sincere
Christian clergyman utilizing conventional means to
satirize fornication, debunk the stale conventions of
love poetry, discourage the romantic idealizing of
women, and recommend moral and intellectual virtues.

330. Ellis, Frank H. "Swift's Seventh Penny Paper." *London
Times Literary Supplement*, 10 May 1974, p. 506.

Swift remarks, in a letter to Stella on 7 August 1712,
that he published "at least 7 penny Papers of my own"
during "the last Fortnight" before the Stamp Tax went
into effect on the first of the month. Five of the
seven titles are mentioned by Swift himself in the
Journal to Stella, and a sixth has been tentatively
identified from advertisements in *The Examiner*. As the
seventh pamphlet, Ellis offers the Tory verses *The
Description of Dunkirk*, which he reprints in full. He
provides bibliographical data on the other six "penny
papers." See the reply by David Woolley, item 425; also
items 304, 456, 482, and 489.

331. Elwood, John R. "Swift's 'Corinna.'" *Notes and Queries*
200 (December 1955): 529-30.

Swift's poem *Corinna*, previously regarded as an attack
on Mrs. Mary de la Rivière Manley probably written in

1711, could not have been written before 1726 and is
probably an attack on Mrs. Eliza Haywood. See the
reply by M. Heinemann, item 348.

332. England, A.B. "Swift's 'An Elegy on Mr. Patrige' and
      Cowley's 'On the Death of Mr. Crashaw.'" *Notes and
      Queries* 218 (November 1973): 412-13.

      The change in Swift's attitude towards the poetry of
      Cowley has for a long time been regarded as an important
      aspect of his development as a poet. Lines 89-90 of
      Swift's mock elegy on Partridge ("*Triumphant* Star!
      Some Pity show / On *Coblers Militant* below") echo lines
      59-60 of Cowley's serious elegy on Crashaw ("Hail, Bard
      Triumphant! and some care bestow / On us, the Poets
      Militant below!"). Probably Swift had other parts of
      Cowley's elegy in mind when he wrote his own poem.

333. Erlebach, Peter. *Formgeschichte des englischen Epi-
      gramms von der Renaissance bis zur Romantik.* Anglis-
      tische Forschungen 131. Heidelberg: Carl Winter,
      1979, pp. 207-12.

      A survey and analysis, in German, of Swift's epigrams.
      These epigrams are occasional poems which express an
      unusual degree of personal antipathy. Often they con-
      sist of puns or similar metaphorical comparisons whose
      meaning is not resolved until the last word. Special
      attention is given to the epigrams against Charles
      Carthy (1734).

334. Esdaile, Katharine A. "The Fairy Feast." *London Times
      Literary Supplement*, 12 February 1931, p. 116.

      Notes that the verses *Mully of Mountown* appear,
      attributed to "the Author of the *Tale of a Tub*," in the
      miscellany *A New Collection of Poems Relating to State
      Affairs*, 1705. Other early texts are discussed. See
      the reply by Harold Williams (item 419), who cites
      conclusive evidence that William King wrote both this
      poem and *The Fairy Feast*.

335. Faber, G.C., ed. *The Poetical Works of John Gay.*
      London: Oxford University Press, 1926, pp. xxiii-
      xxxiv. Reprint. New York: Russell and Russell, 1969.

      Discusses the authorship of several poems possibly
      by Swift, including *Blue-Skin's Ballad* (*Newgate's Gar-
      land*), *A Poem Address'd to the Quidnunc's* (*The Quid-
      nuncki's*), and *Bounce to Fop*.

336. Falle, George. "Divinity and Wit: Swift's Attempted
Reconciliation." *University of Toronto Quarterly*
46 (Fall 1976): 14-30.

   This essay can be read as an elaborate commentary on
   line 12 of *The Author upon Himself*, "He reconcil'd
   Divinity and Wit," from which Falle's title is taken.

337. Ferguson, Oliver W. "The Authorship of 'Apollo's
Edict.'" *PMLA* 70 (June 1955): 433-40.

   This important article dates *Apollo's Edict* at least
   as late as 1724 rather than 1721, the date assigned to
   it in the Williams edition, and suggests that it may
   have been written by Mary Barber, perhaps with revisions
   by Swift.

338. Firth, C.H. "The Canon of Swift." *Review of English
Studies* 3 (January 1927): 73-74.

   Calls attention to a contemporary ascription of *Jack
   Frenchman's Lamentation* to Congreve; see items 311, 415,
   417. Firth also suggests that Swift's "Ballad, full of
   puns, on the Westminster Election," mentioned in a
   letter to Stella in October 1710, may be *An Excellent
   New Ballad, Being the Second Part of the Glorious
   Warrior*; see items 360, 368, 414.

339. Foot, Michael. *The Pen and the Sword*. London: Mac-
gibbon and Kee, 1957, pp. 341-44.

   On *The Windsor Prophecy* and Swift's reasons for
   writing it.

340. Gilbert, Jack G. *Jonathan Swift: Romantic and Cynic
Moralist*. Austin: University of Texas Press, 1966.
Pp. x + 161.

   Although no poems are discussed in detail, Gilbert
   cites a substantial number of them to illustrate Swift's
   concern with ethics (for example, on pp. 65-68).

341. Goldgar, Bertrand A. "Swift's 'Character of Sir Robert
Walpole.'" *Notes and Queries* 221 (November 1976):
492-93.

   Reproducing the satirical lines *The Character of Sir
   Robert Walpole* from a manuscript presumably enclosed by
   Swift in a letter to the Countess of Suffolk in 1731,
   Sir Harold Williams, in his edition, noted that they

were printed in Swift's *Miscellaneous Pieces*, 1789,
and in an earlier, undated slip (see item 16). They
were, however, printed in the anti-ministerial paper
Common Sense in 1739, signed mysteriously "J.C.--Seven's
the Main." Other evidence assembled by Goldgar like-
wise casts doubt on Swift's authorship, including an
apparent reference to the poem by Lord Hervey in a
letter to Stephen Fox in 1731. John Nichols, in 1783,
assigned it to Samuel Wesley the younger or Bishop
Atterbury. See Peter J. Schakel, item 394.

342. Graham, Edward. "Smedley and Swift--'Further Reasons
     for Their Enmity.'" *Philological Quarterly* 48 (July
     1969): 416-20.

     Background for Swift's verse attacks on Smedley, in-
     cluding *His Grace's Answer to Jonathan* (1724). The
     "further reasons" center upon a pamphlet against the
     Sacramental Test published by Smedley early in 1718.

343. Grenfell, Ian. "Swiftian Anecdotes." *American Notes
     and Queries: Supplement.* Vol. 1. Studies in English
     and American Literature. Edited by John L. Cutler
     and Lawrence S. Thompson. Troy, NY: Whitston, 1978,
     pp. 147-50.

     A group of eight anecdotes printed in *Lloyd's Evening
     Post* in 1759 includes four which have not hitherto been
     used by Swift's biographers and editors. One of these
     involves a satirical couplet allegedly written by Swift
     on Delany. According to the anecdote, seeing a Latin
     motto on Delany's coach, "Nam Avos et Proavos et quae
     non fecimus ipsi, / Vix ea nostra voco" ("For to boast
     of birth, and matters in which we have no merit, I
     scarce can call such things mine"), Swift wrote under
     it: "By this grave motto be it known, / Delany's coach
     is not his own."

344. Gückel, W., and E. Günther. *D. Defoes und J. Swifts
     Belesenheit und literarische Kritik.* Palaestra 149.
     Leipzig: Mayer & Müller, 1925. Pp. iv + 117.

     Lists literary allusions in Swift's poems.

345. Hagstrum, Jean H. "Swift's Vanessa and Stella." *Sex
     and Sensibility: Ideal and Erotic Love from Milton to
     Mozart.* Chicago and London: University of Chicago
     Press, 1980, pp. 145-59.

     Comments on much of Swift's sexually oriented verse
     such as the "scatological" poems, the Stella poems, and

Cadenus and Vanessa. With Stella and Vanessa, "Swift's love is rational, sexless, spiritual—based not on physical attraction, ... but on wit, virtue, and charity." Hagstrum's interest lies in the developing relationship between "sex and sensibility" rather than in the interpretation of particular poems.

346. Halsband, Robert. "Jonathan Swift and Swiftiana at Columbia." *Columbia Library Columns* 16 (May 1967): 19-23.

Among several Swift items recently acquired by the Columbia Libraries is the holograph manuscript, dated 18 July 1736 by Swift himself, from which Sir Harold Williams printed the eight-line translation *From Catullus.* A photograph of the holograph text is included.

347. Harper, Charles G. "Swift's Visits to England: The 'Four Crosses' Inn." *Notes and Queries,* ninth ser., 9 (8 March 1902): 186-87.

Reports a version of *At the Sign of the Four Crosses* cut into "an old diamond-shaped piece of green glass" which was allegedly taken from the Four Crosses inn, at Willoughby, near Daventry, on the Holyhead Road. The verses are signed "Swift D. 1730." See the response by John T. Page, item 377.

348. Heinemann, M. "Swift's 'Corinna' Again." *Notes and Queries* 217 (June 1972): 218-21.

In answer to John R. Elwood (see item 331), Heinemann argues that Swift's poem *Corinna* does not specifically satirize Mary de la Rivière Manley, Eliza Haywood, Elizabeth Thomas, or Martha Fowkes, but is a composite description of the women writers, reputedly licentious, who work for Edmund Curll.

349. Hone, Joseph M. "The Story of the Damer Gold." *Studies* 39 (December 1950): 419-26.

Biographical information on Joseph Damer, the subject of Swift's *An Elegy on the Much Lamented Death of Mr. Demar* (1720).

350. Jarrell, Mackie L. "'Jack and the Dane': Swift Traditions in Ireland." *Journal of American Folklore* 77 (April-June 1964): 99-117. Reprint. *Fair Liberty*

Was All His Cry: A Tercentenary Tribute to Jonathan Swift 1667-1745. Edited by A. Norman Jeffares. London: Macmillan; New York: St. Martin's Press, 1967, pp. 311-41.

The Irish traditions recounted by Jarrell include about a dozen scraps of verse attributed to Swift, most of them on doubtful authority.

351. Johnson, Maurice. "'A Love Song. In the Modern Taste.'" *Johnsonian News Letter*, vol. 10, no. 1 (February 1950): 4-5.

Two stanzas in Swift's poem reflect a couplet in *The Rape of the Lock*. Swift may be slyly poking fun at this passage in the work of his friend Pope, or Pope may have had a hand in *A Love Song*.

352. Kelly, Ann Kline. "A Rowlands-Butler-Swift Parallel." *Notes and Queries* 219 (March 1974): 101-02.

In Swift's *Horace, Part of the Sixth Satire of the Second Book Imitated* (1714), the initial couplet, "I often wish'd, that I had clear / For Life, six hundred Pounds a Year," may echo Butler's *Hudibras*, III.i. 1277-78: "*What makes all Doctrines Plain and Clear? / About two Hundred Pounds a Year.*" To this parallel, which was noticed by Ehrenpreis, Kelly adds another from Samuel Rowlands's *Good Newes and Bad Newes*, 1622, lines 13-14: "I might haue had an office, that would cleere / Haue brought me in two hundred pound a yeare." Kelly speculates about who influenced whom.

353. Koon, Helene. "A Lilliputian Poem." *English Language Notes* 7 (December 1969): 107-10.

Prints and claims for Swift's authorship the monometer lines *A Poem to his Majesty King George II on the Present State of Affairs in England* (Teerink 1230). Although attributed to Swift in the Faulkner printing of 1727, it is omitted from the Sir Harold Williams edition (see item 16).

354. Levine, Jay Arnold. "The Status of the Verse Epistle before Pope." *Studies in Philology* 59 (October 1962): 658-84.

In the traditional form of the verse epistle, Swift follows the common rhetorical strategy of using his addressee in order to comment upon the world at large.

As illustrations, Levine discusses *To Mr. Gay on His Being Steward to the Duke of Queensberry* and *An Epistle to a Lady*.

355. Longe, Julia G., ed. *Martha, Lady Giffard: Her Life and Correspondence*. London: George Allen, 1911, pp. 187-90.

Prints the full text of *A Description of Mother Ludwell's Cave*, arguing that "these verses may well be an early effort of Swift's." See also items 302, 373.

356. McElrath, Joseph R., Jr. "Swift's Friend: Dr. Patrick Delany." *Eire-Ireland* 5 (Autumn 1970): 53-62.

An account of the friendship between Swift and Delany, with liberal citation of the poems stemming from this relationship, including Swift's *To Mr. Delany*; *George Nim-Dan-Dean's Invitation to Mr. Thomas Sheridan*; *Apollo, to Dean Swift*; *An Epistle upon an Epistle*; *A Libel on Doctor Delany*; *A Panegyric on the Reverend Dean Swift*; *To Doctor Delany on the Libels Writ against Him*; *To a Friend Who Had Been Much Abused in Many Inveterate Libels*; and also *The Lady's Dressing Room*, lines 99-107. See Jean Agnew, item 432.

357. McGovern, J.B. "Two Epitaphs by Dean Swift." *Notes and Queries* 156 (22 June 1929): 442.

McGovern offers two verse epitaphs, asserted to be by Swift, which were recited to him "some sixty years back" by "a clerical paternal uncle." One begins "Here lies the body of John Shine," the other "Here lies the body of honest Peg." See the reply by V.B. Neuburg, item 375.

358. Mabbot, Thomas. "'Bounce to Fop' by Swift and Pope." *Notes and Queries* 200 (October 1955): 433.

These verses are spoken by "Pope's beloved big dog, mother of many puppies." In the line "Tho' some of J---'s hungry Breed," which the Twickenham editors cannot explain, "J---" presumably refers to "the father of some of the whelps." See items 308 and 359.

359. Macey, Samuel L. "'Bounce to Fop': Alexander Pope and Henry Carey." *Bulletin of the New York Public Library* 79 (Winter 1976): 203-08.

Concludes that the original version of *Bounce to Fop* was composed, not by Pope (or Swift), but possibly by Henry Carey. See items 308 and 358.

360. Main, C.F. "Defoe, Swift, and Captain Tom." *Harvard
     Library Bulletin* 11 (Winter 1957): 71-79.

     Suggests that Swift's lost "Ballad, full of puns,
     on the Westminster Election," mentioned in a letter to
     Stella in October 1710, is *A Dialogue between Captain
     Tom and Sir H[enr]y D[utto]n C[ol]t.* See items 338,
     368, 414.

361. Manch, Joseph. "Jonathan Swift and Women." Monographs
     in English, no. 3. *University of Buffalo Studies*,
     vol. 16, no. 4 (February 1941): 131-214.

     One chapter, "Women in Swift's Verse" (pp. 162-89),
     is an encyclopedic survey of Swift's poems on the sub-
     ject. Manch concludes that Swift "finds women vain,
     foolish, affected, and improperly educated--but not
     hopelessly so. Stella and Vanessa are cases to prove
     that women are capable of living intelligent, construc-
     tive lives...." There are special sections on the
     "scatological" poems, *Cadenus and Vanessa*, and the
     Stella poems.

362. Marshall, George. "Lines on Swift." *Notes and Queries*
     9 s. 6 (1 September 1900): 177-78.

     Responding to M.L.R. Breslar (see item 319), Marshall
     suggests Richard Steele as the author of the verses
     affixed to the door of St. Patrick's Cathedral when
     Swift was installed as Dean in 1713. See the further
     response by John Pickford, item 379, who identifies the
     author as Jonathan Smedley.

363. Mayhew, George P. "Anglo-Latin Games and a Fragment
     of *Polite Conversation*." *Rage or Raillery: The Swift
     Manuscripts at the Huntington Library*. San Marino,
     CA: Huntington Library, 1967, pp. 131-55.

     Prints and briefly discusses three satiric poems in
     Latino-Anglicus on "Dick" Tighe as they appear in Swift's
     hand in MS. HM 14341 in the Huntington Library.

364. Mayhew, George P. "A Draft of Ten Lines from Swift's
     Poem to John Gay." *Bulletin of the John Rylands
     Library* 37 (September 1954): 257-62.

     Prints, from a manuscript in the Rylands Library, a
     holograph draft comprising two versions of lines 61-70
     of Swift's poem *To Mr. Gay on His Being Steward to the
     Duke of Queensberry*. The first version is probably a

rough preliminary draft representing the first stage of
composition, the second a more polished version representing a later stage of composition. Mayhew uses the
two versions to analyze Swift's habits in composing
his poems.

365. Mayhew, George P. "Jonathan Swift's 'On the burning of
Whitehall in 1697' Re-examined." *Harvard Library
Bulletin* 19 (October 1971): 399-411.

Prints and claims for Swift's authorship the unfinished
poem *On the Burning of Whitehall in 1697*. These verses
were printed in Sir Walter Scott's edition but have not
been reprinted by later editors including Sir Harold
Williams (see item 16), although they are accepted as
authentic by F. Elrington Ball (see item 45) and in
Ricardo Quintana's *Mind and Art* (see item 384). The two
points at issue, as Mayhew presents the case, are whether
Scott possessed a manuscript in Swift's own handwriting
and whether the poem expresses approval of the beheading
of Charles I.

366. Mayhew, George P. "A Missing Leaf from Swift's 'Holyhead Journal.'" *Bulletin of the John Rylands Library*
41 (March 1959): 388-413.

Consisting of undated jottings in Swift's handwriting,
the first leaf of British Museum Egerton MS. 201 includes,
in the form of a prose statement translated from Scarron,
what appears to be the beginnings of Swift's poem *The
Power of Time*. This poem occurs in the "Holyhead Journal" in both an intermediate and a final draft, which is
printed in the Sir Harold Williams edition as *Shall I
Repine* (see item 16). See Clive T. Probyn, item 381.

367. Mayhew, George P. "Swift's Manuscript Version of 'On
his own Deafness.'" *Huntington Library Quarterly* 18
(November 1954): 85-87. Reprint (much expanded).
*Rage or Raillery: The Swift Manuscripts at the Hunting-
ton Library*. San Marino, CA: Huntington Library,
1967, pp. 115-30.

Prints, and analyzes at length, a variant version of
Written by Dr. Swift on His Own Deafness found in a
holograph manuscript in the Huntington Library.

368. Mayhew, George P. "Swift's Political 'Conversion' and
His 'Lost' Ballad on the Westminster Election of 1710."
Bulletin of the John Rylands Library 53 (Spring 1971):
397-427.

Agrees with Charles Main (see item 360) that the
anonymous pamphlet *A Dialogue Between Captain Tom and
Sir H[enr]y D[utto]n C[ol]t* is Swift's lost "Ballad,
full of puns, on the Westminster Election," mentioned
to Stella in a letter of October 1710. Additional internal and external evidence of Swift's authorship includes a copy of the ballad, now in the Huntington
Library, which may represent a Dublin reprint. Mayhew
attempts to locate the poem in the context of events
surrounding Swift's "conversion" to Toryism, particularly
his second long private meeting with Harley on 7 October.
Variant texts are reproduced and analyzed.

369. Mercier, Vivian. "Swift and Irish Satire in the English
      Language." *The Irish Comic Tradition*. Oxford:
      Clarendon Press, 1962, pp. 182-209.

Although there is little evidence that the Gaelic comic
tradition influenced Swift directly, his writings display
all of its most strongly marked features: a mastery of
fantasy, macabre and grotesque humor, a passion for word
play, an arrogant sense of the satirist's power and
prestige, a scorn of moderation, and a readiness to en-
gage in a "flyting." Among the poems mentioned in passing are *The Description of an Irish Feast*, the epigrams
on Charles Carthy including *Irish Epigram English'd*,
and *The Legion Club*. Anglo-Irish satire, which virtually
begins with Swift, was deeply indebted to him for a
century afterward, and he was posthumously incorporated
into the Gaelic tradition. See item 370.

370. Mercier, Vivian. "Swift and the Gaelic Tradition."
      A Review of English Literature, vol. 3, no. 3 (July
      1962): 69-79. (Special issue on Swift). Reprint.
      *Fair Liberty Was All His Cry: A Tercentenary Tribute
      to Jonathan Swift 1667-1745*. Edited by A. Norman
      Jeffares. London: Macmillan; New York: St. Martin's
      Press, 1967, pp. 279-89.

Covers some of the same points made in Mercier's *The
Irish Comic Tradition* (see item 369). Swift fits into
the Gaelic tradition in three ways: his conception of
the power and prestige of the satirist, an apparent
direct impact of the tradition upon him, and his influence upon at least two later Gaelic poets, Brian
Merriman and Richard Barret. Among the poems cited are
The Legion Club, *The Description of an Irish Feast*, and
the epigrams on Charles Carthy including *Irish Epigram
English'd*.

371. Miner, Earl Roy. "A Poem by Swift and W.B. Yeats's
      Words Upon the Window-Pane." *Modern Language Notes*
      72 (April 1957): 273-75.

      Suggests that the title of Yeats's play, its fictional
      situation, and part of the conception of its characters
      grow out of one of Swift's half-dozen or so minor poems
      Written upon Windows at Inns, in England.

372. Moore, John Robert. "An Unrecorded Drapier Poem."
      Yearbook of English Studies 2 (1972): 115-17.

      Prints an anonymous broadside, *An Excellent New
      Ballad Upon the New Half-Pence*, undated, from a copy
      in the Lilly Library, Indiana University. It resembles
      A New Song on Wood's Half-Pence, which some editors,
      though not Sir Harold Williams, have attributed to
      Swift.

373. Moore Smith, G.C., ed. *The Early Essays and Romances
      of Sir William Temple.* Oxford: Clarendon Press,
      1930, pp. xxvi-xxxviii, 186-88, 206-07.

      Pointing to resemblances of phrase and imagery in
      acknowledged early poems of Swift, Moore Smith concludes
      "there is considerable probability" that he wrote *A
      Description of Mother Ludwell's Cave.* The opening
      portion of the manuscript is reproduced in facsimile.
      See also items 302, 355.

374. Moskovit, Leonard A. "Pope and the Tradition of the
      Neoclassical Imitation." *Studies in English Litera-
      ture* 8 (Summer 1968): 445-62.

      Contains illuminating comments on Swift's imitations
      of Horace, *Epistles* 1.7 and 1.5 (*Toland's Invitation
      to Dismal*). In terms of Moskovit's two categories,
      Swift's poems belong, not to the more literal "trans-
      lational" kind of imitation, but to the freer "creative"
      kind, in which the imitator aims to interpret his own
      situation rather than Horace's original. Swift follows
      the method of Rochester's *An Allusion to Horace* and
      anticipates Pope's practice. See also Harold F. Brooks
      and Eric Rothstein, items 321, 393A.

375. Neuburg, V.B. "Two Epitaphs by Dean Swift." *Notes and
      Queries* 157 (13 July 1929): 32.

      Asserting that "neither of the epitaphs quoted by
      Mr. J.B. McGovern 'tastes' to me like genuine Swift"

(see item 357), Neuburg supplies another source for the second of the two, a variant version beginning "Here lies Dame Dorothy Peg."

376. Osborn, James M. "Swiftiana in the Osborne [*sic*] Collection at Yale." *University Review* (Dublin) 4 (Spring 1967): 72-83. (Jonathan Swift Tercentenary Issue).

The Swift manuscripts in the Osborn Collection at Yale University include one poem of eighteen lines entitled "Eulogium of A. Pope by Swift" and another of twenty lines entitled "The function of a Vice Roy (or Ld. Lieutt. of Ireland) by Dr. Swift." Both are copied from Swift's *A Libel on Doctor Delany and a Certain Great Lord*. Two manuscripts of *Verses on the Death of Dr. Swift* are mere copies of the third edition of the poem. See item 300 and the correction by James D. Woolley, item 427.

377. Page, John T. "Swift's Visits to England: The 'Four Crosses' Inn." *Notes and Queries*, ninth ser., 9 (19 April 1902): 312.

In response to Charles G. Harper (see item 347), Page supplies background information on the version of *At the Sign of the Four Crosses* which was allegedly cut into a window pane of the Four Crosses inn, Willoughby.

378. Peake, Charles. "Swift's 'Satirical Elegy on a Late Famous General.'" *A Review of English Literature*, vol. 3, no. 3 (July 1962): 80-89. (Special issue on Swift).

Peake's article, though brief, was historically important in demonstrating that Swift's poetry can be understood only by responding to the extreme precision with which it uses language. Taking the *Satirical Elegy* as a "test-piece," this detailed *explication de texte* illustrates Swift's intricate dislocation of the conventional ordering of funeral procedures, his subversion of traditional figures of speech, the resulting tone of bitter irony and moral indignation, and in general the remarkable "crispness and precision" of Swift's seemingly ordinary diction. The poem traces the ritual of a state funeral step by step, parodically translating its elevated but hackneyed metaphors into the prosaic language of reality. "For exact discussion of those very aspects of poetry in which Swift excels,"

observes Peake, "we may still lack adequate critical
tools"--tools which his article helped to provide,
showing in the process how "Swift's poetry has its own
peculiar excellencies."

379. Pickford, John. "Lines on Swift." *Notes and Queries*
9 s. 6 (13 October 1900): 292.

Responding to M.L.R. Breslar and George Marshall concerning the authorship of the verses affixed to the
door of St. Patrick's Cathedral when Swift was installed
as Dean in 1713 (see items 319, 362), Pickford identifies
the author as Jonathan Smedley, as had been pointed out
earlier in *Notes and Queries* 7 s. 10 (18 October 1890):
300.

380. Powell, William S. "A Swift Broadside from the Opposition." *The Virginia Magazine of History and Biography* 67 (April 1959): 164-69.

Prints (from a broadside in the British Museum) and
argues for Swift's authorship of the anonymous burlesque
poem *The Loyal Address of the Clergy of Virginia*,
[London], 1702, which pretends to express support for
William III in opposition to Louis XIV's proclamation
of James II's son as King James III of England. The
argument is ill-informed and unconvincing, although the
poem has also been attributed to Swift by F. Elrington
Ball (see item 45) and by Richmond P. Bond in *English
Burlesque Poetry* (see item 128).

381. Probyn, Clive T. "'The Power of Time': Swift as
Translator." *Notes and Queries* 214 (September 1969):
337.

Swift's verses *The Power of Time* are translated from
a *Sonnet* by Scarron, which is itself an imitation of
Lope de Vega. Hence Swift's much-praised concluding
couplet, "When my old cassock says a Welch divine / Is
out at elbows why should I repine?," illustrates not
only his gift for idiomatic freshness and love of wit,
but also his conciseness in translation. See George
P. Mayhew, item 366.

382. Probyn, Clive T. "The Source for Swift's 'Fable of the
Bitches.'" *Notes and Queries* 213 (June 1968): 206.

Swift's poem has a definite, though hitherto unnoticed,
source in a fable by the sixteenth-century Italian

fabulist Astemio, whose pieces were included in a volume of fables by Aesop and others, well known to Swift in the translation by L'Estrange (1699). An anonymous fable in the same volume is possibly the source for Swift's *A Fable of the Widow and Her Cat*.

383. Quinlan, Maurice J. "Swift and the Prosecuted Nottingham Speech." *Harvard Library Bulletin* 11 (Autumn 1957): 296-302.

    Clarifies the circumstances surrounding the publication and possible prosecution of Swift's *An Excellent New Song, Being the Intended Speech of a Famous Orator against Peace* (December 1711). Besides Swift's ballad, memorable for its use of the pun "*Not in game*" as a rhyme-word, at least two other attacks on Nottingham were published about this same date: another ballad, echoing Swift's phraseology, which survives in a rare copy in the Harvard College Library, and a sham speech by Nottingham in prose. It was the prose speech, not Swift's poem, that was prosecuted.

384. Quintana, Ricardo. *The Mind and Art of Jonathan Swift*. London and New York: Oxford University Press, 1936. Pp. xii + 398. Reprint (slightly revised). London: Methuen; New York: Oxford University Press, 1953. Pp. xvi + 400. Reprint (of rev. ed.). Gloucester, MA: Peter Smith, 1965.

    Includes brief discussions of many of Swift's poems.

385. Rawson, C.J. "'The Vanity of Human Wishes,' Line 73: A Parallel from Swift." *Notes and Queries* 210 (January 1965): 20-21.

    The wording of line 73 in Johnson's *The Vanity of Human Wishes* (1749), "Unnumber'd suppliants croud Preferment's gate," parallels that of line 93 in Swift's *To Doctor Delany on the Libels Writ against Him* (1730), "They croud about Preferment's Gate." See Christopher Ricks, item 390.

386. Real, Hermann J., and Heinz J. Vienken. Correspondence. *The Scriblerian*, vol. 13, no. 1 (Autumn 1980): 51.

    Facetiously offers additional evidence that Frances Harris in the *Petition* is pregnant. See Richard Reynolds, item 388.

387. Real, Hermann J. "Swift's *A Satirical Elegy on the Death of a Late Famous General*." *The Explicator*, vol. 36, no. 2 (Winter 1978): 26-27.

A *Satirical Elegy* portrays Marlborough as the devil. Swift's image of the burnt-out candle alludes to the superstition that "the devil leaves a stink behind." Earlier, in the *Journal to Stella*, Swift had called Marlborough "covetous as Hell, and ambitious as the Prince of it."

388. Reynolds, Richard. "Swift's 'Humble Petition' from a Pregnant Frances Harris?" *The Scriblerian*, vol. 5, no. 1 (Autumn 1972): 38-39.

The argument for Frances Harris's pregnancy is unconvincing. See the response by Hermann Real and Heinz Vienken, item 386.

389. Ricks, Christopher. "A Debt of Pope to Swift." *Notes and Queries* 204 (November 1959): 398-99.

Lines in Pope's *First Epistle of the Second Book of Horace* (to Augustus) and *First Satire of the Second Book of Horace* (to Fortescue) were suggested by passages in Swift's *Directions for a Birth-day Song*.

390. Ricks, Christopher. "Notes on Swift and Johnson." *Review of English Studies* n.s. 11 (November 1960): 412-13.

In the opening lines of *Verses on the Death of Dr. Swift*, what seems a mistranslation of La Rochefoucauld's maxim is actually a conflation of the maxim with a reminiscence of a song by George Granville. Also, Johnson's line "Unnumber'd suppliants croud Preferment's gate" in *The Vanity of Human Wishes* is borrowed from line 93 of *To Doctor Delany on the Libels Writ against Him*, "They croud Preferment's Gate." See C.J. Rawson, item 385.

391. Risk, May H. "'Bradley, the taylor.'" *Hermathena* 108 (Spring 1969): 18-23.

"Bradley the taylor," in line 27 of Swift's poem *The Yahoo's Overthrow* (1734), goes unidentified in the Sir Harold Williams edition (see item 16). Risk identifies him as Richard Bradley, a religious eccentric living in or near Dublin in the early eighteenth century whose aggressively unorthodox views were unacceptable to Protestants and Catholics alike. See also C.M. Webster, item 411.

124   *Miscellaneous*

392. Roberts, Philip. "Swift, Queen Anne, and *The Windsor Prophecy*." *Philological Quarterly* 49 (April 1970): 254-58.

Evidence from the unpublished diary of Sir David Hamilton, physician to Queen Anne, shows that Swift's *The Windsor Prophecy* (1711), his lampoon on the Duchess of Somerset, affected his career more drastically and adversely than was formerly supposed. Largely because of it, not only was the Queen determined that Swift should not obtain preferment in England, but far from becoming a bishop in Ireland, he was lucky even to become Dean of St. Patrick's. See Calhoun Winton, item 421.

393. Rogers, Pat. *Grub Street: Studies in a Subculture.* London: Methuen, 1972, pp. 241-59.

In the wake of Pope's *Dunciad*, references to Grub Street occur increasingly in Swift's poems of the 1730s such as *To Doctor Delany, on the Libels Writ against Him* and especially *On Poetry: A Rapsody*, which provides "a climactic moment in the evolution of Grub Street mythology." The two *Description* poems, as recent criticism has shown, are more than just "engaging travesties of classical originals." *To Charles Ford on His Birth-day* is "a splendid and too little considered poem."

393A. Rothstein, Eric. *Restoration and Eighteenth-Century Poetry 1660-1780.* The Routledge History of English Poetry, general editor R.A. Foakes, vol. 3. Boston, London, and Henley: Routledge and Kegan Paul, 1981, pp. 88-91.

Does not give Swift's poetry nearly the attention it deserves, but comments briefly on six of the Horatian imitations. None of these poems "makes much capital of the originals being Horatian or classical. Any well-known model with the same sentiments would do." Attention is focused upon *Odes* 2.1 (to Steele), 3.2 (to Oxford), and 4.9 (to King); *Epistles* 1.5 (*Toland's Invitation to Dismal*) and 1.7 (to Harley); and *Satires* 2.6 (to Harley). See also Harold F. Brooks and Leonard Moskovit, items 321, 374.

394. Schakel, Peter J. "'The Character of Sir Robert Walpole': A Previously Unnoticed Publication."

Papers of the Bibliographical Society of America 70 (First Quarter 1976): 111-14.

Prints and discusses a hitherto unknown text of *The Character of Sir Robert Walpole* which Schakel discovered in the William Andrews Clark Library in part three of *Robin's Panegyrick. Or, The Norfolk Miscellany*, published *c*. 1733. This text possesses at least as much authority as the manuscript used for the Sir Harold Williams edition (see item 16). See Bertrand A. Goldgar, item 341.

395. Schakel, Peter J. "Swift's *Verses Wrote in a Lady's Ivory Table-Book.*" *The Explicator*, vol. 28, no. 9 (May 1970): item 83.

A detailed interpretation of the poem. Schakel traces the discrepancies implicit in the jottings of the beaux and fops, which represent the internal affectations of romantic love, and those of the lady herself, which reflect the external affectations of physical appearance. He also explores the sexual *double entendre* of the "Gold Pencil tipt with Lead" and the ironical effects of Swift's manipulation of the identities of the "speaking" table-book, the poet, and the reader.

396. Schakel, Peter J. "Virgil and the Dean: Christian and Classical Allusion in *The Legion Club.*" *Studies in Philology* 70 (October 1973): 427-38.

As Schakel's useful discussion shows, the Christian allusions are mostly to the gospels, the classical allusions mostly to Virgil's description of the underworld in Book VI of the *Aeneid*.

397. Segar, Mary G. "Philips or Carey?" *London Times Literary Supplement*, 3 April 1930, p. 298.

Disagreeing with Frederick T. Wood (see item 422), Segar maintains that *A Christmas Box for Namby Pamby* satirizes Philips rather than Carey and, further, that Swift wrote not only these verses but also four lines prefixed to *Namby-Pamby, a Panegyric*, which was ascribed to "Gordon" rather than Carey in the original broadside. Segar adds that Swift invented the name Namby Pamby. See also Segar, Wood, and Arthur E. Case, items 398, 423, 424, 324.

398. Segar, M.G. "Philips or Carey?" *London Times Literary Supplement*, 24 April 1930, p. 352.

      Replying to Frederick T. Wood (see item 423), Segar denies that she misquoted and claims there is other evidence for her belief that Swift invented the name Namby Pamby. See also Segar, Wood, and Arthur E. Case, items 397, 422, 424, 324.

399. Selby, Hopewell R. "The Cell and the Garret: Fictions of Confinement in Swift's Satires and Personal Writings." *Studies in Eighteenth-Century Culture* 6, edited by Ronald C. Rosbottom (Madison: University of Wisconsin Press, 1977): 133-56.

      Numerous poems by Swift are cited in passing to illustrate his "fictions of confinement."

400. Sherburn, George. "The 'Copies of Verses' about *Gulliver*. *Texas Studies in Literature and Language* 3 (Spring 1961): 3-7.

      Raises the possibility that the five burlesque "Copies of Verses Explanatory and Commendatory" prefixed to a second edition of *Gulliver's Travels*, 1727, may have been the product of a typical Scriblerian collaboration which included Swift. They are generally ascribed *in toto* to Pope.

401. Shipley, John B. "A Note on the Authorship of *The Whale*." *Review of English Studies* n.s. 18 (May 1967): 166-69.

      These verses, a coarse satire of 1737 on King George II, Queen Caroline, and his current mistress, Sophie Walmoden, were printed by Sir Harold Williams as possibly Swift's on the basis of a single ascription in the commonplace book where they appear. But they also appear in Lord Hervey's memoirs, ascribed by him to Lord Chesterfield, and other evidence supports this ascription. Shipley supplies some necessary explication of the poem.

402. Shuster, George N. "Ode Writers of the Augustan Age." *The English Ode from Milton to Keats*. Columbia University Studies in English and Comparative Literature, no. 150. New York: Columbia University Press, 1940, pp. 146-85.

      Includes brief, rather contemptuous remarks on Swift's Pindaric odes and *A Cantata*.

403. Sisson, C.H. "The Poetry of Jonathan Swift." *The
      Avoidance of Literature: Collected Essays.* Edited
      by Michael Schmidt. Manchester, Eng.: Carcanet,
      1978, pp. 501-07.

      A slightly altered reprint of the introduction to
      Sisson's edition of *Jonathan Swift: Selected Poems*
      (see item 14). The emphasis is mostly biographical.

404. Smith, David Nichol, ed. *The Letters of Jonathan Swift
      to Charles Ford.* Oxford: Clarendon Press, 1935,
      pp. 179-212. Reprint. Norwood, PA: Norwood Editions,
      1975.

      Prints six of Swift's poems from manuscripts formerly
      owned by Charles Ford. Two of the poems, *The Bubble*
      and *To Charles Ford on His Birth-day*, are in Swift's
      autograph. The remaining four, in Ford's handwriting,
      are *Vanbrug's House*, *Directions for a Birth-day Song*,
      and two poems, *Stella's Distress* and an untitled draft
      beginning "Don Carlos in a meery Spight," which were
      printed together as *Stella at Wood-Park*.

405. Solomon, Harry. "Swift's 'Poeta De Tristibus.'"
      American Notes and Queries: Supplement. Vol. 1.
      Studies in English and American Literature. Edited
      by John L. Cutler and Lawrence S. Thompson.
      Troy, NY: Whitston, 1978, pp. 140-46.

      Claims that several of Swift's poems, dating from
      1693 to 1731, were influenced by the anonymous minor
      poem *Poeta De Tristibus: Or, The Poet's Complaint* (Lon-
      don, 1682). Written in four cantos of octosyllabic
      couplets, *Poeta De Tristibus* laments the misfortune of
      the author having chosen poetry as a profession in an
      age, the Restoration, when only prose is in vogue. In-
      fluence is claimed on *To Mr. Congreve*, *Occasioned by
      Sir William Temple's Late Illness and Recovery*, Frances
      Harris's *Petition*, *Vanbrug's House*, and *Verses on the
      Death of Dr. Swift*.

406. Sterne, Noel. "A Mistaken First Publication Date of a
      Poem by Swift." *Notes and Queries* 214 (September
      1969): 338.

      Swift's imitation of Horace, *Odes* 3.2, *To the Earl of
      Oxford, Late Lord Treasurer. Sent to Him When He Was in
      the Tower, before His Tryal* (1716), which Williams says
      was first printed by Faulkner in 1735, appears in a

miscellany compiled by David Lewis and published in
1730. This miscellany also, as Williams noted, prints
Swift's *Part of the 9th Ode of the 4th Book of Horace,
Address'd to Doctor William King, Late Lord Archbishop
of Dublin* (1720).

407. Thompson, Paul Vern. "The Canon of Swift." *Review of
      English Studies* 14 (April 1938): 182-89.

      Presents information on the lines on Thomas Weaver in
      the *Tripos* speech, given at Dublin University in 1688,
      which has been doubtfully attributed to Swift. Thompson
      argues that Swift may have written *The Fop*, as these
      satirical verses are headed in the variant version
      printed in *The Gentleman's Journal* for August and Sep-
      tember 1694. See the reply by Harold Williams, item 416.

408. Thompson, Paul Vern. "Verses on Blenheim." *London
      Times Literary Supplement*, 22 August 1936, p. 680.

      Among F. Elrington Ball's "Undated Pieces Attributed
      to Swift" (see item 45) are verses "On Blenheim."
      Thompson points out that they were printed in a miscel-
      lany by Edmund Curll at the end of July 1714.

409. Varney, A.J. "Swift's Dismal and Otway's Antonio."
      Notes and Queries 222 (May-June 1977): 224-25.

      Maintains plausibly, though not conclusively, that
      in his portrayal of the Earl of Nottingham as "Dismal"
      in *An Excellent New Song, Being the Intended Speech of
      a Famous Orator against Peace*, Swift probably had in
      mind the character of the speech-making senator Antonio
      in Otway's *Venice Preserved*. See the reply by J.A.
      Downie, item 328.

410. Waller, Charles Thomas. "Swift's Poems on the Wood's
      Halfpence Affair." *South Atlantic Bulletin* 34
      (March 1969): 1-3.

      Although the Drapier's Letters are justly famous,
      readers tend to neglect a group of poems that Swift
      wrote at the time to reinforce his basic arguments.
      Recapitulating the affair of Wood's Halfpence, Waller
      cites *A Serious Poem upon William Wood, An Epigram on
      Wood's Brass-Money, Prometheus, Whitshed's Motto on His
      Coach*, the three *Verses on the Upright Judge* (Whitshed),
      Wood, an Insect, On Wood the Iron-monger, and *A Simile
      on Our Want of Silver*.

411. Webster, C.M. "'The Yahoo's Overthrow.'" *London Times Literary Supplement*, 14 May 1931, p. 390.

    Identifies the fanatics Muggleton and Nayler who are mentioned along with deists and freethinkers in a stanza of Swift's satirical ballad *The Yahoo's Overthrow* (1734). See also May H. Risk, "'Bradley, the taylor'" (item 391).

412. Williams, Aubrey. "Swift and the Poetry of Allusion: 'The Journal.'" *Literary Theory and Structure: Essays in Honor of William K. Wimsatt*. Edited by Frank Brady, John Palmer, and Martin Price. New Haven and London: Yale University Press, 1973, pp. 227-43.

    In Swift's humorous yet telling poem *The Journal*, the ordinary and even autobiographical events of a manorial day, seemingly tranquil and secure amid the patterns of life in rural retreat, are turned into an artful and canny comment on the dissatisfactions inherent in mortal life. In this two-part poem, the second half constitutes a gloss on the first. Lines 1-60, drawing upon the *beatus ille* tradition, especially Book II of Lucretius's *De Rerum Natura*, provide an hour-by-hour record of the felicities of rural retirement. The remaining lines, however, directly challenge any notion that man can achieve perfect tranquillity of mind or indolence of body in this life. Williams's deft analysis shows that "next to Pope, Swift was the best and most subtly allusive poet of his time."

413. Williams, Aubrey L. "'A vile Encomium': That 'Panegyric on the Reverend D--n S---t.'" *Contemporary Studies of Swift's Poetry*. Edited by John Irwin Fischer and Donald C. Mell, Jr., with David M. Vieth, associate editor. Newark: University of Delaware Press; London and Toronto: Associated University Presses, 1980, pp. 178-90.

    Questions the authenticity of *A Panegyric on the Reverend Dean Swift in Answer to the Libel*, which was accepted as genuine by F. Elrington Ball and Sir Harold Williams and has figured in recent critical essays by Robert Uphaus and Louise Barnett (see items 283, 46). The poem was not, however, ascribed to Swift before the twentieth century; the attribution depends solely upon the circumstantial assumption that it is the "Scrubb libel" Swift says he wrote on himself; and in 1768 it was assigned by George Faulkner, Swift's own publisher, to James Arbuckle, an attribution supported by the presence of a copy in a bound collection of Arbuckle's poems mentioned by D.F. Foxon. Stylistically, *A Panegyric* resembles Arbuckle's "Momus Mistaken," which is "a close Imitation of Dr. Swift's manner of writing." The premise that Swift wrote *A Panegyric* implies more ironic complexity in the poem than a reader could fathom. See James Woolley, item 426.

414. Williams, Basil. *Stanhope: A Study in Eighteenth-Century War and Diplomacy.* Oxford: Clarendon Press, 1932, pp. 125-27.

Assumes that Swift's unidentified ballad mentioned in letters to Stella in October 1710 is *An Excellent New Ballad, Being the Second Part of the Glorious Warrior.* See items 338, 360, 368.

415. Williams, Harold. "The Canon of Swift." *Review of English Studies* 3 (April 1927): 212-14.

Moderates Williams's earlier support for Swift's authorship of *Jack Frenchman's Lamentation*, in light of Sir Charles Firth's observation that Lady Cowper assigns this ballad to Congreve. See items 311, 338, 417.

416. Williams, Harold. "The Canon of Swift." *Review of English Studies* 14 (July 1938): 326-27.

In answer to Paul Vern Thompson (see item 407), Williams reaffirms how little support there is for Swift's authorship of the lines on Thomas Weaver or any other part of the *Tripos* speech delivered at Trinity College, Dublin, in July 1688.

417. Williams, Harold. "The Canon of Swift: A Late Addition." *Review of English Studies* 2 (July 1926): 322-28.

Offers evidence and arguments favoring Swift's authorship of the Whig ballad *Jack Frenchman's Lamentation* (1708), which was assigned to him by Sir Walter Scott. See items 311, 338, 415.

418. Williams, Harold. "*A Hue and Cry after Dismal.*" *Review of English Studies* 6 (April 1930): 195-96.

Suggests that six lines of verse, added in a variant broadside of the prose tract *A Hue and Cry after Dismal* (1712), may have been written by Swift. They are, however, relegated to the textual notes in the Herbert Davis edition of Swift's prose works (VI, 211).

419. Williams, Harold. "Mully of Mountown." *London Times Literary Supplement*, 19 February 1931, p. 135.

> In reply to Katharine A. Esdaile (see item 334), Williams reviews the overwhelming case for William King's authorship of *Mully of Mountown* as well as *The Fairy Feast*.

420. Williams, Harold. "A Swift Epitaph?" *London Times Literary Supplement*, 9 May 1935, p. 301.

> Responding to E.L. Allhusen (see item 305), Williams lists other texts of the satirical epitaph on Gilbert Burnet, Bishop of Salisbury, but doubts that Swift wrote it.

421. Winton, Calhoun. "Steele, Swift, and the Queen's Physician." *The Augustan Milieu: Essays Presented to Louis A. Landa*. Edited by Henry Knight Miller, Eric Rothstein, and G.S. Rousseau. Oxford: Clarendon Press, 1970, pp. 144-49.

> The unpublished journal of Sir David Hamilton, one of Queen Anne's physicians, reveals how *The Windsor Prophecy* was used to damage Swift's opportunities for ecclesiastical preferment. See Philip Roberts, item 392.

422. Wood, Frederick T. "Phillips or Carey?" *London Times Literary Supplement*, 27 February 1930, p. 166.

> Argues that *A Christmas Box for Namby Pamby* (1725), which has been doubtfully attributed to Swift, is a satire, not on Ambrose Philips as was formerly thought, but upon Henry Carey's satires on Philips, particularly *Namby-Pamby, A Panegyric on the New Versification, Addressed to A[mbrose] P[hilips], Esq.* (1725). See also Wood, Mary G. Segar, and Arthur E. Case, items 423, 424, 397, 398, 324.

423. Wood, Frederick T. "Philips or Carey?" *London Times Literary Supplement*, 10 April 1930, p. 318.

> Answering Mary G. Segar (see item 397), Wood reviews the extensive evidence that *Namby-Pamby, a Panegyric* was written by Carey rather than by Swift or Thomas Gordon. Citing an alleged misquotation, he challenges Segar's statement that Swift invented the name Namby Pamby and also her confident assumption that *A Christmas Box* was written by Swift against Philips. See also Wood, Segar, and Arthur E. Case, items 422, 424, 398, 324.

424. Wood, Frederick T. "Philips or Carey?" *London Times
      Literary Supplement*, 8 May 1930, p. 394.

      Concedes that Mary G. Segar did not misquote (see item
      398), but does not otherwise alter his position. See
      also Wood, Segar, and Arthur E. Case, items 422, 423,
      397, 324.

425. Woolley, David. "Swift's Seventh Penny Paper." *London
      Times Literary Supplement*, 17 May 1974, p. 528.

      Doubts that Swift wrote *The Description of Dunkirk*,
      as claimed by Frank H. Ellis (see item 330). Woolley
      observes that this verse lampoon, though reprinted by
      F. Elrington Ball (see item 45), was rejected from the
      canon in the editions of Swift's poems by Sir Harold
      Williams and Herbert Davis (see items 16 and 3). See
      also items 304, 456, 482, and 489.

426. Woolley, James. "Arbuckle's 'Panegyric' and Swift's
      Scrub Libel: The Documentary Evidence." *Contemporary
      Studies of Swift's Poetry*. Edited by John Irwin
      Fischer and Donald C. Mell, Jr., with David M. Vieth,
      associate editor. Newark: University of Delaware
      Press; London and Toronto: Associated University
      Presses, 1980, pp. 191-209.

      Beginning with Aubrey Williams's doubts about the
      authenticity of *A Panegyric on the Reverend Dean Swift*,
      which were based partly on internal evidence (see item
      413), Woolley presents external evidence virtually
      proving that the poem was written by James Arbuckle.
      The principal evidence is a bound volume of Arbuckle's
      poems in the National Library of Wales, containing four
      printed poems and thirty-three in manuscript, mostly
      transcribed by Arbuckle himself. One of the four printed
      items is the London edition of *A Panegyric*, with emenda-
      tions in Arbuckle's own hand. Woolley supplies useful
      information on Arbuckle's life and literary career.
      The "Scrubb libel" that Swift wrote on himself, which has
      been confused with *A Panegyric*, may be *An Answer* [to
      Dr. Delany's Fable of the Pheasant and the Lark].

427. Woolley, James D. "Letters." *The Scriblerian*, vol. 3,
      no. 2 (Spring 1971): 81.

      Corrects item 300, "The Osborn Collection at Yale."
      Of the three manuscript poems attributed to Swift in
      the Osborn Collection, one, the "Eulogium" is quoted

from *A Libel on Doctor Delany and a Certain Great Lord*. A second, "The function of a Viceroy," is from the same poem, as James M. Osborn himself had pointed out in print (see item 376).

428. Woolley, James, ed. *"The Place of the Damn'd" by Jonathan Swift & the Devil's Reply*. Dublin: Trinity Closet Press, 1980. Reprint. Easton, PA: privately printed, 1981.

Reprints, from contemporary halfsheets now in the Library of Trinity College, Dublin, Swift's *The Place of the Damn'd* together with an anonymous verse reply, *The Devil's Gratitude* (1731?). The latter poem is not mentioned in the Teerink bibliography, in the Sir Harold Williams edition of Swift's poems, or in D.F. Foxon's *English Verse*. Woolley's headnote explains the circumstances.

429. Woolley, James. "Thomas Sheridan and Swift." *Studies in Eighteenth-Century Culture* 9, edited by Roseann Runte (Madison: University of Wisconsin Press, 1979): 93-114.

A biographical account of Sheridan, giving special attention to his friendship with Swift and useful as background for the many poems the two men addressed to each other. Woolley quotes Swift's *A Portrait from the Life* (of Mrs. Sheridan) and three hitherto unpublished lines he wrote on Sheridan: "Altho a great Dunce I be / Happy if once I be / with my Friend Punsiby."

VI. BACKGROUND

430. Anonymous. "A Note on Samuel Butler (1612-1680) and
      Jonathan Swift." *Notes and Queries* 203 (July 1958):
      294-96.

      Parallels with Butler's prose *Characters*, which existed
      only in manuscript during Swift's lifetime, suggest that
      they might have influenced *Gulliver's Travels*. No direct
      reference is made to the influence of Butler's poems,
      such as *Hudibras*, on Swift's poetry.

431. Acworth, Bernard. *Swift*. London: Eyre and Spottis-
      woode, 1947. Pp. xix + 250.

      Quotes extensively from several of Swift's major poems.

432. Agnew, Jean. "The Delanys and Their Links with Clogher
      and Derryvullan." *Clogher Record* 7 (1970): 221-35.

      Biographical information on Swift's friend Patrick
      Delany, with whom he exchanged poems. See Joseph R.
      McElrath, Jr., item 356.

433. Atherton, James S. "Swift: a Paradigm of a God." *The
      Books at the Wake: A Study of Literary Allusions in
      James Joyce's "Finnegans Wake."* London: Faber and
      Faber, 1959; New York: Viking Press, 1960, pp. 114-23.
      Expanded and corrected ed. Mamaroneck, NY: Paul P.
      Appel, 1974.

      Makes little direct reference to Swift's poems except
      to point out how his *Epigram* on the powder magazine in
      Phoenix Park is parodied in *Finnegans Wake*.

434. Berwick, Donald M. *The Reputation of Jonathan Swift
      1781-1882*. Philadelphia, 1941. Pp. 170.

      While trying to deny that Swift was a poet, critics
      during the century surveyed by Berwick evince more
      interest in his verse than one might expect. A title

that keeps recurring is *Cadenus and Vanessa*. Berwick's
illuminating investigation provides a separate account
of the poetry for each of the four brief chronological
intervals he covers.

435. Brezianu, Andrei. "Swift şi Cantemir sau Gulliver şi
     Licorna" (Swift and Cantemir or Gulliver and the
     Unicorn). *Secolul XX*, vol. 16, nos. 11-12 (1973):
     39-53.

     In Rumanian. "This comparison of *The Beasts Confession
     to the Priest* and *Gulliver's Travels* with the satiric
     tale *The Hieroglyphic History*, written by the Rumanian
     prince Dimitrie Cantemir in the year in which the Dean
     was publishing *A Tale of a Tub*, sheds light on similari-
     ties and disparities of two various cultural traditions.
     Special stress is put upon the different treatment of
     the definition of man as an 'animal rationale' accepted
     by both writers.... " (Quoted from *The Scriblerian*,
     vol. 7, no. 1 [Autumn 1974]: 4-5. See also the abstract
     in vol. 9, no. 2 [Spring 1977]: 92).

436. Broes, Arthur T. "Swift the Man in *Finnegans Wake*."
     ELH 43 (Spring 1976): 120-40.

     A supplement to the article by Mackie L. Jarrell
     (see item 451). Broes cites a few additional allusions
     to Stella and Vanessa in *Finnegans Wake*.

437. Broes, Arthur T. "Swift's Works in *Finnegans Wake*."
     English Studies in Canada 5 (Summer 1979): 167-86.

     Observing that Joyce makes frequent use of Swift's
     poetry in *Finnegans Wake*, Broes documents his claim
     with a series of examples.

438. Bullitt, John M. *Jonathan Swift and the Anatomy of
     Satire: A Study of Satiric Technique*. Cambridge:
     Harvard University Press, 1953. Pp. viii + 214.
     2d printing. 1961.

     Cites ten of Swift's poems, including *An Epistle to
     a Lady*.

439. Dennis, Nigel. *Jonathan Swift: A Short Character*.
     Masters of World Literature. New York: Macmillan;
     London: Collier-Macmillan, 1964. Pp. 160.

     Briefly notices a range of Swift's poems.

440. Dobrée, Bonamy. *English Literature in the Early Eighteenth Century 1700-1740*. Oxford: Clarendon Press, 1959. Pp. xii + 701.

 Comments in passing on many of Swift's poems.

441. Erskine-Hill, Howard. *The Social Milieu of Alexander Pope: Lives, Example and the Poetic Response*. New Haven and London: Yale University Press, 1975, pp. 244-45, 253-55.

 Cites the concept of true and false stewardship developed by Swift in his verses *To Mr. Gay on His Being Steward to the Duke of Queensberry* (1731).

442. Goldberg, Gerald Y. *Jonathan Swift and Contemporary Cork*. Cork: Mercier Press, 1967. Pp. 120.

 References to Swift's poetry figure prominently in this volume.

443. Goulding, Sybil. *Swift en France*. Paris: Champion, 1924. Pp. ii + 210.

 Includes information on translations of Swift's poems into French--for example, by the abbé Yart in his *Idée de la Poésie Anglaise*, published in eight volumes from 1749 to 1756. *Cadenus and Vanessa* was popular in translation.

444. Gunny, Ahmad. *Voltaire and English Literature: A Study of English Literary Influences on Voltaire*. Studies on Voltaire and the Eighteenth Century 177. Oxford: Voltaire Foundation at the Taylor Institution, 1979, pp. 244-70.

 Many of Swift's poems, including *An Elegy on Mr. Patrige*, were translated into French by the abbé Yart and published in his *Idée de la Poésie Anglaise*, which appeared in eight volumes between 1749 and 1756. Voltaire, who probably read Yart's work, called Swift's verses worthy of Horace in their elegance and simplicity.

445. Gwynn, Stephen. *The Life and Friendships of Dean Swift*. London: Thornton Butterworth, 1933. Pp. 319. New York: Henry Holt, 1933. Pp. xi + 362.

 Includes unusually frequent citations of Swift's poems.

446. Hardy, Evelyn. *The Conjured Spirit--Swift: A Study in the Relationship of Swift, Stella and Vanessa.* London: Hogarth Press, 1949. Pp. xii + 266.

Includes many references to Swift's poems.

447. Harrington, John P. "Swift through Le Fanu and Joyce." *Mosaic,* vol. 12, no. 3 (Spring 1979): 49-58.

Records allusions to Swift's poetry in *Finnegans Wake* and Joseph Sheridan Le Fanu's *The House by the Churchyard.* Attention is given to Swift's *Epigram* on the powder magazine in Phoenix Park and *On the Little House by the Church Yard of Castleknock.*

448. Idol, John L., Jr. "Thomas Wolfe and Jonathan Swift." *South Carolina Review* 8 (November 1975): 43-54.

Thomas Wolfe used Swift's *A Beautiful Young Nymph Going to Bed* as his model for a satire on a North Carolina gubernatorial candidate, Preston Carr. In a later work he mentions *An Elegy on Mr. Patrige.* Wolfe's frequent remarks about Swift reveal his keen appreciation of Swift's personality and his enduring respect for Swift's literary achievement.

449. Jackson, R. Wyse. *Swift and His Circle: A Book of Essays.* With a Foreword by Seumas O'Sullivan. Dublin: Talbot Press, 1945. Pp. ix + 112.

Includes many references to Swift's poems.

450. Jacobs, Monty. *Jonathan Swift.* Berlin: Wedding-Verlag, 1948. Pp. 243.

In German. Includes brief discussions of several of Swift's better-known poems.

451. Jarrell, Mackie L. "Swiftiana in *Finnegans Wake.*" *ELH* 26 (1959): 271-94.

The Swiftiana include many allusions to Stella and Vanessa. See also Arthur T. Broes, items 436 and 437.

452. Johnson, Maurice. "A Literary Chestnut: Dryden's 'Cousin Swift.'" *PMLA* 57 (December 1952): 1024-34.

Dryden probably never uttered the often-quoted remark, "Cousin Swift, you will never be a poet." First reported by Theophilus Cibber in 1753, the statement was apparently polished to its now-current form by Dr.

Johnson in his *Life of Swift*, to be subsequently repeated and elaborated by biographers and novelists. The remark has a quality of fictional truth that renders it more convincing than demonstrably authentic pronouncements could be. It cannot be proved that Swift and his elder kinsman ever met or corresponded, and the legend of his "perpetual malevolence" toward Dryden is much exaggerated. Swift's later references to Dryden are canvassed, including two passages in *On Poetry: A Rapsody*. See items 464, 465, 467.

453. Johnson, Maurice. "T.S. Eliot on Satire, Swift, and Disgust." *Papers on Language and Literature* 5 (Summer 1969): 310-15.

Although he never wrote formally on the subject, Eliot mentioned in 1924 that he had earlier projected an essay treating of Jonathan Swift as a poet. He considered Swift's salient characteristic in prose and verse satire to be "disgust."

454. Korn, Max Arnim. *Die Weltanschauung Jonathan Swifts*. Jena: Biedermann, 1935. Pp. 143.

Includes scattered brief discussions of Swift's poems, especially the early odes.

455. Köster, Patricia. "Notes upon Notes: Gulliver and the Pepper-Water-Worms." *The Scriblerian*, vol. 2, no. 1 (Autumn 1969): 29-30.

An addendum to Alan T. McKenzie's note on "vinegar eels" and "Pepper-Water-Worms" in the Scriblerian poem *The Lamentation of Glumdalclitch, for the Loss of Grildrig* (see item 461). The conjunction of these two items, which McKenzie found only in the poem and in a letter of Anthony van Leeuwenhoek, occurs also in *Dr. Gregory's Elements of Catoptrics and Dioptrics*, translated by William Browne (London, 1715).

456. Lavers-Smith, H. "Swift's Political Tracts." *The Athenaeum*, no. 3915 (8 November 1902): 619-20.

Of the "seven penny papers" that Swift told Stella he had published during the fortnight before the Stamp Tax went into effect on 1 August 1712, George A. Aitken maintained that five titles could be ascertained from earlier entries in the *Journal to Stella*, while the remaining two could be conjecturally identified from advertisements in *The Examiner*, even though he had not located a copy of either (see item 304). Lavers-Smith prints the text of one of these two pamphlets, *It's Out at Last; or, French Correspondence Clear as the Sun*, which he confidently attributes to Swift. See also items 330, 425, 482, and 489.

457. Leslie, Shane. *The Skull of Swift: An Extempore Exhumation*. Indianapolis: Bobbs-Merrill; London: Chatto and Windus, 1928. Pp. 347.

Includes numerous references to Swift's poems.

458. Longcore, Chris. "A Possible Echo of Jonathan Swift in Dylan Thomas." *Notes and Queries* 208 (April 1963): 153.

Dylan Thomas's "The hand that signed the paper felled a city," from the poem of that title, may echo a line in Swift's *An Elegy on Demar*, "The Hand that sign'd the Mortgage paid the Shot."

459. Longe, Arthur. *The Old Night-Watchman, the Ghost of Spixworth Hall*. Ipswich, Eng.: W.S. Cowell Ltd., 1950, pp. 39-42. See *London Times Literary Supplement*, 20 October 1950, p. 667.

An eccentric publication attributing to Swift several manuscript poems found in a cabinet at Spixworth Hall, Norfolk. One is *The Vicar of Bray*, including two stanzas said to be unpublished. Another is a lyric titled *On a Lady*, beginning "Laurette has an eye than the halcyon more blue."

460. McKenzie, Alan T. "'The Lamentation of Glumdalclitch for the Loss of Grildrig. A Pastoral': What We Have Been Missing." *Texas Studies in Literature and Language* 12 (Winter 1971): 583-94.

Accepting George Sherburn's suggestion that the five "explanatory and commendatory" poems prefixed to a second edition of *Gulliver's Travels*, 1727, may have resulted from a typical Scriblerian collaboration which included Swift (see item 400), McKenzie subjects one of them, *The Lamentation of Glumdalclitch*, to detailed analysis. Attention is given to such matters as genre (pastoral), details taken from *Gulliver's Travels*, prosody, rhetorical devices, metaphors, poetic diction, and allusions.

461. McKenzie, Alan T. "Lemuel Gulliver and Pepper-Water-Worms." *The Scriblerian*, vol. 1, no. 1 (Autumn 1968): 31-32.

Explicates a puzzling passage in *The Lamentation of Glumdalclitch, for the Loss of Grildrig,* one of five burlesque poems by the Scriblerians prefixed to a second edition of *Gulliver's Travels,* 1727. The term "Pepper-Water-Worms," as well as an allusion to "vinegar eels," comes from the scientific experiments of the Royal Society. The two items are mentioned together in a letter of Anthony van Leeuwenhoek. See also Patricia Köster, item 455.

462. Maxwell, D[esmond] E.S. "The Poetic Inception." *American Fiction: The Intellectual Background.* New York: Columbia University Press, 1963, pp. 19-24.

The cultural disseverance of early American writers is paralleled by Swift's dilemma as an Anglo-Irish poet. He is an exile who can yet do the state some service through his art. His verse is for the most part a ruthless stripping of social and literary artifices. He envisages abstract vice primarily in concrete particulars, not in an intellectual void.

463. Mayhew, George. "Two Burlesque Invitations by Swift." *Notes and Queries* 199 (February 1954): 55-57.

These two brief prose burlesques, addressed to John Rochfort, may relate tangentially to Swift's poem *The Journal.* Mayhew also quotes from *Dr. Swift to Dr. Sheridan* and *Dr. Swift's Answer to Doctor Sheridan.*

464. Moore, John R., and Maurice Johnson. "Dryden's 'Cousin Swift.'" *PMLA* 68 (December 1953): 1232-40.

A four-part exchange between Moore and Johnson, stemming from Johnson's *PMLA* article on the remark attributed to Dryden, "Cousin Swift, you will never be a poet" (see item 452). Conceding most of Johnson's points, Moore nevertheless maintains that Swift displayed unusual animosity toward Dryden which could have resulted from something like Dryden's alleged remark. The exchange, which is more speculative than informative, includes comments by Moore on Swift's opinion of Dryden's use of the triplet and alexandrine and the famous burlesque of this device in *A Description of a City Shower.* See also items 465, 467.

465. Mundy, P.D. "The Dryden-Swift Relationship." *Notes and Queries* 193 (30 October 1948): 470-74.

Clarifies the relationship between the poet-cousins Jonathan Swift and John Dryden—who allegedly remarked, "Cousin Swift, you will never be a poet." See items 452, 464, 467.

466. Newman, Bertram. *Jonathan Swift*. London: George Allen and Unwin; Boston and New York: Houghton Mifflin, 1937. Pp. 432.

Includes references to many of Swift's poems.

467. Novarr, David. "Swift's Relation with Dryden, and Gulliver's *Annus Mirabilis*." *English Studies* 47 (October 1966): 341-54.

Apropos of Dryden's alleged remark, "Cousin Swift, you will never be a poet," Novarr surveys Swift's expressed opinions of Dryden and speculates on the reasons for Swift's dislike, which he finds less conventionally literary and more subtle and complex than Maurice Johnson had concluded. See items 452, 464, 465.

468. Pagetti, Carlo. "Bibliografia." *La Fortuna di Swift in Italia*. Biblioteca di Studi Inglesi 21. Bari: Adriatica, 1971, pp. 275-313.

Lists translations of Swift's poems into Italian. In the eighteenth century, there were translations of *Cadenus and Vanessa*, *A Description of the Morning*, *A Description of a City Shower*, and Frances Harris's *Petition*.

469. Priestley, F.E.L. "Science and the Poet." *Dalhousie Review* 38 (Summer 1958): 141-53.

Quotes ten lines from *On Poetry: A Rapsody*.

470. Quintana, Ricardo. *Swift: An Introduction*. London: Oxford University Press, 1955. Pp. viii + 204. Reissue (Oxford Paperbacks). 1962.

Includes brief accounts of representative poems spaced at chronological intervals.

471. Quintana, Ricardo. *Two Augustans: John Locke, Jonathan Swift*. Madison: University of Wisconsin Press, 1978. Pp. viii + 148.

Includes some illuminating comments on specific poems, but does not discuss any in detail.

472. Rosenheim, Edward W., Jr. *Swift and the Satirist's Art.*
     Chicago: University of Chicago Press, 1963, pp. 234-37.

     Stresses the straightforward, prose-like style of
     Swift's verse. Rosenheim does not discuss any of the
     poems in detail.

473. Rossi, Mario M., and Joseph M. Hone. *Swift, or The
     Egoist.* London: Gollancz; New York: E.P. Dutton, 1934.
     Pp. 418. Reprint. Folcroft, PA: Folcroft Press, 1969,
     1976.

     Includes references to Swift's poems.

474. Rowse, A.L. *Jonathan Swift: Major Prophet.* London:
     Thames and Hudson, 1975. Pp. 240.

     Includes numerous citations of Swift's poems.

475. Rühl, Ernst. *Grobianus in England.* Palaestra 38.
     Berlin: Mayer and Müller, 1904, pp. lxvii-lxxi.

     Inquires whether Swift's ironical satires might have
     been influenced by *Grobianus* (cf. "Grubaean"), the Latin
     satirical poem by the sixteenth-century German poet
     Friedrich Dedekind, which was translated into English
     verse and dedicated to Swift in 1739 by "Roger Bull."
     Rühl cites only one of Swift's poems directly, *Verses
     on the Death of Dr. Swift.*

476. Segar, Mary. "Ambrose Philips." *London Times Literary
     Supplement*, 7 December 1933, p. 875.

     Thinks that Philips's nickname "Namby Pamby" may have
     been invented by Swift rather than by Henry Carey, adding
     that "in the case of the parodies written [by Swift and
     his circle] on Philips's verses to the Carteret and
     Pulteney children it seems possible that no fewer than
     five were written by Swift himself."

477. Selby, Hopewell. "'Never Finding Full Repast': Satire
     and Self-Extension in the Early Eighteenth Century."
     *Probability, Time, and Space in Eighteenth-Century
     Literature.* Edited by Paula R. Backscheider. New
     York: AMS Press, 1979, pp. 217-47.

     Comments briefly on notions of space in several of
     Swift's poems.

478. Sisson, C.H. "Yeats and Swift." *The Avoidance of
     Literature: Collected Essays.* Edited by Michael

Schmidt. Manchester, Eng.: Carcanet, 1978, pp. 271-74. (Reprinted from *Agenda*, Autumn/Winter 1971/72).

Mostly peripheral to Swift's poetry, but there is comment on Yeats's personal application of a quatrain from *The Progress of Beauty* about form and matter.

479. Spillane, James M. "Herder's Translations from Swift." *Kentucky Foreign Language Quarterly* 7 (Third Quarter 1960): 156-64.

Although he was at pains to justify Swift to his German contemporaries both as artist and as man, Herder used two of Swift's poems to counter what he considered the Dean's "fall from humanity" with his own formula of *Humanität*. *Verses on the Death of Dr. Swift* inspired both a translation and an answer. In his rather free rendering of the *Verses* into German, Herder produced "a good translation of a poem that is admittedly fraught with translation hazards." His original poem *Das Mitgefühl*, as its title implies, is a refutation of the cynical amour propre illustrated by the maxim Swift borrowed from La Rochefoucauld. Herder's poem *Himmel und Hölle* combines the two purposes, translating part of Swift's *The Place of the Damn'd* and then "humanizing" it as a foil to expound his own philosophy of life.

480. Staley, Thomas F. "The Poet Joyce and the Shadow of Swift." *Jonathan Swift: Tercentenary Essays*. University of Tulsa Department of English Monograph Series, no. 3. Tulsa, OK: University of Tulsa, 1967, pp. 39-52.

Examines in some detail the resemblances between Swift as poet and Joyce as poet. Joyce consciously imitated Swift in two verse satires written in octosyllabic couplets, *The Holy Office* (1904) and *Gas from a Burner* (1912).

481. Steele, Peter. *Jonathan Swift, Preacher and Jester*. Oxford: Clarendon Press, 1978. Pp. 252.

Comments briefly on Swift's poetry in general and on more than a dozen individual poems.

482. Stephens, John C., Jr. "'7 Penny Papers of My Own.'" *Notes and Queries* 197 (29 March 1952): 139-40.

Swift remarks, in a letter to Stella on 7 August 1712, that he published "at least 7 penny Papers of my own" during "the last Fortnight" before the Stamp Tax went into effect on the first of the month. Five of the seven titles, including the poems *Toland's Invitation to Dismal* and *Peace and Dunkirk*, can be ascertained from earlier entries in the *Journal to Stella*, leaving two in doubt. Stephens presents evidence and arguments that a prose pamphlet sometimes proposed, Swift's *A Letter of Thanks from My Lord Wharton to the Lord Bishop of St. Asaph*, cannot have been one of them, since it was already in print by the first week of July. See the answer by Harold Williams, item 489; also items 304, 330, 425, and 456.

483. Stevick, Philip. "The Augustan Nose." *University of Toronto Quarterly* 34 (January 1965): 110-17.

On the prevalence of references to smells and noses in Swift's poetry and other eighteenth-century literature.

484. Strong, L.A.G. *The Sacred River: An Approach to James Joyce*. London: Methuen, 1949; Theodore Brun, 1949; New York: Pellegrini and Cudahy, 1951, pp. 76-83.

On Swift's influence on Joyce. Stella and Vanessa figure prominently.

485. Torchiana, Donald T. "Jonathan Swift, the Irish, and the Yahoos: The Case Reconsidered." *Philological Quarterly* 54 (Winter 1975): 206-07, 209.

From first to last, Swift's poetry--the *Holyhead Journal*, for example--is almost uniformly derogatory toward that nation of slaves, Ireland.

486. Trowbridge, Hoyt. "Swift and Socrates." *From Dryden to Jane Austen: Essays on English Critics and Writers, 1660-1818*. Albuquerque: University of New Mexico Press, 1977, pp. 81-123.

Comments briefly on *An Answer to a Late Scandalous Poem*, *Stella's Birthday, 1719*, and *To Stella, Visiting Me in My Sickness*.

487. Van Doren, Carl. *Swift*. New York: Viking Press, 1930. Pp. 279.

Includes references to many of Swift's poems.

488. Williams, Harold, ed. *The Correspondence of Jonathan
      Swift*. 5 vols. Oxford: Clarendon Press, 1963-1965.
      Pp. lxx + 427; xx + 475; xviii + 511; xviii + 560;
      xii + 404.

      This is the definitive edition of Swift's correspon-
      dence, which includes numerous references to poems he
      was writing at the time.

489. Williams, Harold. "'Seven Penny Papers of My Own.'"
      Notes and Queries 197 (10 May 1952): 218.

      Suggests that the case against accepting *A Letter of
      Thanks from Wharton* as one of Swift's "seven penny
      pepers" is less conclusive than John C. Stephens, Jr.,
      had supposed (see item 482), since Swift's use of the
      phrase "the last Fortnight" may be inexact. See also
      items 304, 330, 425, and 456.

490. Williams, Kathleen, ed. *Swift: The Critical Heritage*.
      The Critical Heritage Series. London: Routledge and
      Kegan Paul; New York: Barnes and Noble, 1970.
      Pp. ix + 348.

      The primary sources reprinted by Williams reveal that
      as late as 1818, Swift's poetry was widely read and much
      admired, especially for its wit, satire, and humor.
      Few detailed comments have survived, however, apparently
      because the poems were not considered serious literature.
      The gross indelicacy complained of in some poems is
      often excused as a device for moral reform. Among the
      works most frequently mentioned are *Cadenus and Vanessa*
      and *The Lady's Dressing Room*.

491. Wilson, T.G. "Swift's Personality." *A Review of English
      Literature*, vol. 3, no. 3 (July 1962): 39-58. (Special
      issue on Swift). Reprint (expanded). *Fair Liberty
      Was All His Cry: A Tercentenary Tribute to Jonathan
      Swift 1667-1745*. Edited by A. Norman Jeffares. Lon-
      don: Macmillan; New York: St. Martin's Press, 1967,
      pp. 15-41.

      A rather shallow biographical essay that makes some
      use of *Cadenus and Vanessa* and the Stella poems.

VII. THESES AND DISSERTATIONS

492. Bishop, Shirley Wolman. "'Varnish and Tinsel': Linguis-
      tic Perspectives on the Work of Jonathan Swift."
      Ph.D. dissertaion, University of California, San
      Diego; 1974. *Dissertation Abstracts International*
      35 (1974): 3723A.

      Discusses Swift's attitudes toward language and empha-
      sizes the importance of his comments on the subject for
      an understanding of his work as a whole. A section on
      Swift's poetry considers his criticisms both of the
      language of casual conversation and of poetic diction.
      It develops the idea of a linguistic dynamic within the
      poetry, in which a sudden and unexpected freeing of
      vocabulary provides a psychological release for the
      reader.

493. Bjornstad, William Bernard. "A Swift Handbook: The
      Biography (1667-1745) and the Poetry through 1745."
      Ph.D. dissertation, University of Minnesota, 1945.

      The first part of this dissertation, originally in-
      tended as part of a larger book to be entitled *A Swift
      Handbook* but never finished, is concerned with various
      problems of Swift's life. The second part discusses,
      as fully as possible, all of Swift's early verse through
      1714, with attention to all the critical commentary up
      to 1945. This verse is of a practical kind, concerned
      with everyday life, with his own affairs or those of his
      friends, with things external to himself; only in his
      later poems does his satire become universal in its
      application. (WBB)

494. Brengle, Richard Logan. "Very Knowing Americans. Jona-
      than Swift and America: His Reputation and Influence,
      1720-1860." Ph.D. dissertation, Columbia University,
      1962. *Dissertation Abstracts* 23 (1962): 1682-83.

      If Swift was no admirer of America, American writers
      were little influenced during the years 1720-1860 by

                              147

either his prose or his poetry. He was, however, held
in esteem as a public figure or "character," more so
than any other contemporary English author.

495. Briden, Earl F. "The Element of 'Anti-' Poetry in Jona-
     than Swift's Verse Satire." M.A. thesis, Brown Uni-
     versity, 1966.

496. Brodbeck, Betty. "Swift as a Poet: A Critical Survey."
     M.A. thesis, University of Akron, 1969.

497. Cashdollar, Paula Mauro. "'My Female Friends': An Exam-
     ination of Women and Women's Roles in the Writings of
     Jonathan Swift." Ph.D. dissertation, University of
     Rhode Island, 1978. *Dissertation Abstracts Interna-
     tional* 39 (1978): 2950A.

     Claims--astonishingly--that "scant attention has been
     devoted to Swift's attitude toward women," and much of
     it is misleading because directed toward the "scatologi-
     cal" poems. Even though the emphasis in satire like
     Swift's is naturally on the negative, the satirist him-
     self is established, not as a misanthropist or misogy-
     nist, but as a moralist. Swift's works provide a sur-
     prisingly extensive and complete portrait of his ideal
     woman, as well as remarkably advanced ideas regarding
     female education. He values the same virtues in women
     as in men and criticizes both sexes equally for the same
     faults.

498. Chisolm, Marsha Katz. "Portraits of the Artists: The
     Rhetoric of Self-Allusion in the Poetry of Pope and
     Swift." Ph.D. dissertation, Vanderbilt University,
     1977. *Dissertation Abstracts International* 39 (1978):
     892A-93A.

     Analyzes the rhetorical strategies employed by Swift
     and Pope to establish a variety of relationships between
     the reader and the versions of themselves depicted in
     their poems. The rhetoric of self-allusion involves a
     living relationship between poet and audience and con-
     veys an ever-shifting sense of the poet's own presence
     in the work and beyond it.

499. Cobb, Joann Patricia. "Jonathan Swift and Epistemology:
     A Study of Swift's Satire on Ways of Knowing." Ph.D.
     dissertation, Saint Louis University, 1975. *Disserta-
     tion Abstracts International* 37 (1975): 3647A.

     Includes references to the poems. Swift's satire on
     epistemological "systems," exposing the inadequacies of

preconceived abstract theories which attempt to impose
order upon human experience by ignoring some aspect of
man's real confrontation with his world, shows him to be
an acute critic of the dangers inherent in the philosophical and scientific revolutions of the seventeenth
and eighteenth centuries.

500. Comeau, Paul M. "Swift's Poems to Stella." M.A. thesis,
Simon Fraser University, [1977-78?].

501. Compean, Richard Edward. "Swift and the Lucianic Tradition." Ph.D. dissertation, University of California,
Davis, 1976. *Dissertation Abstracts International*
37 (1976): 3638A.

Recognizes, as too few Swiftians have done, the importance for Swift's best works of the Renaissance tradition of paradox and nonsense that begins with Lucian and
includes Erasmus, More, Rabelais, Montaigne, Cervantes,
and Burton. Besides its influence on *A Tale of a Tub*
and *Gulliver's Travels*, the Lucianic tradition attracted
Swift strongly for *Verses on the Death of Dr. Swift*, a
complex Lucianic *apologia*.

502. Cormick, Jean Ann Dwyer. "Humor at the Expense of Shame:
Swift, the Athenian Society, and *A Tale of a Tub*."
Ph.D. dissertation, University of California, San
Diego, 1972. *Dissertation Abstracts International*
33 (1972): 303A-04A.

Although primarily a psychoanalytical account of the
composition of *A Tale of a Tub*, this study provides
background on Swift's *Ode to the Athenian Society*.

503. Coshow, Betty G. "The Dramatic Method in Swift's Verse."
M.A. thesis, University of Oklahoma, 1957.

504. Cox, Mary Elizabeth. "Realism and Convention: A Study
of the Poetry of Prior, Swift, and Gay." Ph.D. dissertation, Ohio State University, 1960. *Dissertation
Abstracts* 21 (1961): 2272-73.

In spite of the "neoclassical" belief that the real
was the universal and that particulars falsified the
truth, realism based on details was conspicuous in the
poetry of the first quarter of the eighteenth century.
The best poems of Prior, Swift, and Gay combine concrete-
ness and particularity with conventions traditionally
associated with neoclassicism.

505. Crow, Nora Frances. "The Poetry of Jonathan Swift."
     Ph.D. dissertation, Harvard University, 1972.

     This dissertation sets out a program for reading Swift's
     poetry that minimizes emphasis on allusion, image, and
     most poetic devices and directs attention to the poet's
     control of the reader's response through self-portraiture,
     rhetorical manipulation of trust, and rhythm. The poems
     are discussed in groups: "The Early Odes," "The Stella
     Poems," "The Excremental Poems," "The Poems of Daily
     Social Life," and "The Political Poems." Also included
     are a chapter on Swift's view of poetry as a calling and
     another relating his verse to the work of Butler, Roch-
     ester, Donne, and Marvell. (NFC)

506. Day, William Harry. "Swift's Political Verse." Ph.D.
     dissertation, University of South Carolina, 1975.
     Dissertation Abstracts International 36 (1976): 7434A.

     Swift's views on the purposes of satire tend in two
     seemingly contradictory directions: toward general satire
     that exposes the vices of all men while sparing the names
     and persons of particular men, and toward specific and
     personal attacks on his political enemies. In Swift's
     prose and his political verse satire, however, these two
     opposed tendencies are complementary. Whereas in his
     prose he often seeks to present his political principles
     and positions rationally and convincingly, in his verse
     libels he seeks to discredit his political antagonists
     individually and personally. The poems are carefully
     and skillfully crafted, and though they have the single
     primary purpose of attacking particular men, are sur-
     prisingly various in tone and technique.

507. De Woody, Florence H. "Treatment of Women in Swift's
     Poetical Works." M.A. thesis, Hardin-Simmons Univer-
     sity, 1962.

508. Dickey, Alice K. "An Undismayed Flaying: Comment on
     Several Poems by Jonathan Swift." M.A. thesis, Uni-
     versity of Nebraska, 1965.

509. Edman, John H. "Jonathan Swift and the Muse of Poetry:
     The Years of His Youth." M.A. thesis, Syracuse Uni-
     versity, 1952.

510. Ellenbogen, George. "'I the Lofty Stile Decline': An
     Approach to Swift's Poetry." Ph.D. dissertation,

Tufts University, 1969. *Dissertation Abstracts
International* 31 (1970): 1270A.

Uses Swift's failures in his Pindaric odes as a key
to his later practice in his satiric poetry. Unable to
give the ungrudging praise that the Pindaric form demands,
Swift is uncertain in his handling of imagery and spatial
relationships. He cannot take at face value either peri-
phrasis specifically or poetic diction generally. In
the later poems, Swift's view of mankind as depraved is
more successfully expressed in the low mimetic mode
(Northrop Frye's term), carefully crafted couplets, and
the use of himself as a participant in his poems.

511. England, Anthony Bertram. "The Rhetoric of *Don Juan*
and Some Aspects of Eighteenth Century English Literature." Ph.D. dissertation, Yale University, 1969.
Dissertation Abstracts International 31 (1970):
1270A-71A.

The style of *Don Juan* is most characteristically
related to that of English burlesque, especially as
manifested in the poetry of Swift and Butler. Byron's
style is perhaps most vividly continuous with that of
Swift's poetry in its tendency to imitate a disordered
external reality by accumulating miscellaneous particulars without organizing them into coherently thematic
shapes.

512. Fischer, John Irwin. "The Echoic Poetry of Jonathan
Swift: Studies in its Meaning." Ph.D. dissertation,
University of Florida, 1968. *Dissertation Abstracts
International* 30 (1969): 278A.

Fischer undertakes to indicate the character and range
of Swift's poetic achievement by studying four of his
major poems: *Ode to Dr. William Sancroft*, *Cadenus and
Vanessa*, *On Poetry: A Rapsody*, and *Verses on the Death
of Dr. Swift*. These poems testify to the broad scope
of Swift's reading and also to his penchant for redirect-
ing much of what he read back into his own lines. The
world of Swift's poetry, although divinely ordained and
sustained, is a world in which man's struggle for truth
must be just such a continuous process of recollection,
adjustment, and balancing.

513. Fletcher, Paul A. "The Hardship Put upon Ladies: A
Study of the Women in Swift's Poetry." M.A. thesis,
University of Virginia, 1967.

514. Fricke, Donna Gillespie. "A Critical Study of the Poetry
      of Jonathan Swift." Ph.D. dissertation, Pennsylvania
      State University, 1971. *Dissertation Abstracts Inter-
      national* 32 (1972): 6425A.

      Urges a variety of more up-to-date approaches to the
      whole range of Swift's poetry. Swift should, for example,
      be considered as a healthy Christian moralist rather
      than as a unique, neurotic scatologist.

515. Friedman, Anabel H. "Delusion at Wit's End: Aspects of
      Jonathan Swift's Singularity as Revealed in His Poetry."
      M.A. thesis, University of Maryland (College Park),
      1966.

516. Friedman, Anabel H. "Perspective: A Study of the Poetic
      Art of Jonathan Swift." Ph.D. dissertation, Univer-
      sity of Maryland, 1971. *Dissertation Abstracts Inter-
      national* 32 (1972): 5181A.

      Criticism of Swift's poetry during the eighteenth,
      nineteenth, and twentieth centuries has suffered from
      recurring patterns of eccentric attempts to force it
      into irrelevant or incomplete contexts. Rational evalu-
      ation is possible only if the poetry itself is made the
      focus for critical analysis. Placed in proper perspec-
      tive, the elements of Swift's life, thought, and literary
      art which most offended earlier readers, including those
      inherent in his view of life as a "ridiculous tragedy,"
      emerge as the qualities he shares with modern existen-
      tialist and absurdist writers.

517. Fuller, Gerry William. "Twentieth-Century Criticism of
      Swift's Poetry." M.A. thesis, University of Maine
      (Orono), 1969.

      Beginning as biographical interest, twentieth-century
      attention to Swift's poetry led to critical study.
      Analysis centered on three characteristics of the poems--
      technical ease, abundant detail, and dramatic intensity--
      and on Swift's use of satire and anti-poetry. Special
      attention was given to the "scatological" verse and to
      a few of the more popular works, notably *Verses on the
      Death of Dr. Swift*. Fuller includes a useful bibliogra-
      phy.

518. Garland, Robert. "The Horatian Imitations of Pope and
      Swift." M.A. thesis, University of New Mexico, 1961.

519. Hall, Inez Jean. "The Poetry of Jonathan Swift: Myth and Matter." Ph.D. dissertation, Ball State University, 1974. *Dissertation Abstracts International* 35 (1975): 6693A-94A.

Investigates myth-making in two areas of Swift's career: by Swift himself in his poems, and by his biographers and critics. The poetic myth proves characteristically consistent in illustrating Swift's philosophy and intent. The biographical myth, on the other hand, proves characteristically confusing, illustrating opposing and questionable theories. The poetic matter tends to dispel many of the biographical myths.

520. Hansen, Jens Viggo. "Morality and Society in Swift's Verse." Ph.D. dissertation, University of Colorado, 1972. *Dissertation Abstracts International* 34 (1973): 727A.

Focuses upon Swift's verse as a dissection of Augustan society. Professional and social leaders are portrayed in Swift's poems as hopelessly self-seeking and avaricious, with only the truth-seeking poet and the abnegating clergyman offered as infrequently found norms. The dismissal in Swift's prose of general social and professional types is complemented in his verse by a similar denigration of specific leaders of his time. He discounts any theory of social improvement or perfectibility.

521. Hayman, John Griffiths. "Raillery during the Restoration Period and Early Eighteenth Century." Ph.D. dissertation, Northwestern University, 1964. *Dissertation Abstracts* 25 (1965): 4146-47.

During the period considered, the word raillery "was most frequently used to refer to a sort of mockery or reproach which might have either a frivolous and affable nature or a serious intention, but which was always characterized by adroitness and urbanity." The increasing influence of Voiture is traced. See the articles on raillery by John M. Bullitt, Eugene Timpe, and David Sheehan (items 129, 136, and 185).

522. Hee, Carol Lynn. "The Living Word: Attitudes toward Language in the Works of Jonathan Swift." Ph.D. dissertation, Yale University, 1977. *Dissertation Abstracts International* 39 (1978): 1588A-89A.

Explores two separate but related topics: Swift's opinions on language and style, and the metaphoric

quality of his thought. The two are integrated in
Swift's own use of language, in particular his penchant
for metaphor, his tendency to reify abstractions, and
his frequent reference to words, letters, and books as
if they were things, even living things. This reflex-
ivity of language, this relevance of form to content,
is a pervasive element in Swift's writings.

523. Hersey, William R. "The Political Satire in Jonathan
      Swift's Poetry." M.A. thesis, Boston College, 1966.

524. Huebner, Wayne Vincent. "Convention and Innovation in
      the Satirical Treatment of Women by the Major Satirists
      of the Early Eighteenth Century." Ph.D. dissertation,
      University of Minnesota, 1964. *Dissertation Abstracts*
      25 (1964): 2961.

      Defends the treatment of women in Swift's satires
      (also in those of Addison, Steele, Young, and Pope)
      against adverse responses resulting from subsequent
      changes in social conditions and the loss of historical
      perspective. Swift's view has been termed unwholesome
      and misogynic, but much of the seemingly pathological
      turns out to be Christian or merely conventional.

525. Hunter, Barbara Caroline. "Vision and the Satiric Glass:
      Visual and Conceptual Patterns in the Major Satires
      of Jonathan Swift." Ph.D. dissertation, Northwestern
      University, 1975. *Dissertation Abstracts International*
      36 (1976): 4510A-11A.

      Identifying Swift's analogy between satire and a mirror
      as a conceptual model in his thought, this study explores
      the discrepancy between the limited perceptions of his
      unreliable narrators and the larger perspective a reader
      is ideally expected to "see."

526. Jelinek, Mariann. "'Poison in Jest': The Central
      Ambiguity of Jonathan Swift's Satiric Stance." Ph.D.
      dissertation, University of California, Berkeley, 1973.

527. Johnson, Donald Ray. "Plowshares, Politics and Poetry:
      The Georgic Tradition from Dryden to Thomson." Ph.D.
      dissertation, University of Wisconsin, 1972. *Disser-
      tation Abstracts International* 33 (1973): 6314A.

      In Gay's *Trivia* and Swift's *Description of a City
      Shower*, Virgil's precepts for plowing and harvesting
      and his descriptions of rural occupations are trans-
      formed into rules for walking city streets and accounts
      of urban diversions.

528. Johnson, Maurice. "The Sin of Wit: Jonathan Swift as
      a Poet." Ph.D. dissertation, Columbia University,
      1951.

529. Keegan, Timothy Leonard. "The Theory and Practice of
      Swift's Poetry." Ph.D. dissertation, University of
      Virginia, 1979. *Dissertation Abstracts International*
      40 (1980): 5064A.

      Discusses, in wider contexts than have normally been
      applied, four genres of Swift's poetry: poems of praise,
      "dirty poems," political satires, and self-portraits.
      Swift's successful poems of praise, as opposed to his
      imitative panegyrics, adopt a down-to-earth manner. His
      "dirty poems" are not only conventional for the period
      but conventionally Swiftian in their attitudes and
      techniques. His political satires exploit the wild,
      self-evident exaggeration, extravagant insult, religious
      and sexual imagery, and images of violence, death, and
      madness that are ubiquitous in Augustan political poetry;
      this poetry characteristically poses the sort of chal-
      lenges to ingenious elaboration that Swift relished.
      The self-portraits, like that in *Verses on the Death of
      Dr. Swift*, are more straightforward than is usually
      supposed, although they fail when they are too straight-
      forward.

530. Kelly, Ann Cline. "Swift's Use of Conversation as a
      Thematic and Stylistic Element in His Poetry." Ph.D.
      dissertation, University of Pennsylvania, 1972. *Dis-
      sertation Abstracts International* 33 (1972): 1687A.

      Swift's concept of real-life conversation provides a
      useful organizing point for a study of his verse because
      his concern with human communication underlies many of
      his poems, and because much of his poetry is conveyed
      in a conversational style. This style draws the reader
      into the conversational dynamics of a poem, acts as a
      positive norm in poems where explicit or implicit dis-
      cussion occurs, and exploits the resources of the rhymed
      couplet to transmit the sound of authentic voices. The
      poems analyzed in detail include *The Journal of a Modern
      Lady*, *The Dean's Reasons for Not Building at Drapier's
      Hill*, *To Stella: March 13, 1723-4*, *The Grand Question
      Debated*, *Mad Mullinix and Timothy*, *On Poetry: A Rapsody*,
      and *Apollo, to Dean Swift*.

531. Kimble, Mark Wilson. "The Scatological Poetry of Swift
      and Pope: Intention and Technique." Ph.D. disserta-

tion, University of Virginia, 1970. *Dissertation Abstracts International* 31 (1971): 4722A.

The scatological idiom of Swift and Pope is a legitimate product of conscious choice, and as such, must be explained in rhetorical rather than psychoanalytic or sociological terms. Swift's distinctive procedure is to present the coarsest material in the most explicit and unmitigated way. By consciously emphasizing filth, he attempts to appeal directly through the offended sense to ladies of quality and men of fashion whose affected delicacy denied the evidence of the senses, and to expose the falsehood of their prurient euphemisms and "gallant" manner.

532. Kirchmeir, Wolfe E. "The Major Themes of Swift's Satiric Verse." M.A. thesis, University of Alberta, 1965.

533. Koger, James Alfred. "The Personal and Literary Relationship of Matthew Prior and Jonathan Swift. Ph.D. dissertation, Rice University, 1971. *Dissertation Abstracts International* 32 (1971): 2058A.

Swift and Prior were close friends from the time they met until Prior's death, although their correspondence became their only connection for most of their relationship. The differences in their temperaments are the differences that appear in their poetry: Swift's is satirical, didactic, and powerful, whereas Prior's avoids satire, cultivates aesthetic enjoyment, and is lighter in tone. Their similarities are essentially technical and stylistic, illustrating the power of poetry in the plain style during the early eighteenth century. As the older man, Prior probably influenced Swift rather than vice versa.

534. Korshin, Carolyn. "A Study of Swift's Verse as Formal Verse Satire." M.A. thesis, Queen's College, 1969.

535. Kulisheck, Clarence Louis. "A Critical Appraisal of the Poetry of Jonathan Swift." Ph.D. dissertation, University of Washington, 1949.

Because surprisingly little criticism of Swift's poetry has resulted since the publication of Sir Harold Williams's definitive edition in 1937, Kulisheck concentrates upon critical appraisal, omitting summaries of the contents of the poems and barely suggesting their

social, political, and biographical background. Swift's
poems have fallen into neglect for three reasons: lack
of good editions, a narrowed sense of literary propriety,
and a Romantic conception of the nature of poetry that
excludes Swift's kind of verse. Kulisheck surveys the
poetry under the headings of "Variety and Range,"
"Texture and Form," and "The Problem of the Scatological,"
giving special attention to metrics and prosody.

536. Lee, Jae Num. "Swift and the Tradition of Scatological
    Satire." Ph.D. dissertation, University of New Mexico,
    1968. *Dissertation Abstracts* 29 (1969): 4459A-60A.

    In contrast to the psychological or biographical em-
    phasis of earlier studies, Lee's essay examines Swift's
    uses of scatology in his verse and prose works from a
    literary point of view that analyzes its rhetorical
    functions and the thematic purposes it serves. Swift
    rarely employs scatology without making some satiric
    point.

537. Levensohn, Alan Mark. "Swift against Madness: The Early
    Years." Ph.D. dissertation, Brandeis University, 1974.
    Dissertation Abstracts International 35 (1974): 1050A.

    Among the experiences and influences that shaped
    Swift's concept of madness during the years 1667-1696
    are the poems of his Pindaric-Cowleyan phase.

538. Lindstrom, James David. "Metaphoric Structure in the
    Verse Fables and Horatian Imitations of Jonathan Swift:
    An Introduction to His Poetic Style." Ph.D. disserta-
    tion, University of California, Los Angeles, 1969.
    Dissertation Abstracts International 30 (1969) 2489A-
    90A.

    Analyzes Swift's technique in his imitations and fables
    in terms of the two components of a metaphor, the vehicle
    and the tenor. Attention is given to the imitations of
    Horace's *Epistles* 1.7 and *Satires* 2.6, *The Fable of Midas*,
    The Faggot, and *The Beast's Confession to the Priest*.

539. McKenzie, Alan Taber. "The Scriblerus Club Poems to
    Gulliver's Travels." Ph.D. dissertation, University
    of Pennsylvania, 1968. *Dissertation Abstracts* 29
    (1969): 3615A-16A.

    A detailed analysis of almost all conceivable aspects
    of the five burlesque poems by the Scriblerians which

were prefixed to a second edition of *Gulliver's Travels*,
1727. Attention is given to such matters as the connections of the five poems with *Gulliver*, the genres to
which they belong--ode, epistle, pastoral, and two formal
addresses, one epideictic, the other forensic--various
other poetic devices, authorship, and textual and bibliographical information. Like George Sherburn (see item
400), McKenzie suspects that Swift, as well as Pope and
other Scriblerians, had a hand in these verses.

540. Metcalfe, Joan Elizabeth. "Jonathan Swift and the Stage
of the World: A Study of Swift's Poetry, with Particular Reference to the Poems about Women." Ph.D. dissertation, University of Florida, 1974. *Dissertation
Abstracts International* 35 (1975): 5417A.

Although he wrote no plays and was alienated from the
contemporary theater, Swift possessed dramatic powers
which find expression both in the play-like structures
of his poems and in orthodox beliefs such as the traditional metaphors of the stage of the world and the Chain
of Being, defining the duties of human beings to one
another and to God. Swift uses both contexts to show
concern at woman's inadequacy in performing the human
role--because of trivial-mindedness or deficient educa-
tion or because of men's failure to remember the place
of Man in the Chain of Being. Men treat women as goddesses to be worshipped or beasts to be used. Women
who rise above their disadvantages, however, are characterized by the reasonableness that to an orthodox
Christian is the essence of human virtue.

541. Migliaccio, Ernest A. "Swift's Scatological Poetry:
Purpose and Rhetoric." M.A. thesis, Columbia University, 1968.

542. Miller, Stephan Alan. "The Satiric Rhetoric of *Poems
on Affairs of State, 1660-1714*: The Schooling of Swift
and Pope." Ph.D. dissertation, Vanderbilt University,
1976. *Dissertation Abstracts International* 37 (1976):
2201A.

Swift may have imbibed much of the octosyllabic tradition begun by Butler from works like those in *Poems on
Affairs of State*. Tom Brown is a likely forerunner of
Swift's verse. Swift's poetry makes extensive use of
personae which resemble those in *Poems on Affairs of
State*. Possibly Swift's term "Yahoo" derives from the
biblical "Jehu" who achieved prominence in these volumes.

543. Munker, Dona Feldman. "'To Set Your Thoughts upon Their Mettle': A Study of Swift's Major Verse Satire." Ph.D. dissertation, New York University, 1976. *Dissertation Abstracts International* 38 (1977): 810A.

Under the camouflage of a deceptively simple style, Swift's poetry offers the reader specious arguments, ambiguous rhetoric, and illogical or unsatisfying conclusions designed to stimulate a critical evaluation of the ethical attitudes being satirized. The ultimate intent of this use of ironic viewpoint is to make the reader more conscious of the complex nature of normal human experience—to make the point that final truths about a confused human reality are not available to reason that is limited by mortality. Swift's achievement is both rhetorical and aesthetic. Munker analyzes more than twenty poems in detail.

544. Okada, Victor Noburu. "A Critical Study of Jonathan Swift's Poetry." Ph.D. dissertation, Ohio State University, 1973. *Dissertation Abstracts International* 34 (1973): 2574A.

Analyzes the poetic techniques in a selected variety of Swift's encomiastic and satiric poems. The emphasis is on such elements as structure, imagery, and tone rather than on biographical and historical background. The encomiastic poems consist of the poems to Stella, *Cadenus and Vanessa*, and the poems to Robert Harley, Earl of Oxford. The satiric poems include satires on individual targets, such as *A Satirical Elegy*, *The Description of a Salamander*, and *Mad Mullinix and Timothy*, and the more impersonal satires, such as *The Beast's Confession to the Priest*, *On Poetry: A Rapsody*, and *The Legion Club*.

545. Patterson, Anne Elizabeth. "Descartes' Animal-Machine and Neoclassical Satire: Animal Imagery in Selected Works of La Fontaine and Swift." Ph.D. dissertation, University of Wisconsin, 1973. *Dissertation Abstracts International* 34 (1974): 6601A-02A.

In rejecting Descartes' theory of the animal-machine, La Fontaine and Swift were able to give new dimensions to the traditional use of the animal as an image of man. Patterson cites Swift's verse as well as *Gulliver's Travels* and other prose works.

546. Pearlman, Mari Ann. "Swift's Poetry: The Art of Vexa-
     tion." Ph.D. dissertation, Rutgers University, 1980.
     Dissertation Abstracts International 41 (1981): 4046A.

     Adopting the view that Swift's poetry in its totality
     resists attempts to fix patterns or formulate critical
     generalizations, Pearlman investigates the nature of
     this fragmentation. The cause, she finds, is the absence
     of a consistent, identifiable satiric voice which could
     establish some stable satiric perspective; Swift trans-
     forms himself and alters his voice from one occasion to
     another. After a chapter examining three of Swift's most
     characteristic satiric roles--actor, scourge, and proph-
     et--one chapter each is devoted to *On Poetry: A Rapsody*,
     The Legion Club, and the "scatological" poems.

547. Pierre, Gerald John. "The Influence of Sir William
     Temple upon the Mind and Art of Jonathan Swift."
     Ph.D. dissertation, University of Minnesota, 1970.
     Dissertation Abstracts International 32 (1971): 1484A.

     Examines Temple's influence in Swift's poems written
     before 1694.

548. Pollak, Ellen M. "Perspectives on a Myth: Women in the
     Verse of Swift and Pope." Ph.D. dissertation, Columbia
     University, 1979. *Dissertation Abstracts International*
     40 (1980): 5878A.

     Modern criticism, such as the New Criticism, has tended
     to emphasize the similarities rather than the differences
     between Pope and Swift and has tended to rate Swift as
     a poet below Pope. The balance alters, however, when the
     two are seen in relation to the "myth of passive woman-
     hood" that developed as a part of English culture by the
     1680's. Whereas Pope emerges as an eloquent justifier
     of the sexual norms of his society, Swift proves to be
     one of their most interesting critics.

549. Potter, Lee Harris. "Walter Scott's Edition of Jonathan
     Swift's Works." Ph.D. dissertation, University of
     North Carolina, Chapel Hill, 1954.

     Includes detailed consideration of Scott's editorial
     labors on Swift's verse. Potter concludes that "Scott's
     decisions as to the authenticity of the poems which he
     first published as Swift's do little credit to his record
     as an editor. For of the total number of his ascriptions
     only a few have survived the tests of modern scholar-
     ship."

550. Rainbolt, Martha Marple. "Jonathan Swift's Nonsense
and Whimsey: The Man and the Mode." Ph.D. dissertation, University of Missouri-Columbia, 1977. *Dissertation Abstracts International* 38 (1978): 4852A.

Describes the lighter writings of Swift, in order to
reach a more balanced view of his personality, and draws
together and defines the modes of his light humor. Nonsense and whimsey, well known in the works of Lewis
Carroll and Edward Lear, were first fully explored by
Swift. Nonsense is characterized by its intellectual
quality, concern with language, incongruity, and illogical logic. The elements of whimsey are spontaneity,
participation in make-believe, freedom and intimacy, and
delight in language. Rainbolt concludes by focusing
upon Swift's self-directed laughter.

551. Rodino, Richard Hodge. "Swift's Poetry: Motive and
Structure." Ph.D. dissertation, Harvard University,
1976.

This dissertation has two principal concerns: Swift's
development as a poet, and his "vexatious" poems.
"Development," defined as changes in what Swift tried
to accomplish by his poems and in the tactics he employed, is traced from the early odes through what Rodino
calls "Whig and Tory" poems of 1696-1714, a group of
descriptive and deliberately non-conclusive poems in
1708-1714, through the varied but orthodox poetry of
1714-1729, to the "vexatious" poems of the early 1730s.
Examination of the "vexatious" poems--which seek to trap,
disconcert, disrupt complacency--is focused by analyzing
Swift's handling of important themes through 1733: poems
about women and marriage, poems about Swift himself,
fables and animal images, and others. There is a final
chapter on Swift's poems after 1733. (RHR)

552. Rogers, Katharine Munzer. "Jonathan Swift's Attitude
toward Women." Ph.D. dissertation, Columbia University, 1957. *Dissertation Abstracts* 17 (1957): 1767-68.

Swift's attitude toward women in his life and works
displays a pattern of approach and avoidance, a self-
contradictory combination of admiration and deflation.
Swift enjoyed the society of women and felt exceptional
respect for their development. Yet he guarded himself
against sexual involvement with them and attacked them
with conspicuous bitterness. Unlike earlier misogynists,
Swift found even the female body nauseating and dispar-
aged woman as a mother.

553. Schakel, Peter James. "Method and Meaning in the Poems
     of Swift." Ph.D. dissertation, University of Wiscon-
     sin, 1969. *Dissertation Abstracts International* 30
     (1969): 1182A.

     Instead of merely summarizing their content, or ana-
     lyzing style apart from content, Schakel examines Swift's
     poems as complex, unified works of art in which content
     and theme interact with style and method to create the
     total meaning. The poems examined include the early
     odes, *Verses Wrote in a Lady's Ivory Table-Book*, *Baucis
     and Philemon*, the Vanessa and Stella poems, the "scato-
     logical" poems, *On Poetry: A Rapsody*, *The Legion Club*,
     and *Verses on the Death of Dr. Swift*.

554. Schoppe, Linnea Pearson. "The Hound and the Hare, the
     Rebel and the Fair: Four Critical Approaches to the
     Love and Anti-Love Poetry of Jonathan Swift." Ph.D.
     dissertation, Northern Illinois University, 1973.
     Dissertation Abstracts International 34 (1973): 1868A.

     Examines Swift's love and anti-love poetry in terms
     of four critical approaches: (1) the roles in the poems
     of the archetypal figures of the Good Mother and the
     Terrible Mother, which evoke powerful emotional responses
     in the reader; (2) the influence on Swift's writings of
     the social milieu, which sought to dehumanize women and
     place them in stereotyped feminine roles; (3) the alleged
     misogyny of Swift's poetry in relation to the satiric
     tradition, the traditional anti-feminism of the Church,
     Swift's literary forebears, and Swift's own moral intent;
     (4) the psychological forces at work in Swift's life,
     which account for the form and content of his poetry
     about love, sex, and women. These four approaches are
     used to analyze *Strephon and Chloe* and *To Stella, Who
     Collected and Transcribed His Poems*. Schoppe concludes
     that Swift was not a misogynist.

555. Scruggs, Charles Watkins. "The Bee and the Spider:
     Swift's Aesthetic and His Role as a Literary Critic."
     Ph.D. dissertation, University of Wisconsin, 1965.
     Dissertation Abstracts 26 (1966): 5417-18.

     Includes treatment of Swift's theory of language in
     the light of his attack upon trite poetic diction and
     metaphor.

556. Selkin, Michael. "The Conscious Muse: A Study of Some
     of Swift's Major Poems." Ph.D. dissertation, Columbia

University, 1975. *Dissertation Abstracts International* 36 (1975): 2856A.

Consists of detailed critical analysis of *Cadenus
and Vanessa, Strephon and Chloe,* and some related poems
by Swift.

557. Selleck, William Robert. "A Study of Images in the
     Poetry of Jonathan Swift." Ph.D. dissertation, Uni-
     versity of Southern California, 1970. *Dissertation
     Abstracts International* 31 (1970): 768A.

     Predictably, this systematic study reveals that except
     for the purpose of parody, Swift avoided conventional
     poetic images, preferring the familiar, the ordinary,
     and the ugly to the remote, the exotic, and the beauti-
     ful. He employs an enormous quantity of physical imagery
     derived from the human environments, the human body, and
     the animal world. The man-animal metaphor so basic to
     Swift's prose satire is pervasive in his poetry. Images
     of human and animal violence are probably more numerous
     and varied than in the work of any other English poet.

558. Seymour, Mary H. "'That Ridiculous Passion': A Commen-
     tary on Five Marriage Poems by Jonathan Swift." M.A.
     thesis, University of Delaware, 1967.

559. Sharp, James A. "*Smoaking* Swift's *Description of the
     Morning.*" M.A. thesis, Louisiana State University,
     [1977-78].

560. Sheehan, David Reynolds. "Private and Public Modes in
     the Poetry of Jonathan Swift." Ph.D. dissertation,
     University of Wisconsin-Madison, 1974. *Dissertation
     Abstracts International* 35 (1975): 5363A-64A.

     Concentrating on Swift's social verse, Sheehan describes
     its patterns and purposes, which not only increase our
     understanding of Swift's achievement in private modes of
     poetry, but also provide important contexts for reading
     his more public, political poems. Successive chapters
     discuss the failure of the early odes to combine private
     and public verse, the success of the two imitations of
     Horace written in 1713 and 1714, raillery in the poems
     to Stella, the verse trifles, the comic quality of the
     "scatological" poems considered in light of the Market
     Hill poems, and the combination of private and public in
     major poems from Swift's mature poetry.

164   *Theses and Dissertations*

561. Sinclair, Reid Baytop. "'What the World Calls Obscene':
     Swift's 'Ugly' Verse and the Satiric Tradition." Ph.D.
     dissertation, Vanderbilt University, 1965. *Dissertation Abstracts* 26 (1965): 1028-29.

     Argues that the coarse, scurrilous, "ugly" elements in
     Swift's verse can be properly understood only in relation
     to the satiric tradition and in relation to their artis-
     tic and thematic function in the poems themselves.
     Obscene and scatological imagery frequently attributed
     to some neurotic condition in Swift in seen to be char-
     acteristic of conventional satirical art.

562. Slepian, Barry. "Jonathan Swift and George Faulkner."
     Ph.D. dissertation, University of Pennsylvania, 1962.
     Dissertation Abstracts 23 (1962): 1689.

     An account of the business and personal relationship
     between Swift and Dublin printer George Faulkner.
     Slepian attempts to prove that the two men cooperated
     in the preparation of the early volumes of Faulkner's
     editions of Swift's *Works*, including Volume II, which
     contains the poems.

563. Smith, Frederik Northrop. "Dramatic Elements in the
     Satire of Jonathan Swift." Ph.D. dissertation, Univer-
     sity of Virginia, 1970. *Dissertation Abstracts Inter-
     national* 32 (1971): 933A.

     Drama and satire developed simultaneously in Swift's
     writings and are inherently related in all that he wrote.
     The term "dramatic elements" includes Swift's techniques
     of reader-involvement and cuts across various generic
     and rhetorical boundaries to focus on the immediacy of
     Swift's common satiric devices, at whatever level.
     Smith devotes one chapter to elements of fable, scene,
     and dialogue in Swift's poetry, and another to the self-
     dramatization that predominates in his loosely struc-
     tured, very personal imitations of Horace.

564. Solomon, Harry Miller, Jr. "The Poetry of Jonathan
     Swift." Ph.D. dissertation, Duke University, 1973.
     Dissertation Abstracts International 34 (1973): 1255A.

     This study investigates the influence of specific poems
     and authors on various poems by Swift, the general liter-
     ary context in which he wrote various poems, his method
     of composition, his poetic development, and the conti-
     nuity implicit in that development. Repeatedly it is

demonstrated how Swift, strongly influenced by the
traditions in which he was writing, always managed to
fashion new forms of poetic art.

565. Spillane, James Maurice. "Herder and Swift." Ph.D.
dissertation, Cornell University, 1958. *Dissertation
Abstracts* 19 (1958): 141.

Investigates the very considerable impact, positive
and negative, of Swift's writings on Johann Gottfried
Herder. For example, Herder was horrified at the lack
of "Humanität" in Swift's sardonic *Verses* on his own
death and countered with *Das Mitgefühl*, a lengthy refutation of the cynical amour-propre which is the basis of
the Swift poem. There are affinities between the basic
ideas of the two men both early and late in their careers.

566. Stephens, Patricia Carol. "Jonathan Swift's Poetry."
Ph.D. dissertation, University of North Carolina at
Chapel Hill, 1970. *Dissertation Abstracts Interna-
tional* 31 (1971): 6023A.

Because Swift's poetry is highly rhetorical, it elicits
an interest more in what it does than in what it is; that
is, the poems are not so much objects of aesthetic con-
templation as artistically structured instruments of
communication. Among the most important choices that
constitute stylistics in this kind of poetry are the role
of the fictive audience, the use of demonstrative devices
from logic or dialectics, and the characterization of
the persona. Swift's poetry does not include a synthetic
resolution of opposing values, but rather demonstrates
through relentless pursuit of its own logic of exposure
that diametrically opposing views include aspects of one
another, by a kind of reciprocal interference, which the
poet can transform into a new contradiction or paradox.
Considered together, Swift's poems dramatize man's
bondage as a largely self-constructed web of words.

567. Sterne, Noel Dorothea. "Jonathan Swift's Imitations of
Horace." Ph.D. dissertation, Columbia University,
1969. *Dissertation Abstracts International* 30 (1970):
4426A-27A.

Although recent criticism has seen Swift as almost
exclusively Juvenalian, contemporaries likened him instead to Horace. Both Horace and Swift cultivated a
conversational style, Horace in his satires and epistles
and Swift in his mature poems. Horace was the only

ancient writer Swift imitated more than once. Sterne analyzes in detail all nine of Swift's imitations of Horace.

568. Thompson, Paul Vern. "The Canon of Swift, 1674-1714." Ph.D. dissertation, Northwestern University, 1937.

See item 32 for further information.

569. Tichy, Henrietta. "The Bible in the Poetry of Pope and Swift." Ph.D. dissertation, New York University, 1942.

Swift's poetry contains about fifty allusions to the Scriptures, considerably more than appear in Pope but a meager collection for a Church of England divine. Swift's allusions, usually a brief mention of a biblical event or name with little development of any kind, occur in a variety of poems, humorous, satirical, serious, and are varied in type. Swift's diversity of New Testament allusions contrasts with Pope's avoidance of the Christian gospels.

570. Tweedle, Mary C. "A Study and Evaluation of the Comic Techniques in the Satiric Poetry of Dryden, Swift, and Pope." M.A. thesis, University of Denver, 1968.

571. Tyne, James Lawrence, S.J. "The Misanthrope and the Muse: Swift's Lapidary Verse." Ph.D. dissertation, Yale University, 1962.

Beginning with an examination of Swift's initial poetic attempts, the curiously uncongenial Pindaric odes, Tyne traces the evolution of Swift as poet and moralist. In both roles the Dean gradually learns to lower his sights. Instead of endeavoring to compose great poetry, he is content with writing correct poetry; instead of exhorting the reader to strive for lofty moral ideals, he tauntingly demonstrates that human nature is capable of achieving only a limited, patchwork goodness. This dual thesis is buttressed by constant references to Swift's poetry, particularly to the scatological poems, the verses to Stella, *Cadenus and Vanessa*, and *Verses on the Death of Dr. Swift*. (JLT)

572. Uphaus, Robert Walter. "'The Narrow Path of Sense': A Study of Jonathan Swift's Poetry." Ph.D. dissertation, University of Washington, 1969. *Dissertation Abstracts International* 30 (1969): 2502A.

Swift's poetry uses "sense" (both physical sensation and self-knowledge) as a mode of awareness urging the

primacy of experience and the need for empirical
analysis as the ultimate source of judgment.

573. Vifian, John L. "An Examination of the Critical Reac-
tion to Swift's Poetry." M.A. thesis, Washington
State University (Pullman), 1956.

574. Waite, Gerald Phillip. "The Creative Impulse behind
the Poetry of Jonathan Swift." Ph.D. dissertation,
University of Wisconsin–Milwaukee, 1974. *Dissertation Abstracts International* 35 (1975): 4461A-62A.

Explores Swift's attitudes toward his own poetry.
Verse writing for him was an earnest activity that he
pursued carefully despite the appearance of careless-
ness, but his chief motive was to entertain rather than
instruct. His poems tend to employ mechanical structures
which are, however, subverted by a recognition of the
absurdity of such structures. The truest key to Swift's
poetics is his playfulness, his passion for pretense,
his delight in fancy that frequently ran away with his
judgment.

575. Wallace, Joel Wise. "The Augustan Poets and the Fair
Sex." Ph.D. dissertation, Columbia University, 1954.
Dissertation Abstracts 14 (1954): 1736-37.

Swift's poetics had no place for lyricism or idealism.
Unusually conscious of the less pleasant side of femi-
ninity, he called attention in his poems to feminine
attitudes and manners that he believed in need of correction. Stella pleased him because, as her tutor and
friend, he had molded her into the kind of woman he
wanted her to be.

576. Waller, Charles Thomas. "The Political Poetry of Jonathan Swift: A Critical Study." Ph.D. dissertation,
University of Pittsburgh, 1965. *Dissertation Abstracts* 26 (1966): 3966.

Swift's political poetry, which has been overshadowed
by his prose, deserves to be better known. Waller
examines three of its aspects: as an expression of the
Augustan Age and of Swift's genius; as satire, similar
in technique to his prose; and as commentary on the contemporary political scene. The poems discussed include
An Epistle to a Lady, *On Poetry: A Rapsody*, and *The
Legion Club*.

577. Weber, Harold Morton. "The Accents of Satire: Comic
      and Tragic Voices in the Poetry of Pope and Swift."
      Ph.D. dissertation, University of Virginia, 1978.
      Dissertation Abstracts International 40 (1979): 3326A.

      Studies the poetry of Pope and Swift in terms of the
      polarities between tragic and comic, Juvenalian and
      Horatian satire. Weber confronts two questions: what
      did these polarities mean for the eighteenth century,
      and how were they applied in practice?

578. Wells, Peter Hamlin. "The Poetry of Swift: Dialectical
      Rhetoric and the Humanist Tradition." Ph.D. disserta-
      tion, New York University, 1971. *Dissertation Ab-
      stracts International* 32 (1972): 3969A.

      Swift's poetry often confuses and disturbs the modern
      reader because it is a combination of moral commentary
      and artistic design. The moral commentary relates to
      the most transient aspects of eighteenth-century life
      and thought, which are the aspects least familiar in the
      twentieth century. Once the context of Swift's moral
      purpose is recognized and understood, the reader is
      freed to undertake close critical analysis of the poems.

579. White, Robert Ogden. "The Importance of Verse Fable in
      Swift's Poetic Achievement: 'In Proper Terms to Write
      a Fable.'" Ph.D. dissertation, Boston University,
      1976. *Dissertation Abstracts International* 36 (1975):
      2794A.

      Among Swift's many verses that parody or burlesque
      traditional "kinds" are approximately forty verse fables.
      These fables illustrate Swift's special combination of
      the imitative and innovative, most of them are occasion-
      al, they convey moral insights and instruction, and each
      of them tells a vivid story. Most of them employ octo-
      syllabic couplets, an unreliable narrator, literaliza-
      tion of metaphor, and vigorous colloquial speech. White
      analyzes a score of Swift's fables, including *The Faggot*,
      Baucis and Philemon, and *The Beast's Confession to the
      Priest*.

580. Woolley, James David. "Swift's Later Poems: Studies in
      Circumstances and Texts." Ph.D. dissertation, Uni-
      versity of Chicago, 1972.

      These essays and notes treat the contexts or the pub-
      lication histories, or both, of several poems from

Swift's last decade as a poet. Woolley discusses
Verses on the Death of Dr. Swift and *On Poetry: A
Rapsody* as well as lesser poems, among them *On Paddy's
Character of the Intelligencer*, *The Parson's Case*,
and the coinage poems of 1737. (JDW)

Miner, Earl Roy, 371
Mitford, John, 13
Moore, Harry T., 224
Moore, John Robert, 372,
  464
Moore Smith, G.C., 373
Moskovit, Leonard A., 321,
  374
Motto, Anna Lydia, 158
Mundy, P.D., 465
Munker, Dona F., 132, 134,
  138, 543
Murry, John Middleton, 89;
  mentioned, 202, 204,
  206, 213, 215, 278, 279,
  285, 288, 302, 329
Murtuza, Athar, 228

Naumov, Nićifor, 90
Nemoianu, Virgil, 91
Neuburg, V.B., 357, 375
Newman, Bertram, 466
Nokes, David, 68
Novak, Maximillian E., 91A,
  96
Novarr, David, 467
Nussbaum, Felicity, 229

O Hehir, Brendan, 156, 159
Ohlin, Peter, 172, 174,
  179
Okada, Victor Noburn, 544
Olive, William John, 182
Orwell, George, 230, 329
Orwell, Sonia, 230
Osborn, James M., 300,
  376, 427
Östman, Hans, 160

Page, John T., 347, 377
Pagetti, Carlo, 468
Palmer, John, 412
Papajewski, Helmut, 16
Parkin, Rebecca Price, 92,
  166
Parrish, Stephen M., 17
Patterson, Anne Elizabeth,
  545

Paulson, Ronald, 93
Peake, Charles, 378
Pearlman, Mari Ann, 546
Perri, Carmela, 105
Peterson, Leland D., 293,
  296
Pickford, John, 319, 362,
  379
Pierre, Gerald John, 547
Pinto, V. de Sola, 235
Piper, William Bowman, 6,
  135
Poirier, Richard, 83
Pollak, Ellen, 217, 231,
  548
Pollard, Arthur, 11
Pons, Emile, 16, 45
Potter, Lee Harris, 549
Potter, Stephen, 16
Pottle, Frederick A., 16
Powell, William S., 380
Praz, Mario, 16
Price, Martin, 91, 94,
  161, 412
Priestley, F.E.L., 469
Probyn, Clive T., 49, 69,
  95, 232, 256, 366, 381,
  382

Quinlan, Maurice J., 383
Quintana, Ricardo, 16, 39,
  87, 91, 365, 384, 470,
  471

Rainbolt, Martha Marple,
  550
Rawson, Claude J., 62, 78,
  80, 96, 233, 234, 257,
  258, 385, 390
Raymond, John, 10, 97
Read, Herbert, 98, 99
Real, Hermann J., 162, 235,
  236, 245, 386, 387, 388
Rees, Christine, 237, 246
Reeves, James, 10, 12
Reichard, Hugo M., 274
Reynolds, Richard, 386,
  388

INDEX OF POEM TITLES